Falling in Love with Jesus' People

Falling in Love with Jesus' People

STUDIES IN THE BOOK OF ACTS
RUBEL SHELLY

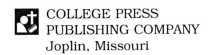
COLLEGE PRESS
PUBLISHING COMPANY
Joplin, Missouri

Cover Design: Mark A. Cole

Library of Congress Cataloging-in-Publication Data

Shelly, Rubel.
    Falling in love with Jesus' people: studies in the Book of Acts / Rubel
Shelly.
      p.   cm.
    Includes bibliographical references.
    ISBN 0-89900-803-8 (pbk.)
    1. Bible. N.T. Acts—Commentaries. 2. Bible. N.T. Acts—Study and
teaching. I. Title.
BS2625.3.S48 1998
226.6'07—dc21   98-3062
                                                    CIP

Preface

Paul once gave this charge to church leaders: "Keep watch over yourselves and all the flock of which God has made you overseers. Be shepherds of the church of God, which he bought with his own blood" (Acts 20:28). The shepherds of the congregation of which I am a part take this responsibility seriously and believe that it begins with a plan to nourish the church with a healthy diet from the Word of God.

The gospel is taught in our public assemblies and in Bible classes for all ages. We have missionary outreach around the world. Tapes and written materials from this congregation literally go around the world for the sake of making known the truth of the Word of God. One of the most effective things that has happened in our church life recently is the widespread commitment by hundreds of our members to small-group Bible study and interaction.

Our overseers have charged a member of our staff with coordinating the small groups. No one "controls" them or dictates what will happen in them. Each group is free to select its own material for study. No one attempts to monitor the groups to see that people think and say only what someone here wants said. The confidence of our elders is that the Holy Spirit will be active in these groups to nurture people and bring them where Christ wants each participant to be.

In order to encourage the groups to maintain their focus on Christ, the shepherds commissioned the church's ministry staff to prepare materials that could be used widely in the chuch. The outcome of this charge is in your hands in the form of a study guide for The Acts of the Apostles. This was preceded by a similar guide for the Gospel of Luke. Falling in Love with Jesus' People has been prepared with every member of the church in mind. Young and old, single and married, new convert and mature believer — all can benefit from its use.

Introduction

Acts of the Apostles has been studied carefully by Christians since it first became available in the early 60s of the Christian Era. It tells of the establishment and early growth of the church. It tells of individuals whose zeal for the Lord caused them to sacrifice on behalf of the gospel. Thus, whether focusing on a person (e.g., Peter, Paul) or a particular congregation of believers (e.g., Jerusalem, Antioch) or the general situation of the body of Christ, Acts is thrilling reading for anyone who wants to understand how God works in the world.

There are several legitimate ways to approach the study of Acts. The approach to be taken in this series is fully consistent with the original text and purpose of the book. It focuses on the building of community among the disciples of Jesus.

Falling in Love with Jesus is the theme we used for the study of the Gospel of Luke. Those lessons revealed Jesus as the Son of God, Son of Man, and Savior of All. *Falling in Love with Jesus' People* is the theme we will use in exploring Acts. We will watch God build a worldwide faith community of people more notable for their differences than their similarities. We will encounter Jews and Gentiles, peasants and Roman officials, males and females, prisoners and their jailers; all were taken by God and molded into the spiritual body of Christ in the world.

Our world is still remarkable for its differences and barriers. Economic, racial, educational, and other distinctions keep people isolated from one another. Yet God's announced intention is to bring all things in heaven and on earth together under one head, even Christ (Eph. 1:10b). As we study God's work of creating oneness among humankind in the first century, we should expect to gain insights into how he would like to work among us today.

Specific Objectives of This Study

As we invite the entire Family of God into a fresh study of Acts of the Apostles, we hope to facilitate several things. Here are at least four goals to keep in mind as we move through Luke's narrative of the early church.

♦ We want to build community among members of the church. Just as the first believers learned to love one another because of their mutual love for and commitment to Christ, we believe the best way to grow in our love for one another is to deepen our shared experience of Jesus. These notes will be most useful to those who work through them in small groups of believers who are seeking the Lord together and sharing their experiences along the way.

♦ Acts serves to ground the church in every generation. It reminds us of our theological roots and calls us anew to find our identity under the authority of Christ. Salvation is not only a personal experience to each believer. It is also a community experience that is learned and lived among others. The Acts holds that ideal before us.

♦ Acts is important to understanding the New Testament. One is simply not prepared to launch into a study of Romans, Hebrews, or Revelation without a mastery of the contents of this book. It is incredibly important, for example, to study the New Testament epistles against the time-line of events in Acts.

♦ Challenges abound to the people of God who study Acts. Too few Christians seem to feel the need to tell their unsaved neighbors about Jesus. Acts stirs hearts to evangelism. Some have not outgrown their national and racial prejudices. Acts forces us to see the church in larger dimensions than most of us have experienced. And almost all of us want our faith made easy and rewarding. But what about the struggle, persecution, and sacrifice demanded of those earliest saints? Do we have no share in them?

How to Use *Falling in Love with Jesus' People*

These notes must not be given priority over the text of the Bible itself. They are designed to encourage you to read Scripture and think deeply about its content. The notes are based on the New International Version, and all verses quoted directly from the text are from the NIV unless otherwise indicated. Whatever translation you are reading, feel free to underline key words and phrases, jot helpful notes in the margins, and otherwise personalize your study Bible.

The notes here will give you background to Acts, an outline of the book, historical data, and other helpful materials to make your reading of Luke's second volume on the history of early Christianity meaningful. Because he wrote in a language and culture so different from our own, the goal in these notes is to fill in the gaps on places, events, and terms so your reading will be more profitable.

The notes in this study guide avoid trying to draw conclusions for you about the meaning of what the Holy Spirit led Luke to record. That is your job.

You may choose to use these notes for personal study and quiet time with the Word of God. Here is a plan you might find helpful:

1. *Before beginning to read,* pray for God to cleanse your heart of anything that would keep you from receiving his instruction. Ask him to guide your reading to show you if there is (a) some sin you need to confess to him, (b) a promise for you to claim, (c) a command for you to obey, or (d) an example for you to imitate.

2. *As you start to read,* read the section of Acts for study that day aloud. Forming the words with your mouth and actually saying them impresses each one more deeply on your heart. Then read the suggested daily text (i.e., Day One, etc.) aloud.

3. *Reflect on the five questions* supplied for each day. These are issues for your personal reflection and will lead you to ask God how the material from Acts applies to your personal life. Here you will need to be introspective and honest about your spiritual life.

4. *End your quiet time with a prayer* that asks God to shape your life by the things you have just studied. Something may impress you powerfully later in the day or week and call this study time back to your consciousness, although you did not realize its significance in your few minutes of study. This is the work of the Holy Spirit in you.

5. [Optional] *You may want to keep a personal journal* of your thoughts, insights, or prayers that relate to this study. You could get either a loose-leaf notebook or spiral-bound notebook for your notes. These notes will trace your spiritual journey over several months.

Many of you will use *Falling in Love with Jesus' People* as a member of a small group that meets regularly. Ideally, these groups should have four to ten members. Keeping each group small allows everyone to participate and keeps it from becoming a lecture class. Small-group studies should be interactive and include everyone.

Each member of the group will find the suggestions outlined for personal study and quiet time ideal for daily preparation. Then, when the group meets, you may decide collectively how to use the study guide. You may review the block of text for that week or concentrate on one or two of the sets of questions for daily reflection. Here is a plan you may wish to try and then adapt to your group:

1. *As members of your group assemble*, greet each other warmly and move to your study location. It will be best to meet at the same time and place. Each person needs to commit to promptness so the group can use its time well.

2. *Ask someone to read aloud the entire text* that is being studied this time. This will focus everyone's thoughts on the same events and issues.

3. *Have someone lead a prayer* for the group to be open to God's voice. God speaks to his seeking children from Scripture, but our hearts must be prepared to hear him.

4. *Conduct your group study* by whatever method you choose. Either work through the verses that have been read or focus on one or more of the sets of reflection questions in the margins. Do not let one or two people dominate the study. The leader's task is to make sure everyone has the opportunity to join the discussion.

5. *Relate your personal experiences and questions* to the issues on the floor. Each group is to be a safe place where people can talk without fear of being set upon by others or having their confidence betrayed to people outside the group.

6. *Close with prayer*. Feel free to share special prayer needs with others in your group as they are called for. Pray about people and issues that have surfaced in the discussion time.

Additional Study Resources

If you wish to build your personal Bible study library and get useful tools that will help you in future study, here are a few recommendations that might be helpful.

The basic study tool everyone needs is a Bible dictionary. It provides an alphabetical index to the persons and places of the Bible. It also provides helpful data on key words and doctrines of the Bible. The best one-volume dictionaries on the market are *The New Bible Dictionary*, 2nd ed., edited by J.D. Douglas, et al. and published by Tyndale House Publishers and the *New Illustrated Bible Dictionary* edited by Ronald F. Youngblood and published by Nelson.

A Bible atlas is particularly helpful in the study of the Gospel of Acts. It provides maps, photographs, and other details that help you understand how the geography of Paul's travels and the early church affected what happened then. *The Rand McNally Bible Atlas*, edited by Emil G. Kraeling, is probably the best of its class. Less expensive but still very helpful is *The New Bible Atlas* by J.J. Bimson and J.P. Kane from Tyndale. *The Oxford Bible Atlas* (Oxford University Press) is also good.

If you wish to purchase a commentary, you might examine William Neil's volume on Acts in *The New Century Bible Commentary* (Grand Rapids: Eerdmans, 1988), William Larkin's *Acts* in the InterVarsity New Testament Commentary Series (Downers Grove, IL: InterVarsity, 1996), or Dennis Gaertner's *Acts* in the College Press NIV New Testament Commentary Series (Joplin, MO: College Press, 1995).

A Final Word

May God bless your study of Acts of the Apostles. As you witness it happen among first-century converts to Jesus, may it also happen in your Christian life that you find yourself falling more deeply in love with Christ and the people he has collected with you to be the Family of God at your church.

RUBEL

Outline

I. Prologue. 1:1-2.
II. The Establishment of the Church. 1:3–2:47.
  A. The events of preparation. 1:3-26.
    1. A summary of post-resurrection events. 1:3-5.
    2. Jesus' ascension. 1:6-11.
    3. Waiting at Jerusalem. 1:12-14.
    4. Matthias appointed to apostleship. 1:15-26.
      a. The fate of Judas. 1:15-20.
      b. Selecting his successor. 1:21-26.
  B. The events of fulfillment. 2:1-47.
    1. The arrival of the Holy Spirit. 2:1-4.
    2. The amazement and bewilderment of the crowd. 2:5-13.
    3. Peter's sermon concerning the Christ. 2:14-36.
      a. His response to the charge of drunkenness. 2:14-21.
      b. His affirmation about Jesus of Nazareth. 2:22-35.
      c. His conclusion. 2:36.
    4. The response to the gospel of Christ. 2:37-41.
    5. A general description of the life of the earliest Christians. 2:42-47.
III. Progress and Perils at Jerusalem. 3:1–8:3.
  A. The healing of a lame man. 3:1-10.
  B. Peter's sermon in Solomon's portico. 3:11-26.
    1. The incident of healing attributed to Jesus. 3:11-16.
    2. A call for faith in Jesus based on the prophets. 3:17-26.

Use this space for notes

11

1. A brief description of Simon and his past. 8:9-11.
2. His conversion and association with Philip. 8:12-13.
3. Peter and John visit Samaria. 8:14-24.
    a. They give the Holy Spirit by laying on of hands. 8:14-17.
    b. Simon the sorcerer's lapse. 8:18-19.
    c. His stern rebuke by Peter. 8:20-24.
4. Peter and John return to Jerusalem via many preaching stops in villages of the Samaritans. 8:25.

C. Philip and a man from Ethiopia. 8:26-39.
1. The two are brought together. 8:26-29.
2. Philip preaches Christ from an Old Testament text. 8:30-35.
3. The baptism of the Ethiopian. 8:36-39.

D. A final comment on Philip's activity. 8:40.

V. The Conversion of Saul of Tarsus. 9:1-31.

A. Events on the road to Damascus. 9:1-7.
1. The purpose of the journey. 9:1-2.
2. The journey interrupted by the Lord. 9:3-7.

B. Saul's three-day wait at Damascus. 9:8-9.

C. Ananias instructs and baptizes Saul. 9:10-19a.
1. Ananias' hesitation about going to Saul. 9:10-14.
2. An explanation of the situation by the Lord. 9:15-16.
3. Ananias' message and Saul's response. 9:17-19a.

D. Saul preaches at Damascus and arouses Jewish opposition. 9:19b-25.
1. His proclamation concerning Jesus. 9:19b-22.
2. His escape from a plot against his life. 9:23-25.

E. Saul's return to Jerusalem. 9:26-30.

1. Skepticism among the disciples. 9:26.
2. The gracious act of Barnabas. 9:27.
3. More bold preaching and more Jewish opposition. 9:28-29a.
4. Another plot against him and his escape. 9:29b-30.

    F. A further Lucan observation on the general status of the church. 9:31.

VI. An Enlargement of the Ministry of Peter. 9:32–11:18.

    A. The healing of Aeneas at Lydda. 9:32-35.

    B. The raising of Tabitha at Joppa. 9:36-43.
      1. A description of this good lady. 9:36.
      2. Her death and a summons to Peter. 9:37-38.
      3. Her return to life and the response to this miracle. 9:39-43.

    C. The conversion of Cornelius. 10:1-48.
      1. Background events which set the stage for a Gentile conversion. 10:1-16.
        a. Cornelius' vision. 10:1-8.
        b. Peter's vision. 10:9-16.
      2. Messengers from Cornelius are sent to bring Peter. 10:17-23a.
      3. Peter goes to the home of Cornelius. 10:23b-33.
      4. The gospel is preached to Gentiles for the first time. 10:34-43.
      5. The Holy Spirit poured out upon the Gentiles. 10:44-46a.
      6. Peter commands baptism in water for the Gentiles. 10:46b-48.

    D. Peter's report of Gentile conversions before the Jerusalem church. 11:1-18.
      1. Criticism from an element of the church. 11:1-3.
      2. His explanation and defense of the episode. 11:4-17.
      3. A positive reaction to his defense. 11:18.

VII. The Gospel Comes to Antioch. 11:19-30.
    A. Circumstances of the church's establishment at Antioch. 11:19-21.
    B. Barnabas and Saul at Antioch. 11:22-26.
        1. Barnabas sent by church at Jerusalem. 11:22-24.
        2. Secures the assistance of Saul. 11:25-26a.
        3. Their work together at Antioch. 11:26b.
    C. Famine relief to Judea through Barnabas and Saul. 11:27-30.
VIII.   Perils for the Saints from Herod. 12:1-24.
    A. Herod's violence against the church. 12:1-5.
        1. James murdered. 12:1-2.
        2. Peter arrested. 12:3-5.
    B. Peter's rescue from prison by a miracle. 12:6-19.
        1. His deliverance. 12:6-11.
        2. His report of it to certain of the saints. 12:12-17.
        3. Herod's punishment of Peter's guards. 12:18-19.
    C. The miserable death of Herod. 12:20-23.
    D. Another observation about the growth of the church. 12:24.
IX. The First Missionary Tour. 12:25–14:28.
    A. Barnabas and Saul set apart for a special work. 12:25–13:3.
        1. Their return from the relief mission to Judea. 12:25.
        2. The Holy Spirit makes the divine purpose known. 13:1-3.
    B. Preaching on Cyprus. 13:4-12.
        1. Their arrival and initial preaching in the synagogues. 13:4-5.
        2. Their encounter with a false prophet at Paphos. 13:6-12.
    C. Their ministry in Antioch of Pisidia. 13:13-52.

       1. John Mark leaves the company at Perga. 13:13.
       2. Paul's sermon in the synagogue at Antioch. 13:14-41.
       3. The interest created by the sermon. 13:42-43.
       4. Jewish jealousy and a turn to the Gentiles. 13:44-52.
    D. The work at Iconium. 14:1-7.
    E. Their work and persecution at Lystra. 14:8-20a.
       1. A miracle performed and an unfortunate response. 14:8-18.
       2. Paul stoned by his enemies. 14:19.
       3. His deliverance from death. 14:20a.
    F. The work in Derbe and a retracing of their route to Antioch in Syria. 14:20b-28.
       1. Encouraging the young churches. 14:20b-23.
       2. Preaching as they travel. 14:24-25.
       3. A report to the church at Antioch on their work. 14:26-28.
X. The Gathering at Jerusalem. 15:1-35.
    A. A threat to further missionary work among the Gentiles. 15:1-5.
       1. Troublesome teachers from Judea visit Antioch. 15:1-2.
       2. Paul and Barnabas go to Jerusalem over the question. 15:3-5.
    B. A speech by Peter. 15:6-11.
    C. Barnabas and Paul relate their experiences among the Gentiles. 15:12.
    D. The speech of James. 15:13-21.
    E. A letter written to the Gentile churches. 15:22-29.
    F. Reception of the letter by the church at Antioch. 15:30-35.
XI. The Second Missionary Tour. 15:36–18:22.

A. The proposal for the second tour. 15:36-39.
　1. The purpose of Paul. 15:36.
　2. A dispute between Paul and Barnabas separates them. 15:37-39.
B. Events in Asia Minor. 15:40–16:10.
　1. Paul and Silas begin the new effort. 15:40-41.
　2. Selection of Timothy as a co-worker. 16:1-4.
　3. Luke notes the continued progress of the church. 16:5.
　4. A vision and a new field of labor. 16:6-10.
C. The ministry in Macedonia. 16:11–17:15.
　1. The work at Philippi. 16:11-40.
　　a. The conversion of Lydia. 16:11-15.
　　b. Paul and Silas imprisoned after a miracle. 16:16-24.
　　c. The conversion of the jailer. 16:25-34.
　　d. Paul and Silas depart the city. 16:35-40.
　2. The work at Thessalonica. 17:1-9.
　　a. Conversions. 17:1-4.
　　b. Difficulties. 17:5-9.
　3. The work at Berea. 17:10-15.
D. The ministry in Greece. 17:16–18:17.
　1. The events in Athens. 17:16-34.
　　a. Paul's daily argumentation with the people. 17:16-21.
　　b. His sermon before the Areopagus. 17:22-34.
　2. The events at Corinth. 18:1-17.
　　a. His arrival and association with Aquila and Priscilla. 18:1-4.
　　b. An eighteen-month period of teaching the gospel. 18:5-11.
　　c. Paul brought before Gallio. 18:12-17.
E. The return to Antioch of Syria. 18:18-22.
XII. The Third Missionary Tour. 18:23–21:16.
A. Strengthening the disciples of Galatia and Phrygia. 18:23.

1. He receives permission to speak. 21:37-40.
2. He relates his background and conversion to the people. 22:1-16.
3. He tells of his commission to preach to Gentiles. 22:17-21.
4. The crowd again enraged and Paul rescued by his captors. 22:22-29.

D. Paul examined before the Sanhedrin. 22:30–23:10.
E. A communication from the Lord. 23:11.
F. A plot against Paul's life is thwarted. 23:12-30.
1. The scheme formulated. 23:12-15.
2. The plan found out and told to Paul's captors. 23:16-22.
3. Preparation for Paul's safe conduct to Caesarea. 23:23-30.

XIV. Paul a Prisoner at Caesarea. 23:31–26:32.
A. Paul's delivery to Caesarea under Roman guard. 23:31-35.
B. Paul before Felix. 24:1-27.
1. The accusations made against him. 24:1-9.
2. His defense. 24:10-21.
3. Felix discontinues the case. 24:22-23.
4. Another interview before Felix. 24:24-26.
5. Festus succeeds Felix with no disposal of Paul's case. 24:27.
C. Paul and Festus. 25:1-12.
1. Festus visits Jerusalem and hears charges against Paul. 25:1-5.
2. Festus returns to Caesarea and examines Paul. 25:6-9.
3. Paul appeals to Caesar. 25:10-12.
D. Paul and Agrippa. 25:13–26:32.
1. Agrippa and Bernice visit Festus and learn of Paul's case. 25:13-22.
2. Paul brought before Agrippa. 25:23-37.
3. Paul's defense and presentation of the gospel. 26:1-29.

a. His address to the group. 26:1-23.

b. Some personal exchanges. 26:24-29.

4. Private reaction of Roman officials to Paul's defense. 26:30-32.

XV. The Prisoner's Journey to Rome. 27:1–28:10.

A. Initial incidents of the voyage. 27:1-8.

B. Paul's counsel to the men in charge. 27:9-12.

C. The storm at sea. 27:13-38.

1. The ship in a violent storm. 27:13-20.

2. Paul encourages the men aboard the ship. 27:21-26.

3. The ship approaches land. 27:27-32.

4. More encouragement from Paul. 27:33-38.

D. The shipwreck. 27:39-44.

1. The vessel runs aground and breaks up. 27:39-41.

2. All the ship's passengers escape to land. 27:42-44.

E. The time spent at Malta. 28:1-10.

1. The group is warmly received. 28:1-2.

2. Paul is bitten by a viper. 28:3-6.

3. Numerous healings at the hand of Paul. 28:7-10.

XVI. The Prisoner's Arrival at Rome. 28:11-31.

A. Arrival and reception by the disciples. 28:11-15.

B. Paul's situation under a Roman guard. 28:16.

C. An initial meeting with Jews at Rome. 28:17-22.

D. Great numbers of the Jews hear Paul again. 28:23-29.

E. The progress of the gospel at Rome during Paul's two-year imprisonment. 28:30-31.

Week One

Introduction to the Gospel;
Acts 1:1-2 (Point I of outline)

Whether tracing the general situation of the body of Christ, describing a church in a particular city, or telling the story of a particular believer, Acts is thrilling reading. It shows how people who had fallen in love with Jesus lived the meaning of that love among themselves. It tells how believers in community with one another evangelized the world, challenged one another to faithfulness to their common calling, and stood together against the forces of Satan set against them.

Literary Genre: What Is a *Praxeis*?

"The Acts of the Apostles" is the name traditionally given to the second volume of a two-book set that tells how Christianity began. Volume One relates the coming of a Redeemer who died for sin, rose in triumph over death, and looks to the time when all people could share in the salvation he had purchased with his own blood. Volume Two takes up the narrative at this point and shows how the gospel went from Jerusalem to Antioch to Rome in approximately 30 years through the ministry of Jesus' apostles. It is even possible to outline the book in light of Acts 1:8. "You will be my witnesses in Jerusalem (Acts 1:1–8:3), and in all Judea and Samaria (Acts 8:4 11:18), and to the ends of the earth (Acts 11:19–28:31)."

The two books by an early church historian are properly regarded as companion volumes. The Luke-Acts materials originally circulated as one complete writing.

In the late first or early second century, the first

Day 1
Daily Time with God's Word

Read Psalm 119:97-112 for an affirmation of love for the Word of God.

1. What method do you use to stay in the Word of God regularly?
2. What difference does daily time with Scripture make in your life? What happens when you neglect it?
3. How do you expect this study of Acts to assist you in going deeper into the Word of God?
4. Summarize David's statements about God's precepts from Psalm 119:97ff.
5. Write a prayer for God to give you the discipline to spend daily time with him.

Use this space for your own notes

Day 2
Acts of the Apostles

Read Luke 1:1-4 to help you remember Luke's purpose in writing his previous volume.

1. Why is Acts an important book to the total NT message?
2. What sources did Luke use to write Luke and Acts?
3. Discuss the title of this book. What title would you suggest for it?
4. Why do you think Luke wanted to write this book as a follow-up to his Gospel?
5. React to this possibility for a title: Acts of the Holy Spirit.

Day 3
Dr. Luke

Read 2 Corinthians 12:1-10 about Paul's bodily ailment and its impact.

1. Summarize what the NT tells us about Luke.
2. What is the picture you get of the man from this information?
3. Why do you think Luke attached himself to Paul?
4. Have you ever seen anyone sacrifice his or

volume of the Luke-Acts materials became associated with the writings of Matthew, Mark, and John. Thus we are accustomed to speak of the "fourfold Gospels." When the separation of our materials took place, the second volume received its present title.

The word "acts" (*praxeis*) refers to movements, heroic exploits, and defining events. It is appropriate as a designation of the book which tells of the gospel's *movement* from Judea to Antioch to Rome, the *heroic exploits* of the apostles and evangelists of the early church, and the *defining events* of the believing community's early life.

There is a problem with the traditional title "*The Acts of the Apostles*." Obviously the book doesn't tell all the acts of any one apostle. Much less does it tell all the acts of all the apostles. It doesn't even tell some of the acts of all the apostles. Peter and Paul are the primary apostolic figures of the book, with occasional references to perhaps three others within the group. A more precise title then would be "*Some of the Acts of Some of the Apostles.*"

"Acts of the Apostles" is probably the best way to title the book, and this is the designation assumed throughout these notes. More commonly still, the book's title is shortened simply to "Acts."

Authorship of Acts of the Apostles

In view of the fact that Acts of the Apostles is an unsigned document — as is its companion Gospel — how may we have confidence that we know the identity of its author?

First, the external evidence from early Christian writers uniformly refers to Luke as the writer of the Luke-Acts material. The Anti-Marcionite Prologues (c. 160-180) attribute both books to Luke. The same source also says that he was a native of Antioch, that he was a physician, and that he died unmarried and childless at the age of 84. The Muratorian Fragment (i.e., a list of books accepted as part of the NT canon by Christians around Rome in the period 170-190) also attributes both volumes to Luke.

Irenaeus [I-rĭ-nē´-əs] of Lyons (died c. 202) and Clement of Alexandria (died c. 212) both explicitly name Luke as the author of Acts. Tertullian [Tər-tŭl´-yən] (died c. 220), Origen [Or´-ĭ-jən] (died 253/254), Eusebius [Yo͞o-sē´-bē-əs] (died 339/340), Jerome (died 419/420), and many others bear witness to the same. In fact, no writers during the first few centuries of the Christian era challenged Lucan authorship or posited a rival suggestion for the third Gospel and Acts.

Luke was not a person of great notoriety and prominence in the early church. If people were merely guessing at the authorship of Acts, could so large and important a section of the New Testament materials be universally attributed to him without good reason? The external evidence of Luke's authorship is very credible.

Second, the internal evidence concerning authorship points directly to Luke. That the man who wrote Acts of the Apostles was a traveling partner and co-worker with Paul is evident from what are called the "we-sections" of the volume. The writer shifts from third-person narrative (i.e., "he" or "they") to a very interesting first-person plural (i.e., "we") in three sections of the book — 16:10-17, 20:5–21:18, and 27:1–28:16. The most obvious and reasonable explanation for this phenomenon is that the writer is incorporating eyewitness materials from a personal travel diary in these places.

These three sections reveal the following pattern of events. The first tells how the author joined Paul, Silas, and Timothy at Troas [Trō´-ăs] on the second missionary tour [note: some have conjectured that he may have been the man Paul saw in his dream, cf. 16:9] and remained at Philippi to continue the work

her career and personal freedom to minister to another person? To serve the Lord?

5. How did Luke's personal experiences with Paul qualify him to write Acts?

when the Pauline party left. The second tells how he rejoined the group when they came back through Philippi on the third tour and went with them to Jerusalem where Paul was arrested. The third has the author joining Paul at Caesarea [Sĕ-sə-rē´-ə] and staying with him throughout the perilous journey to Rome. The vocabulary and writing style of these sections are indistinguishable from those of the remainder of Acts. The third-person and first-person narratives are clearly from the same pen.

By a process of elimination, the evidence of the "we-sections" brings one to Luke. Luke 1:1-4 clearly implies that the writer of Luke-Acts was not an eyewitness to the life of Christ. This fact alone eliminates all the apostles and several others. Next, by excluding all those associates of Paul who are mentioned as distinct from the writer in the "we-sections," Silas, Timothy, Tychicus [Tĭkh´-ĭ-kŭs], Trophimus [Trŏf´-ĭ-mŭs], and a few others are ruled out. Finally, there is the fact that the writer of Acts was with Paul at Rome during the apostle's first imprisonment there. Since there is no evidence that Luke was an eyewitness to the life of Christ, he is not named in the "we-sections," and he was at Rome during Paul's house arrest there (Col. 4:14; Phlm. 24), he is the best candidate for authorship.

Additional factors favoring Lucan authorship from the writer's medical interest will be noted later. To say the very least, the burden of proof is on anyone who would deny the traditional view that Luke wrote the third Gospel and Acts of the Apostles.

New Testament Information about Luke

Luke is named only three times in the New Testament. From Colossians 4:10-14, we learn that he was a Gentile physician. In Philemon 23-24, he is referenced by Paul during his Roman imprisonment (A.D. 60–62) as one of "my fellow-workers." Then,

---

Day 4
Along for the Ride

Read Paul's reference to Luke at Colossians 4:7-18.

1. What are the so-called "we-sections" of Acts?
2. What is the importance of the "we-sections"?
3. When you travel, do you keep a diary or journal? Why do you think Luke kept one?
4. How do you see Luke contributing to Paul's evangelistic work?
5. What are some important "support roles" in Christian ministry today? How difficult is it to get those roles filled in most churches?

when 2 Timothy 4:11 was written, Paul was in prison at Rome for a second time. This jailing would not end as the first one had in freedom but in the apostle's execution under Nero. During these final days, Paul wrote Timothy and said, "Only Luke is with me."

Luke was the only New Testament writer who was a non-Jew. That he was a trusted and competent fellow-worker to Paul is evident from the close association they had in the "we-sections" of Acts. And Paul's tender reference to him as "the *beloved* physician" in Colossians forces us to suspect that Luke ministered to Paul's health problems. With his "thorn in the flesh" (2 Cor. 12:7-10), our physician-writer may have felt a particular attachment and obligation to the Apostle to the Gentiles.

That Luke was a physician also raises the matter of an alleged medical vocabulary in the third Gospel and Acts. In 1882 W.K. Hobart published *The Medical Language of St. Luke* and argued the case for Lucan authorship was supported strongly by the presence of language that a physician might have been expected to use. The same thesis was advanced a bit more cautiously by Adolf Harnack (*Luke the Physician*, 1907). It would be claiming too much to say that Lucan authorship can be proved by such an argument. At the very least, however, there is nothing inconsistent with the view that the author of Luke-Acts was a physician.

Purposes Served by Acts of the Apostles

Acts of the Apostles was written for a reason. In fact, it seems to serve several purposes in the New Testament canon.

First, Luke explicitly affirms his sense of need to commit to writing the events involved in the beginning and spread of Christianity at Luke 1:1-4. Acts 1:1 links this volume with the Gospel (i.e., "my former book") and implicitly renews the author's

Day 5
A Few Faithful Friends

Read Proverbs 17:17 and 18:24 for biblical comments about friendship.

1. Luke was clearly a faithful friend to Paul. Name three or four other famous friendships from the Bible.
2. What is the value of Christian friendship to the development of faith and character?
3. Who is your best friend? Why?
4. Is there someone who would call you his or her best friend? Explain your relationship.
5. Someone has said: "The best anyone can hope for in this life is to make a few faithful friends among the many people to cross his or her path in a lifetime." React to this statement.

purpose of writing "in order" (*kathexes* = in sequence, whether chronological or topical) concerning the basic facts of the Christian religion.

Both Luke and Acts are addressed to "Theophilus" [Thē-ä´-fī-ləs] (Luke 1:3; Acts 1:1). The name means "Lover of God" and may be a symbolic reference to all those Gentiles who would be willing to read Luke's presentation of the basic facts about Jesus and the church. That he is given the title "most excellent" (*kratistos* = a designation used in Acts to indicate a person of rank or official status, cf. 23:26; 24:3; 26:25) at Luke 1:3 makes it more likely that the Gospel was written to a man of substance who was not yet a convert to Christ. The absence of an honorific title in Acts 1:1 has been taken by some to imply that he had become a believer in the interval between the writing of the two volumes.

Second, Acts is designed to show the universality of the new Christian faith. This is certainly consistent with a major motif in his Gospel. It carefully traces the spread of the gospel from an exclusively Jewish period in the first seven chapters of Acts through its spread to the Samaritans in chapter eight and to the Gentiles in chapter 10. The Antioch church and its missionaries receive special attention.

Third, many students of Acts of the apostles believe they see an apologetic motive behind the writing of the book.

Were Jews hostile to Christianity? Luke is careful to show the relationship between the two religions. Christianity is not a repudiation of or an attack against the Law and its institutions. Stephen's long speech at Jerusalem (7:1ff) argues this point in detail. The gathering at Jerusalem (15:1ff) stresses it again.

Were officials of the Roman Empire worried about this new movement? Luke stresses that the church is neither a political rival to Rome nor the source of unrest in the empire. While certain people have instigated uproars involving Christians (e.g., the mob that attacked Paul at Jerusalem, 21:27ff), the followers of Christ were not behind such events. Furthermore, Luke tends either to state explicitly (e.g., Gallio, 18:12-17) or to imply (e.g., Festus, 25:14-21) the fairness of Roman authorities toward the Christians. Some have suggested that Acts might have served as a "defense brief" for Paul's trial at Rome.

Fourth, Acts shows the triumph of the gospel in a hostile world. God purposed to save mankind through Christ, and this book tells how that purpose was being worked out in human history regardless of unbelief among many and the opposition of some. A reader of Acts can hardly fail to notice Luke's periodic progress reports on the spread of the Word of God (2:47b; 6:7; 9:31; 12:24; 16:5; 19:20; 28:30-31).

I. Prologue. 1:1-2.

Luke ties together the third Gospel and the present volume in the opening two verses of Acts of the Apostles. In the former book, he had written Theophilus (cf. "Purposes Served by Acts of the Apostles") about the things Jesus "began to do and to teach until the day he was taken up to heaven." In this book, he shows how this redeeming ministry was continued in the power of the Holy Spirit through "the apostles [Jesus] had chosen."

Week Two

Acts 1:3-14 (II A 1 to II A 3 in Outline)

Day 1
The Resurrection

Read Luke 23:50–24:12 for an account of the Lord Jesus' resurrection.

1. What sort of "convincing proofs" did Jesus provide about his resurrection?
2. Why do you think Luke ended his Gospel and opened Acts with the same event?
3. How central is the doctrine of the resurrection to Christian faith? Why is it so critical?
4. What does the word "ascension" mean? How are Christ's resurrection and ascension linked together?
5. What perspective on Christ's return to heaven does Dan.7:13-14 provide you?

II. The Establishment of the Church. 1:3–2:47.

The first two chapters of Acts tell the story of the coming of the Holy Spirit and the establishment of the church. They set the stage for all that follows in Luke's account of the events following on Christ's ascension and the coming of the Holy Spirit.

During his personal ministry, Jesus had promised an inbreaking of the kingdom of God during the lifetime of his contemporaries. "I tell you the truth, some who are standing here will not taste death before they see the kingdom of God," he had said (Luke 9:27). Yet the Savior's earthly life and ministry ended with that event still in anticipation. It is Luke who tells us that Joseph of Arimathea [Ar-ĭ-mə-thē´-ə] was still "waiting for the kingdom of God" when he received permission from Pilate to remove Jesus' body from the cross for burial in his own new tomb (Luke 23:50-53).

The waiting ends in the opening paragraphs of Acts. The first Pentecost Day following the resurrection of Christ became the birthday of the church.

A. The Events of Preparation. 1:3-26.

1. A summary of post-resurrection events. 1:3-5.

Luke begins his second volume on the history of early Christianity with a reference to the death and resurrection of Christ. The resurrection of Jesus from the dead will be the primary message of the apostles and evangelists in the pages to follow, so it is only right that the book should begin with a reference to it. There is no better-attested fact of ancient history than the resurrection. Everything involved in the Christian faith is joined together by this keystone doctrine. It is no myth projected backward onto Jesus; it is the solid fact that reassembled his dispirited followers, emboldened them to the point that they would henceforth be willing to die for Jesus, and provided them the substance of the gospel message they would take to the whole world.

There can be no doubt of the reality of the bodily resurrection of the Son of God, for Jesus "showed himself to [the apostles] and gave many convincing proofs that he was alive." Only Luke informs us that these appearances took place "over a period of forty days." The subject matter of Jesus' conversations with the apostles focused on "the kingdom of God."

Luke makes no attempt in the opening verses of Acts to catalog the various times when Jesus showed himself to humans during the interval between his resurrection and ascension. For his purposes in setting the stage for what will be chronicled in Acts, he summarizes the post-resurrection events in only a few words. He is particularly interested in only one of those occasions — the final one. That appearance took place on the Mount of Olives, just outside Jerusalem in the direction of Bethany (cf. Luke 24:33-53).

In his various meetings with his apostles over a forty-day period, Jesus "opened their minds so they could understand the Scriptures" (Luke 24:45). With their minds enlightened with insight and their hearts burning with passion for their risen Lord, the apostles must have been chomping at the bit to tell what they knew. Travel plans for getting back to Galilee as soon as possible may have been forming in their heads when they heard Jesus say, "Wait!"

"Do not leave Jerusalem," Jesus told his chosen ones, "but wait for the gift my Father promised, which you have heard me speak about. For John

Day 2
Do You Understand God's Ways?

1. What question did the apostles ask Jesus in their last visit with him?

2. What do you think they had in mind? Did they understand the true nature of the kingdom?

3. How did Jesus respond? Explain his reaction.

4. Was it necessary for them to understand

God's ways? The nature of the kingdom?

5. What work of God or biblical doctrine causes you the greatest perplexity? Does your lack of understanding limit God in any way?

baptized with water, but in a few days you will be baptized with the Holy Spirit." The Father had promised (Joel 2:28), John the Baptist had repeated (Matt. 3:11), and Jesus himself had affirmed (John 14:16-17) that the Holy Spirit would come to teach and empower God's people. So great a task lay before the apostles that they would need the Spirit's presence and strength to enable them to carry out their task of evangelizing the Roman Empire.

2. Jesus' ascension. 1:6-11.

In what would turn out to be his final time with the apostles on Earth, Jesus was with them on the Mount of Olives (cf. 1:12). With the group assembled, someone spoke for the group and asked him, "Lord, are you at this time going to restore the kingdom to Israel?" With all the explanation of the Law and Prophets they had been given over the past six weeks, the apostles were still thinking of the kingdom of God in narrow, material terms. They were still envisioning a Jewish kingdom, and they were still thinking in terms of the glories of David and Solomon. It still awaited the coming of the Holy Spirit before they would grasp that the kingdom (i.e., sovereign rule) of God would be offered to Gentiles and Jews alike.

Jesus did not rebuke their lingering wrong impressions. He simply said that it was not for them to "know the times or dates the Father has set by his own authority." In other words, it was not important for them to figure out the timing or, at this point at least, even the nature of the kingdom of God. It was their duty simply to wait for the coming of the Holy Spirit and to be open to his leading. In the New Testament's fourth record of what we call the Great Commission, Luke summarizes Jesus' final instructions to his apostles in these words: "But you will receive power when the Holy Spirit comes on you; and you will be my witnesses in Jerusalem, and in all

Judea and Samaria, and to the ends of the earth."

At this point in the New Testament's only narrative account of the ascension, Jesus disappeared from the apostles' view for the final time. "After he said this, he was taken up (i.e., enveloped) before their very eyes, and a cloud hid him from their sight." In the Old Testament, the majesty and glory of God were represented among the people by the cloud that accompanied Israel during the wilderness wanderings (Exod. 40:38). Called the *shekinah*, it was a visible manifestation of God's presence and approval. Upon being enveloped in the shekinah cloud, Jesus was received into the glory he had prior to his incarnation for our sakes (cf. John 17:5).

Referring back to Luke's Gospel, the detail is added that Jesus "lifted up his hands and blessed them" as he disappeared from their view (Luke 24:50b). There is a sense of finality about this departure that the apostles sensed. It was not merely that he disappeared briefly as before during the forty days. He had gone from the sight of the apostles until his appearance in triumph at the end of time. Yet, if there was a note of finality and sadness among the apostles as they viewed his departure from Earth, there must have been a chorus of cheers as that same event was witnessed from heaven. The eternal Word who had emptied himself to become flesh was returning to his home and to a great coronation scene (cf. Dan. 7:13-14).

The apostles stood staring after their Lord. They caught no further glimpse of him, but they did see "two men dressed in white." These heavenly messengers (cf. Matt. 28:3), promised that Jesus would come again. They did not specify the time of that return, for angels do not know the day or hour of it (Matt. 24:36). However, they did assure the apostles, "This same Jesus, who has been taken from you into heaven, will come back in the same way you have

Day 3
Keeping Promises

Read Hebrews 10:19-39 about the faithfulness of God.

1. Give some biblical examples of promises that God has kept.
2. Human *faith* is grounded in divine *faithfulness*. Explain.
3. In Acts 1, what promise did Jesus give the apostles about the Holy Spirit?
4. Did the apostles understand the promise? Did their lack of understanding keep Jesus from honoring his word to them?
5. How important is promise-keeping to you? Is your word dependable?

Day 4
He's Coming Back!

Read John 14:1-14 for a personal promise of his return from Jesus' lips.

1. What is the significance of Jesus' being received into a cloud?
2. When Jesus disappeared from the apos-

31

tles' view, who appeared to them?

3. What message did they deliver?

4. Explain why it was important for the apostles to know Jesus would return. For you to know it.

5. What difference does the knowledge of Christ's Second Coming make in your daily life?

Day 5
Waiting

Read Psalm 27 and pay particular attention to verse 14.

1. What commandment about "waiting" did Jesus give his apostles?

2. Why did he order them to wait about telling what they knew?

3. Do you think it was hard for them to obey this order? Explain.

4. Have you ever acted prematurely in some important matter? Failed to wait for God's timing?

5. Is there some important issue in your life that is tempting you to impatience today? How is God helping you to wait for his timing in the matter?

seen him go into heaven." In other words, his Second Coming will be visible, bodily, and glorious.

The apostles apparently took great comfort in the assurance of Jesus' return. In addition, they had the promise of the Holy Spirit to anticipate and a mission of worldwide witness to fulfill. Thus they went back to the city not in despair but "with great joy" (Luke 24:52), spending at least a part of their waiting time "at the temple, praising God" (Luke 24:53).

The apostles were now without the presence of their leader for the first time since the beginning of his personal ministry over three years before. Only a few days would pass between the ascension of Jesus and the descent of the Holy Spirit. These days would be spent in eager waiting and expectant prayer.

3. Waiting at Jerusalem. 1:12-14.

The apostles retraced their path into Jerusalem. The trip was a short one of just over a half mile (i.e., "a Sabbath day's walk") from the Mount of Olives to the upstairs room where they were staying. This may have been the same upper room where Jesus was with the apostles the night before his death (cf. Luke 22:12), but we cannot be certain.

What we do know about the time of waiting until Pentecost Day is that it was a time of obedience, close fellowship, and prayer. The group was in Jerusalem only because of the command of Jesus for them to wait there. Their commitment to be obedient to their Lord now outweighed their fear of danger at the hands of the same people who had put him to death. Their fellowship in his absence was distinctly focused around thoughts of Jesus and anticipation of the future he had in store for them. Both in their upstairs room and in the larger temple precincts where they spent their time, they were in continual prayer to God.

Even prior to seeing the church take life in Acts 2, believers today should see a model for our life together. The obedience of faith, loving fellowship, and believing prayer are the hallmark qualities of kingdom life. These three traits must be present among us if we are to recognize and benefit from the promise of the Holy Spirit in our lives. They are the foundation of ministry and evangelism. Perhaps the powerlessness of many Christians can be traced to their absence.

Luke gives a list of the names of the apostles (cf. Matt. 10:2-4; Mark 3:16-19), and there is a glaring omission. The name missing from the original list of The Twelve is Judas Iscariot. He had vacated his office by apostasy, and Luke will shortly tell of the selection of someone to take his place.

In addition to the apostles, Luke informs us that certain other believers were joined with the apostles in prayer. These included "the women" (likely Mary Magdalene, Joanna, Susanna, and others who followed Jesus' ministry closely, cf. Luke 8:2-3), "Mary the mother of Jesus," and "his brothers" (James, Joses, Judas, and Simon, Mark 6:3). Interestingly, Jesus' four brothers had refused to accept his messianic claims prior to the resurrection (John 7:5). But the resurrection had convinced his half-brothers of his divine nature and rights. It made them willing participants in the worship of Jesus as Lord.

A single event — the resurrection — molded the apostles into a solid band of loyal followers, convinced Jesus' brothers of his true identity, and set the stage for the coming of the Holy Spirit. It remains the defining event of the Christian faith for all who embrace it with authenticity.

Week Three

Acts 1:15-26 (II A 4 in Outline)

Day 1
The Apostles

Read Matthew 10:1-16 about the selection of The Twelve.

1. Can you name the apostles from memory? How many appear in the Acts narrative?

2. Which apostle do you admire most? Identify with?

3. What was the nature of the apostolic ministry?

4. Do we need apostles today? Explain your answer.

4. Matthias appointed to apostleship. 1:15-26.

During the ten days of waiting between Jesus' ascension and the arrival of the Holy Spirit on Pentecost, there was one notable event that has no New Testament parallel. A successor was chosen for the apostolic office vacated by Judas. Approximately fifteen years after this, for example, James the son of Zebedee will be executed by Herod Agrippa I (cf. 12:1-2). But there will be no account of someone being selected to fill his office. Why the difference between the two situations? The answer to our question seems to come in two parts: (1) the significance of a twelvefold witness for the early Jewish church and (2) the nature of the apostolic work.

First, the New Testament consistently presents Christianity as an extension and fulfillment of the Abrahamic promise. Nowhere does either Jesus or any evangelist of the early church repudiate the Law of Moses and the messianic hope of Israel. To the contrary, the church was seen as the outcome of both. The motif of "fulfillment" is used throughout the New Testament to describe not only the personal activities of Jesus of Nazareth but the corporate life of his church. Justification for the choosing of a replacement for Judas is sought by Peter in citing Old Testament texts (1:20; cf. Psa. 69:25; 109:8). Jesus had promised that in the great messianic feast the apostles would "sit on thrones, judging the twelve tribes of Israel" (Luke 22:30). Indeed, the first-century church saw itself as the Israel of God (Gal. 6:16). For the apostles to represent themselves to fellow-Jews as the fulfillment of Israel's hope, they saw an implicit need to bring their number back to twelve.

Second, by the time of the death of James in A.D. 44, the primary work of the apostles was finished and no successor would be needed. As will be seen from the text of Acts 1, the fundamental requirements for Judas' replacement had nothing to do with administrative skills or church government. The apostolic role was to bear witness to the resurrection of Jesus from the dead and to ground the gospel message of repentance and faith in that attestation. The apostles were not an ecclesiastical body but a witnessing nucleus around whose testimony the church would form. The church is "built on the foundation of the apostles and prophets, with Christ Jesus himself as the chief cornerstone" (Eph. 2:20). The foundation of apostolic witness was already well in place by the time of the death of James, so no suggestion of a replacement for him was forthcoming at his death.

a. The fate of Judas. 1:15-20.

Peter, as was his custom, took the lead among the group — a group that included for this purpose not only the eleven remaining apostles but a larger group of disciples that numbered approximately 120. He saw what Judas had done when he "served as guide for those who arrested Jesus" as a fulfillment of Old Testament prophecy. Specifically, he cited two Davidic psalms. From Psalm 69:25, he found a reference to enemies who turned against King David and deserted their place at his table. From Psalm 109:8, he cited a text about the desirability of an evil man's place being taken by a good man. Putting the two passages together, he urged the 120 to select someone to replace Judas.

The verses Peter cited are not messianic predictions and had not been understood as such by either the rabbis or the disciples prior to Jesus' betrayal and death. In typical Jewish hermeneutical style, the apostle cited texts that contain principles he saw being played out in the events surrounding him and his colleagues. Interestingly, Psalm 69:25 points explicitly to leaving the traitor's place vacant. A second text had to be produced to propose the selection of a twelfth person to fill out the ranks of the apostles.

Day 2
Hearing God

Read John 8:31-47 and pay attention to the issue of listening to God.

1. What is the primary means by which God speaks to his people today?
2. Anything we suspect God is saying to us must be examined in light of Scripture. What other means does God use to speak to people?
3. What is the role of the Holy Spirit in communicating with persons in Acts? Today?
4. Can you recall a situation in which God revealed his will to you in a particularly emphatic way?
5. How does God speak to us through the living community of Jesus' people, the church?

We must be careful in developing our own hermeneutical rules not to come up with such rigid principles that we disallow apostolic interpretations. One could have argued with Peter that his use of Psalm 69 "clearly implies" the necessity of leaving Judas' office vacant and unfilled. But neither Peter nor his brothers and sisters present that day were committed to such rigidity. They informed and guided their actions by the total body of Scripture they knew and proceeded in good faith to search for a replacement.

With a two-verse parenthesis (i.e., 1:18-19), Luke interrupts his narrative of the proceedings at hand to let his readers know what had become of Judas after the betrayal event. The information he gives creates some confusion and has been used by some of the Bible's critics to show how inconsistent and contradictory some of the scriptural record is. In Matthew 27:3-10, we are told that Judas was "seized with remorse," returned the 30 silver coins he had been paid to betray Jesus to the Sanhedrin, and "went away and hanged himself." The Sanhedrin then took the money and bought a potter's field that was henceforth used as a burial site. Yet Luke says "Judas bought a field" in which "he fell headlong, his body burst open and all his intestines spilled out." Both Matthew and Luke say the field was known to everyone in Jerusalem as "Field of Blood" and that "foreigners" were buried there.

The difficulties with these accounts are similar to those we encounter with the Gospel narratives of the resurrection or the three accounts of the conversion of Saul of Tarsus in Acts (9, 16, 22). Negative critics of the Bible see contradictions whenever the narratives vary. (On the other hand, they are quick to allege artificial harmonizations when the language is very similar or identical. You just can't win with some people!) Conservative scholars incline to what is sometimes called the "principle of charity" and insist that a genuine contradiction exists only where harmonization is impossible.

Taking the latter view of things, the following sequence of events emerges as the most likely: (1) Judas was grieved beyond the possibility of being comforted when he saw the events he had set in motion leading to Jesus' death, (2) he went back to the Jewish authorities and returned the money they had paid him, (3) he committed suicide by hanging himself, (4) the unclaimed body fell from its makeshift gallows into a potter's field, (5) the decomposing body burst from the impact of the fall, (6) the owner of the potter's field sold it to the authorities for 30 pieces of silver [note: since blood money could not be put back into the sacred treasury, the field technically belonged to Judas and his heirs!] (7) the field came to be known as the Field of Blood for the twofold reason that it was both bought by blood money and defiled with the blood of the traitor Judas, and (8) the field was used as a burial place for the unclaimed bodies of strangers who died in Jerusalem.

Suicide is a tragic thing in any setting, whether ancient or modern. Because it was regarded as such a morally hateful thing by the Jews, Matthew would have needed to tell no more than he did to communicate to his readers that Judas came to an awful end. The Greek view of suicide was very different, however. They viewed it as a morally neutral event, and some ancient writers — including Plato — recom-

Day 3
Suicide

Read the account of Judas's death at Matthew 27:1-10.

1. In your opinion, why has the suicide rate jumped in the past several years?
2. Have you followed the

recent discussions of euthanasia and physician-assisted suicide? What is your reaction?

3. Do you distinguish between a suicide of rational choice (i.e., Judas) and suicides of despair? Explain your view.

4. What contribution can the church make to the ongoing discussion of these issues?

5. The study notes say: "Compassionate care and support for the sick or despairing within a community of people who love Christ and one another is the Christian alternative to The Hemlock Society." What is your reaction to that statement?

mended it under certain circumstances as a noble alternative to burdening one's family or larger community. In order for the Gentile Luke to convey the appalling nature of Judas' fate to his Gentile readers, he added details of the suicide that would produce the same basic negative reaction among his readers that Matthew's terse account would among his.

Most of us likely believe that suicide is a highly complex issue to be approached with appropriate humility. Many would hold that suicide is not necessarily a "mortal sin," for it most often happens when someone suffering severe emotional or physical pain goes over the edge to despair. The impaired thinking and desperate behaviors of such persons are very different from something urged or approved for rational people. The modern right-to-die movement that advocates personal or physician-assisted suicides crosses a line that horrifies Christians. Compassionate care and support for the sick or despairing within a community of people who love Christ and one another is the Christian alternative to The Hemlock Society. In the case of despair brought on by sin, Peter embraced the alternative of confession and forgiveness that Judas refused. The rational choice of suicide has moral implications that suicide under thinking-impaired situations does not. In this case of suicide, at least, Peter had no doubt that Judas "left [the apostolic ministry] to go where he belongs" (1:25) — a euphemism for going to hell.

b. Selecting his successor. 1:21-26.

There were two qualifications potential candidates had to meet. First, he had to have had unhindered and frequent access to Jesus during the period of the Messiah's earthly ministry. Second, he had to have been a "witness with us of his resurrection." These two qualifications point to the real task of an apostle. He was an eyewitness guarantor for the gospel message.

On the basis of their own powers of reason and judgment, the 120 could look among themselves to determine who among them best satisfied the basic requirements of the apostleship. They came up with two candidates and advanced their names. Either of them was apparently fit to fill the role. The men were "Joseph called Barsabbas (also known as Justus) and Matthias." Moving beyond their own powers of reason and judgment, the group then chose between the two on the basis of prayer and casting lots.

Prayer is the communication to God of the praise, confession, and desires of his people. Thus we understand the part of this process that asked God to make his will known in this selection process. We do the same in our contemporary selection of church shepherds, for example. But should we also cast lots? This is not the only time the Bible speaks of it, for Proverbs 16:33 says: "The lot is cast into the lap, but its every decision is from the Lord." We are not even sure what this involved. Most scholars think it was the throwing of some sort of marked objects that were read in terms of revealing the will of God. Several ancient cultures, including the Jewish people, used it. By this process, Matthias was chosen.

As we study this book over the next several months, we will discover that Acts both *is* and *is not* a pattern for the modern church. Here is a good example of the fact that we distinguish binding and nonbinding things in Luke's narrative. We use reason and prayer to select our church leaders, but we do not (to my knowledge at least) cast lots. Casting lots was a cultural phenomenon that the early Christians believed God would use in answering their prayers for guidance. Today we believe he guides congregational voting or some other procedure that we have in place within our culture. Both then and now, we believe that God honors the requests of his people and answers our prayers for

Day 4
Handling Disappointment

Read Psalm 42 and hear the lament of a "downcast" man.

1. Who were the men offered as candidates to replace Judas? Who was chosen?

2. Pretend you are Justus when the selection is announced. How do you feel? What do you say?

3. What is the most disappointing thing that has happened to you recently?

4. How did you feel? What did you say? What did you do?

5. Explain how God has helped you get past your disappointment.

guidance through appropriate cultural means. Acts is principally a book of historical narrative, not doctrinal statements. It tells what happened in a particular time and place, with the hand of God overruling all to his glory. Thus we should be very careful about making fun of or otherwise discounting a judgment one comes to on the basis of a dream, "chance" conversation, or other sign he or she believes has come from God. If it has been thought through carefully and prayed over thoroughly, God will *somehow* fulfill his promise to guide his people (cf. Jas. 1:5-8). As John Wesley cautioned: "Do not hastily ascribe things to God. Do not easily suppose dreams, voices, impressions, visions, or revelations to be from God. They may be from [God]. They may be from nature. They may be from the devil." Openness to God's leading must include caution against deception.

Some students of Acts have been critical of this episode. They insist that Peter and the others were presumptuous in this choice of a successor to Judas. After all, they are quick to point out, Matthias is never again mentioned in the text. That is not quite correct, for Luke lets us know that in the functioning church in Acts "the Eleven" (1:26; cf. 2:14) are henceforth known as "the Twelve" (6:2). If one means that he is never again singled out from the Twelve, that is correct — as it is also correct of well over half of the original band.

Perhaps the criticism of Matthias's selection stems from the belief by some that Paul was the Lord's later choice to take the place of Judas. This is hardly the case, however, for the simple facts that Paul's was a special apostleship to the Gentiles, he refers to himself as an apostle "abnormally born" (1 Cor. 15:8), and never counts himself among the Twelve (Gal. 1:19).

Our method of advancing candidates and selecting leaders for our churches is different from the

Day 5
Selecting Leaders

Read 1 Timothy 3 about overseers and ministers.

1. React to this statement: "No church rises above its leaders." Do you agree? Explain.
2. What is the role of an elder-shepherd?
3. Explain the function of a deacon-minister in the church.
4. How are leaders chosen in your church? Critique the process. How would you change it?
5. What is the most important thing you look for in a leader? Do you have that quality?

one used here in some ways, and we certainly do not select modern apostles to fill that unique role. Yet, in the most critical aspects, it must be the same. It must be done with careful deliberation and in much prayer. Only then may we be assured, as these early believers were, that the leaders are in place that God has appointed.

Week Four

Acts 2:1-41 (II B 1 to II B 4 in Outline)

Day 1
The Holy Spirit

Read John 16:5-16 for Jesus' promise of the Spirit to the Twelve.

1. Why was it necessary for Jesus to send the Holy Spirit?
2. Why were the apostles ordered to wait for the Spirit's arrival before beginning their work?
3. What is the "gift of the Holy Spirit" received by all believers?
4. How does the Spirit enrich your Christian life?
5. What happens in your life that would not be happening without the Spirit's presence?

Still meeting daily on the temple grounds for prayer, the apostles — possibly still accompanied by some or all of the larger group of 120 — were all together on the day of Pentecost. This feast day of the Jews was a joyous harvest celebration in Israel. The firstfruits of the harvest were offered to the Lord. One of Judaism's three annual pilgrim feasts, Pentecost brought huge numbers of people to the city. Jerusalem was filled with people from all over the known world and must have been buzzing with conversation about what had taken place seven weeks earlier when Jesus was crucified and a series of strange reports filtered back to town. This day would turn out to be Christianity's first great ingathering of souls to Jesus.

Pentecost fell fifty days (i.e., seven Sabbaths plus one day, Lev. 23:15ff) after Passover. This means the events of Acts 2 took place on a Sunday. Following the chronology of Finegan (*Handbook of Biblical Chronology*) for A.D. 30, Pentecost Day that year fell on May 28.

B. The Events of Fulfillment. 2:1-47.

1. The arrival of the Holy Spirit. 2:1-4.

Jesus' promise concerning the arrival of the Holy Spirit was fulfilled on the first Pentecost following his resurrection from the dead. The outward manifestation of the Spirit's coming was both audible and visible. There was "a sound *like* the blowing of a violent wind" and the apostles "saw what *seemed* to be tongues of fire that separated and came to rest on each of them." There was neither wind nor fire, but the noise and radiant tongues were symbols of the presence of the Holy Spirit.

"The whole house where they were sitting" was not the upper room where the apostles were lodging but a chamber or portico of the temple grounds. After all, thousands heard the sound created by the Spirit's advent and came together to inquire, "What does this mean?"

2. The amazement and bewilderment of the crowd. 2:5-13.

Another sign of the Spirit's presence that day was tongues-speaking by the apostles. They spoke the languages (*glossa*, 2:4,11) and dialects (*dialektos*, 2:6,8) of the many language groups assembled at Jerusalem for Pentecost (2:8-11). In this instance of tongues-speaking, at least, the miracle consisted of the Spirit-given ability to communicate in a human language or dialect the speaker had not mastered by ordinary means of language study. Apparently it was only The Twelve — not the larger group of 120 disciples — who were baptized with the Holy Spirit and spoke in tongues that day. This seems evident from the fact that Peter defended only himself and eleven others against the charge of drunkenness when some in the crowd tried to explain their unusual speech with that explanation (cf. 2:13-15).

The gift of tongues in this setting was like all other biblical miracles. It was both a sign of God's power and a gift of grace designed to meet a need. While we cannot be sure how many language groups were included among the people drawn together, the Galilean apostles were able to address every person there "in his own language." Each apostle may have preached in a language different from every other, or some of them may have preached in the same language to different assemblies.

Whatever the details of the occurrence, the magnitude of the miracle was obvious to the assembled multitude. Seeking to make sense of what was going

Day 2
Confusion Among Onlookers

Read 1 Corinthians 1:18-31 about the world's attitude toward things of God.

1. What was the reaction of the temple crowd to the Spirit's arrival?
2. How did some of them explain the apostles' ability to speak foreign languages?
3. What aspects of the church's life are typically misunderstood or misrepresented by outsiders today?
4. Why do these misunderstandings and misrepresentations occur?
5. How should the church respond to these situations?

on, people turned to one another and asked, "What does this mean?" A few scoffers in their midst suggested that the Twelve had probably been celebrating the feast with a drinking bout. "They have had too much wine," they said.

3. Peter's sermon concerning the Christ. 2:14-36.

Day 3
Preaching Christ

Read 1 Corinthians 2:1-10 for Paul's summary of his preaching.

1. What was the theme of Peter's Pentecost sermon?

2. What supporting evidence did he offer for his thesis about Jesus?

3. If we preach Christ to our world, what themes will we emphasize?

4. Do you think the modern church keeps its focus on Christ in its teaching ministry? Explain your answer.

5. What was the most recent sermon you have heard? Did it focus clearly on Christ?

Peter, along with the other apostles, took advantage of the curiosity created by the events in which they had been central figures to preach their first sermon under the Great Commission. On this first Pentecost following the resurrection of Jesus, repentance and forgiveness of sins began to be preached at Jerusalem and would eventually spread to the remainder of the inhabited world. Only the sermon of Peter is recorded by Luke, but his was surely representative of those preached by all the other apostles.

a. His response to the charge of drunkenness. 2:14-21.

Peter made only a passing reference to the charge of drunkenness. After all, what sort of charge was that? Being drunk typically makes people slur their speech, but it certainly doesn't give them unprecedented linguistic skills! His brief response is merely to suggest the improbability that he and eleven other pious men come to Jerusalem for a holy festival would be drunk so early in the day (i.e., "It's only nine in the morning!").

To the contrary, Peter insisted that Scripture had predicted these events in Joel 2:28ff. Yahweh had promised to pour forth his Spirit "in the last days." The Old Testament frequently uses the expression "last days" to mean nothing more than sometime in the future (cf. Isa. 2:1-2, et al.). Most often in the New Testament, however, the same expression embraces the period between Christ's ascension and his Second Coming.

But what of the promise that the Spirit would come upon "all flesh"? The reference is obviously not to every single individual on the planet, saint and sinner alike. It must be understood in some qualified sense. To the Jewish mind, there were two and only two types of human creatures — Jews and all non-Jews (i.e., Gentiles, pagans, the uncircumcised). The prophecy in Joel may therefore be understood as a promise that God would signify his acceptance of "all flesh" in the last days by an outpouring of the Holy Spirit on both Jews and Gentiles. Indeed, Acts shows Jews receiving that promise here (in the representative persons of the apostles) and Gentiles receiving the same thing a few years afterward (in the representative persons of Cornelius and his household, cf. 11:15). Everything necessary to the fulfillment of Joel's prophecy is found in these two events.

The visions, dreams, and prophecies that were to issue from the pouring out of the Spirit are recorded throughout Acts of the Apostles. The wonders and signs mentioned at verses 19-20 may be largely figurative, although one cannot but recall that the sun was "turned to darkness" less than two months previous on the day when Jesus died (Matt. 27:45).

b. His affirmation about Jesus of Nazareth. 2:22-35.

The primary point of that Pentecost Day was not the signs but the sermon. For the first time ever, the gospel message was preached in fullness as a completed event. Salvation was offered to anyone who would turn to Jesus Christ. "No modern preacher can claim such divine inspiration as Peter enjoyed; yet one who would be used by the Spirit should imitate him in at least two particulars: he preached Christ and he expounded the Scriptures." [Charles R. Erdman, *The Acts: An Exposition* (Philadelphia: Westminster Press, 1966), p. 38.]

The thesis of the Pentecost sermon is *Jesus of Nazareth is Lord and Christ.* Drawing heavily from Old Testament texts his hearers would have known

Day 4
The Gospel

Read 1 Corinthians 15:1-11 for a summary of the gospel message.

1. The word *gospel* means "good news." How is the Christian message a good-news message?
2. How is the gospel the power of God for salvation? Cf. Rom. 1:16.
3. Under what circumstances did you first learn the gospel?
4. Why is it important for the gospel message to

be shared with every-
one?

5. What is the best
method for teaching the
gospel to our contem-
poraries?

and accepted as divine authority, Peter offered three
lines of proof for his claim for Jesus.

First, Peter affirmed, "Jesus of Nazareth was a
man accredited by God to you by miracles, wonders
and signs, which God did among you through him,
as you yourselves know." The people were asked to
draw the logical conclusion that followed from their
firsthand knowledge about Jesus, that no man could
have done such supernatural deeds except by the
power and approval of God (John 3:2).

Second, Peter appealed to the resurrection of
Jesus from the dead as proof of his thesis. David had
prophesied of the Messiah and said that his soul
would not be left "to the grave" (i.e., *hades*, the
unseen world) and his flesh would not be allowed to
"decay" (Psa. 16:8-11). David could not have been
speaking of himself, Peter argued, for his tomb was
still occupied. To the contrary, he was speaking of a
descendant of his whom God had sworn to set upon
his throne (cf. 2 Sam. 7:12-13). This coronation took
place in connection with the resurrection and ascension of Jesus. [Note: The King James Version incor-
rectly translates *hades* with the English term "hell."
The Greek word refers to the place where all disem-
bodied spirits reside between physical death and the
resurrection of the body. The word does not signify
a place of fiery torment, for the place of everlasting
torment threatened for the unbelieving in Scripture
is designated by the word *gehenna*.]

Third, Peter said his claims about Jesus were
proved by the phenomena that had been witnessed
by the multitude hearing him. The pouring forth of
the Holy Spirit and the signs accompanying it were
directly related to Jesus. The Father had not only
raised him from the dead but had also exalted him
(cf. Dan. 7:13-14). He is now "seated at the right
hand of the mighty God" (Luke 22:69). David had
prophesied of this exaltation but, again, had obvi-

ously been speaking not of himself but of the Messiah. The Lord (i.e., Yahweh) had said to David's Lord (i.e., Messiah), "Sit at my right hand until I make your enemies a footstool for your feet" (Psa. 110:1; cf. Mark 12:35).

c. His conclusion. 2:36.

The sermon's crescendo and grand conclusion has been reached: "God has made this Jesus, whom you crucified, both Lord and Christ." This statement from the apostle involved both a claim and a charge. The *claim* about Jesus is that he is divine (i.e., Lord = God, divine being, master) and the one anointed by Yahweh to bring Israel's hope to fulfillment in delivering humankind from sin's captivity (i.e., Christ = Messiah, anointed one). The *charge* against Peter's hearers was that they had murdered the Holy One.

4. The response to the gospel of Christ. 2:37-41.

What conviction was created in the heart of many who heard the Spirit-given message of that Pentecost Day! They were "cut to the heart" and pleaded with the apostles to tell them if there was any hope for people who had committed so awful a crime against the divine Christ. They were told to repent and submit to baptism "in the name of Jesus Christ" — to do something on the authority of and trusting the power of the very one they had rejected and murdered.

Repentance is a change of heart that subsequently shows itself in a changed life; it is a contrite turning of one's entire being from the love and practice of sin to the love and service of God (cf. Luke 3:8ff). Baptism is the immersion of a man or woman in water; it is one's personal confession of the death, burial, and resurrection of Jesus as Savior (cf. Rom. 6:1ff). One's changed behavior doesn't undo the harm already done, and his baptism doesn't literally wash away either the guilt or consequences of his sin

Day 5
Responding to the Gospel

Read a parable at Luke 18:1-15 about different responses people make to the gospel.

1. What was the response to Peter's presentation of the gospel on Pentecost Day?
2. How many people publicly accepted Christ that day? How did they indicate their change of attitude toward him?
3. How did you initially respond to the gospel when you learned of Christ?
4. How is your life affected daily by the gospel?
5. In what ways are you trying to encourage others to respond to the gospel?

(cf. 1 Pet. 3:21). Forgiveness comes only through the shed blood of Christ (cf. Heb. 9:22; 10:4,10). Repentance and baptism confess one's trust in and willingness to take salvation as God's free gift from Jesus.

One who comes to Christ by this faith-process not only receives forgiveness of sins but the "gift of the Holy Spirit." Just as the New Testament knows no such thing as an unbaptized Christian, neither does it know of a disciple faithfully serving his God apart from an empowerment by the Holy Spirit. The saved person's body becomes a temple for the Holy Spirit (1 Cor. 6:19-20). By the power of the indwelling Spirit, he or she exhibits the distinctly Christlike traits of love, joy, peace, and the like (Gal. 5:22-23).

On that day, an incredible 3,000 Jewish souls took the bold step of acknowledging Jesus of Nazareth as their Messiah, confessing him to be divine, and appealing to him for the forgiveness of their sins. The infant church went from 120 "charter members" to 3,000 baptized believers.

Week Five

Acts 2:42-47 (II B 5 in Outline)

5. A general description of the life of the earliest Christians. 2:42-47.

Once the marvelous events of Pentecost Day had passed, what did the 3,000 who had been converted to Christ do? What did God do with the apostles after they had experienced the striking gifts of that day? Luke knew that his readers would be curious about these very things, so he follows the account of the church's birthday with a summary of what life was like among those earliest believers.

In the paragraph at hand, Luke names four elements that were conspicuous among the disciples. He then lets us know the combined effect these ingredients had not only on the young Christians but on the outsiders who observed them. According to his account: "They devoted themselves (1) to the apostles' teaching and (2) to the fellowship, (3) to the breaking of bread and (4) to prayer."

"The apostles' teaching" is the essential foundation on which the church is built (Eph. 2:20). Since many of these people had only recently been shouting for the death of Jesus and because even those who had perhaps once been his disciples were still locked into the misunderstandings the apostles had held themselves until the 40-day period just past in which Jesus had taught them more fully, teaching was the first thing they needed. Furthermore, the arrival of the Holy Spirit meant that even the apostles would be receiving more and more insight yet into the things of Christ and the kingdom (John 16:12-15). As those revelations and insights came, they shared them with the young believers who

Day 1
The Jerusalem Church

Read an Old Testament prediction about Jerusalem from Isaiah 2:1-5.

1. Why is Jerusalem such an important city in biblical history?
2. Why do you think God chose Jerusalem as the birthplace of the church?
3. What is the best thing you know about the Jerusalem church? The worst?
4. In what ways do you consider the Jerusalem church a model for us?
5. How long did Jerusalem remain the center of activity in Acts?

49

Day 2
Apostolic Teaching

Read Ephesians 2:19-22
about the importance of the
apostles to Christ's church.

1. What is meant by the term "apostles' teaching"?
2. Why is their teaching so critical to the life of the church?
3. How does the teaching of the apostles extend to us?
4. How may an individual root himself or herself deeply in the Word of God?
5. Describe your personal commitment to the Word of God.

looked to them for understanding and guidance in their new life.

The knowledge that makes one a Christian or makes a group of Christians into a church is not a particular set of facts or doctrines. A Christian is someone who is in Christ and in whom Christ lives. He or she follows Christ in daily obedience to please him and lives in loving relationships with others who follow him (cf. 1 John 3:21-24). Yet all this is grounded in and grows from the teachings of prophets, apostles, and evangelists as preserved for us in Holy Scripture. It will always be imperative for those who are seeking Christ to root themselves deeply in the Word of God.

"The fellowship" that was a hallmark of the first church was an awareness of, sympathy for, and life involvement with others for Christ's sake. Just as league bowling or political campaigning puts one in company with people he might never have known otherwise, so does one's being in Christ put her or him into a relationship with new and different people. The uniqueness of Christian fellowship lies in the fact that one finds a reason for being involved with others for the sake of Jesus alone and not on the basis of social position, common interests (other than Jesus!), or common concerns (other than the kingdom of God!).

First-century fellowship in Christ's church would eventually include not only Jews from far-flung nations of the diaspora but Jews with Gentiles and masters with slaves. We should not confuse occasional church meals or pleasant time with our friends from church with what the New Testament means by fellowship. This important biblical concept (Gk. *koinonia*) affirms the existence of a relationship with others that exists solely on the basis of a common relationship with Jesus. One of the members of that first church would later explain it this way: "We proclaim to you what we have seen and heard, so that you also may have fellowship with us. And our fellowship is with the Father and with his Son, Jesus Christ" (1 John 1:3).

Christians need each other. We need not simply the companionship and friendship that unbelievers need because humans are social creatures but, more urgently, the challenge, encouragement, and shared experiences of God that produce spiritual growth. We need to band together as a body for worship and ministry opportunities that cannot be generated in private or as a small group (Heb. 10:24-25). Yet there are some needs for sharing and confession that are inappropriate to a large body and that need the option of small-group or one-on-one intimacy (Jas. 5:13-16). Every believer needs both these forms of Christ-focused fellowship in his life. "Just as each of us has one body with many members, and these members do not all have the same function, so in Christ we who are many form one body, and each member belongs to all the others" (Rom. 12:4-5).

"The breaking of bread" named here is almost surely a reference to the Lord's Supper rather than common meals (cf. v. 46). The covenant meal of Christ's body and blood binds the body together with its constant reaffirmation of the cross. Eating the bread with other Christians both affirms the reality of the historical event and shows the world one of its abiding consequences (i.e., the church, Christ's spiritual body).

Luke does not answer some of the questions we have put to this text about the frequency or precise manner of the observance of this meal in the early church. The believing community may have eaten the Lord's Supper daily for a time. Whether it was eaten en masse or in small groups is another question without an answer. The one thing that is certain about the event is that it served as a dramatic and

Day 3
The Lord's Supper

Read Matthew 26:17-30 for background to the Lord's Supper.

1. The Lord's Supper is sometimes called "communion." Why? What special communion is shared by people who eat this meal?

2. What are some of the other terms we use to designate the Lord's Supper? What is the meaning of each?

3. What is the central meaning of the Lord's Supper for you?

4. How do you assure that your participation in the Lord's Supper is meaningful each time you eat it?

5. Imagine that you have been asked to present a brief communion devotional for next Sunday. In no more than 100 words, write what you would want to say.

tangible call to all the young church to keep its focus on Christ's atonement as the ground of its identity.

"Prayer" is the final of the four central components of the first church identified by Luke. As we continue to work through the text of Acts, it will be practically impossible to miss the significance the earliest church attached to prayer. It was the throbbing heart of all the church's life — whether apostolic ministry (6:4), benevolence (6:6), standing faithful under persecution (7:59-60), personal devotion (10:9), preaching (13:3), or any other facet of life and ministry.

It is a terrible mistake for the church in any generation to neglect prayer. Committees ought not become the modern alternative to congregational prayer, and any decision or action that comes from a committee should be undergirded by much prayer. Devotional reading and meditation are helpful spiritual disciplines for the individual in his or her spiritual life, but they ought to remain secondary to prayer. Prayer is the church's most direct link to the heart of God. He graciously accepts and even desires our praise. He hears our confession and faithfully pardons our transgressions. He allows us to cast all our cares upon him and promises to act in our life circumstances to perfect our spiritual maturity.

As the church at Jerusalem devoted itself to these holy things, God was free to move freely and powerfully among the disciples. Indeed, the great number of miracles done at the hands of the apostles produced a sense of great "awe" throughout the believing community. Then, appropriately overwhelmed with God's presence in their midst, the disciples exhibited the changed lives that always result from a saving relationship with Jesus Christ.

Faith shows itself to be genuine when it moves beyond words to actions. The apostle John may have remembered the Jerusalem example when he wrote these words more than 60 years later: "This is how we know what love is: Jesus Christ laid down his life for us. And we ought to lay down our lives for our brothers. If anyone has material possessions and sees his brother in need but has no pity on him, how can the love of God be in him? Dear children, let us not love with words or tongue but with actions and in truth" (1 John 3:16-18).

Contrary to the claims of some, there is no evidence that the Jerusalem church practiced a form of "communism" or "communal life." What happened among those people was far more beautiful as a demonstration of Christian love. Various members of the body began "selling their possessions and goods." From the proceeds, they met the needs of the poorer people among them.

The "temple courts" — a compound of more than 25 acres — continued to serve as the focal point for the church's daily life. There were obviously no church buildings for them to use. Various open courts, porches, and wide stairway areas provided places in the temple compound for men and women to congregate. As they met together, the apostles continued to instruct and encourage their spiritual charges. At this point, no open conflicts had erupted between the apostles and the temple authorities that made such meetings subject to interruption or challenge. We cannot be certain how long this situation lasted.

In addition to their regular meetings for instruction, fellowship, the Lord's Supper, and prayer in the temple precincts, those eager disciples also sought out each other for times of small-group sharing in their homes. Times in each other's homes included the sharing of ordinary meals as they "ate together with glad and sincere hearts" — as well as the repetition of the public acts they had come to associate with their new faith.

Day 4
Fellowship

Read Psalm 133 about the precious nature of spiritual fellowship.

1. Define the term "fellowship" in your own words.
2. How is fellowship different from mere association?
3. What is the most meaningful thing to you about Christian fellowship?
4. How has the fellowship of other believers had a positive impact on your spiritual life?
5. Write a prayer for God to help you experience a deeper level of fellowship in Christ.

At this early stage of the church's life, there was not only no tension between Jesus' people and the Jewish authorities but an atmosphere of goodwill toward the Christians. Luke informs us that those early days saw the church "enjoying the favor of all the people." It is not wrong for a church to have a good name in a community and to use that approbation as a base for telling the story of Jesus. Indeed, both common sense and this biblical precedent combine to say that is the ideal situation. A church ought to take its public image and its relationship to the entities and individuals around it very seriously. In every way that is holy and effective, Christians should show themselves to be the sort of people one would want to have as neighbors. Separation from the world's evil (cf. 1 Cor. 15:33) ought never to be confused with isolation from the world's inhabitants.

The church's worshiping, sharing, and congenial life appears to have been its initial evangelistic strategy. To say the least, there is no separate mention of an evangelistic crusade beyond its daily life of devotion to Jesus and one another. That powerful witness was enough to attract others, so that "the Lord added to their number daily those who were being saved."

One author has written on this section of text that describes the life of the earliest church: "In all these activities of teaching, fellowship and sharing, breaking of bread, and praying we see a well-rounded picture of the church, the marks of authentic embodiment of the Spirit in the community's life, a canon for the measurement of the church's activity today. As one views modern congregations, many with their hectic round of activities — yoga, ceramics, basketweaving, daycare — one suspects that socialization is being substituted for the gospel, warm-hearted busyness is being offered in lieu of Spirit-empowered community." [William H. Willimon, *Acts* (Atlanta: John Knox Press, 1988), p. 42.]

Day 5
Prayer

Read some warnings about prayer found at Matthew 6:5-8.

1. Why do you think the early church was so prayerful?
2. How do you think today's church compares with the first-century church in this matter of diligent prayer?
3. What situations remind you most pointedly of your need for prayer?
4. What situations hinder you most in your prayer life?
5. Name the things you need to be most prayerful about today.

What an appropriate warning is found in those words. Simply to have activities going on is not proof of the presence of the Holy Spirit. The distinctive features of a Christian community as described in Acts are the ones we must perpetuate with deliberate effort. Nothing will substitute for faithful adherence to the teaching of the apostles. And that teaching will most naturally show itself in the fellowship, worship, and constant prayer that were in evidence among the disciples at Jerusalem.

In the first century, the people who had fallen in love with Jesus naturally found themselves falling in love with the rest of his people and living out the implications of that love in practical ways. May it always be so among the people of God.

Week Six

Acts 3:1-26 (III A to III B in Outline)

Day 1
Spiritual Disciplines

Read Psalm 63 about the dearness of God to his people.

1. The Jews had three set times for prayer each day. How disciplined are you in your personal spiritual life?
2. What spiritual disciplines do you practice regularly?
3. How do you keep these disciplines from becoming legalistic requirements?
4. What benefits have come to you from the spiritual disciplines?
5. What advice would you give someone just beginning to practice these disciplines?

III. Progress and Perils at Jerusalem. 3:1–8:3.

The material in this five-chapter section of Acts tells about the "progress and perils" of the Jerusalem church. Activity centers around the preaching of the apostles and the miracles God performed at their hands. These events cover a period of two to three years.

The first event of this section sets the outline for the ones to follow: (1) an opportunity to preach results in numerous conversions, (2) the conversions precipitate conflict between the church and the Jewish authorities, and (3) the conflict makes the church even bolder in its preaching of the gospel.

A. The Healing of a Lame Man. 3:1-10.

Peter and John were "going up to the temple at the time of prayer — at three in the afternoon." This was the second of three regular times for prayer in Judaism. In the early morning when sacrifices were being offered, at the mid-afternoon time of sacrifice here, and at sunset, observant Jews paused for prayer. That these apostles were still following this scheme after the establishment of the church shows how gradually the break between Judaism and Christianity came about. The earliest believers were Jews by birth and habit, regarded their new faith as the fulfillment of Jewish hope rather than its repudiation (cf. Matt. 5:17-18), and characteristically began their earliest evangelistic efforts in Acts at the temple and synagogues of the Jews by presenting

Jesus as the Messiah. It would not be until the destruction of Jerusalem in A.D. 70 that a final separation was recognized between the two religions.

At one of the large gates leading into the temple compound, Peter and John encountered "a man crippled from birth" who regularly begged help from people passing his way. The man asked them for money. They stopped, Peter told him to look at them, and the man "gave them his attention, expecting to get something from them."

Peter's first words to the beggar must have dashed his hopes: "Silver or gold I do not have." What he said next must have bewildered him: "But what I have I give you. In the name of Jesus Christ of Nazareth, walk." The fisherman-apostle then took the beggar by his right hand and helped him to his feet. For the first time in his life, the congenitally crippled beggar was able to support his weight with his own limbs. His healing was neither partial nor accomplished in stages over time. The beggar was healed "instantly" and "jumped to his feet and began to walk." Overjoyed by what had happened to him, the man not only exercised his legs by leaping but also exercised his voice in "praising God."

Being the afternoon hour of prayer, a large crowd was naturally on the temple grounds. For someone in their midst to be jumping and shouting at such a holy hour would certainly call attention to himself. When various ones recognized the man as "the same man who used to sit begging at the temple gate," they were understandably "filled with wonder and amazement at what had happened to him."

B. Peter's Sermon in Solomon's Portico. 3:11-26.

The outer court of the temple (i.e., Court of the Gentiles) was surrounded by a porch inside the walls. Along the east wall, two rows of columns

**Day 2
Compassion**

Read Psalm 118 about the mercy and compassion of the Lord.

1. Have you ever seen a street beggar in a Third World country? What was the life situation of a beggar in ancient times?

2. What is your first reaction when you see someone begging?

3. Imagine you are the beggar in this story. What things do you say while praising God?

4. What compassion ministry is nearest to your heart today?

5. Is there a suffering person you need to phone or see today?

extended the length of the wall and supported a wide roof that created a three-aisled portico called Solomon's Colonnade. Here people could be sheltered from sun or rain (cf. John 10:23). Such colonnades completely surrounded the temple area, and it was in them that the money changers had their stalls and the scribes did their teaching.

Day 3
Credit Where
Credit Is Due

Read 1 Kings 8:14-30 and notice the credit Solomon gave God at the dedication of the temple he had built.

1. How did Peter disclaim credit for the healing of the lame man? Why?
2. Reflect on the meaning of the phrase "in the name of Jesus" in the NT.
3. How natural do you find it to give God the glory for good things in your life?
4. Have you ever been tempted to take credit for something that was clearly a work of God?
5. How do you guard yourself in this matter of giving God the glory he is entitled to have in your life?

1. The incident of healing attributed to Jesus. 3:11-16.

As the crowd gathered in Solomon's Colonnade, Peter seized the opportunity to preach Jesus. As at the moment of the healing, he disavowed personal responsibility for the cure of the lame man. Peter told the beggar: "*In the name of Jesus Christ of Nazareth, walk.*" Shortly he would explain to the larger group: "By faith *in the name of Jesus*, this man whom you see and know was made strong. It is *Jesus' name* and the *faith that comes through him* that has given this complete healing to him, as you can all see." Whether the beggar even knew who Jesus was is unclear from the text. The ones who had faith in Jesus and worked this miracle in his name were his servants Peter and John. But they were not about to take credit for the wonderful thing that had happened.

It must have been a great temptation for men such as Peter and John to make themselves the center of attention in situations like this. After all, we know the human factor called "pride" and know how easy it would be for us to take credit, build a ministry-enterprise, and get a heady sense of our own importance. But Peter would have none of that and gave all the glory to God. "Why do you stare at us as if by our own power or godliness we had made this man walk?" he asked. What had been done was attributed to the powerful name of Jesus — the one who is Yahweh's "servant" (v. 13; cf. Isa. 53), "the Holy and Righteous One" (v. 14), "the author of life" (v. 15). Human piety does not command divine healing; such events are acts of divine sovereignty and grace.

With the crowd looking to the two men for an explanation, Peter spoke to them. Following the pattern of his sermon on Pentecost, he accused his hearers of bearing direct responsibility for Jesus' death at the hands of the Romans. They had "handed him over to be killed" and had "disowned him before Pilate." When Pilate was convinced of Jesus' innocence and tried to release him, "you disowned the Holy and Righteous One and asked that a murderer (i.e., Barabbas, Luke 23:18-25) be released to you." Still following the Pentecost precedent, Peter moved immediately to affirm the fact of the resurrection: "God raised him from the dead. We are witnesses of this."

2. A call for faith in Jesus based on the prophets. 3:17-26.

The preaching of the early church was apologetic in tone. It consisted of presenting arguments that proved Jesus was the Messiah and Son of God to whom men must turn for salvation. To the Gentiles, the arguments in Acts are based on natural theology — God's revelation of himself in nature (14:14-18; 17:22-31). To the Jews, the arguments are rooted in the Old Testament — God's revelation of himself to Israel through Moses and the prophets (2:22-36).

Peter granted that the people who had crucified Jesus "acted in ignorance." But it was an inexcusable ignorance, for God had prophesied about the Christ throughout the Holy Scriptures the Jews had in their possession. From their knowledge of the Old Testament, they should have recognized and accepted Jesus of Nazareth as their Messiah.

Peter quoted a messianic prophecy from Moses to show that Jesus' work was the fulfillment of Judaism rather than a rejection of it. The great Lawgiver of Sinai had predicted (Deut. 18:15-18) that Yahweh would raise up "a prophet like me from among your own people; you must listen to everything he tells you." Not only Moses but also "all the

**Day 4
Credibility for
Preaching**

Read John 9:1-21 for the account of a miracle by Jesus and the reaction to it.

1. Why did the miracles of Jesus and his apostles cause trouble for them?
2. How did those miracles confer credibility on them?
3. Explain the meaning of Nicodemus's comment at John 3:2.
4. Describe a situation from your own experience of how someone's act of compassion conferred credibility for him or her to share the gospel.
5. What happens when we try to preach Christ without first imitating his example of caring about people?

prophets from Samuel on, as many as have spoken, have foretold these days."

Indeed, Peter continued, Jesus of Nazareth was the one Yahweh had in mind when he entered a covenant with Abraham and promised, "Through your offspring all peoples on earth will be blessed" (cf. Gen. 12:3; 22:18; 26:4; 28:14). The New Testament consistently interprets this promise of a special offspring (i.e., "seed," KJV) as an anticipation of Jesus Christ (cf. Gal. 3:16). The promised Messiah had come as God's "servant" (cf. Isa. 53; Acts 8:30-35); he was put to death but was "raised up" by the Lord. That servant's work has been intended to bless Israel "by turning each of you from your wicked ways."

This sermon is enough to prove that the earliest Christians were not antisemitic. They were Jews themselves and were claiming Christ as the fulfillment of their long-cherished hopes that were grounded in the Law and the Prophets. The antisemitism that has periodically emerged in Christian history is an evil perversion of the gospel. Christianity was born in the womb of Judaism.

The means by which people could find release from their sins is stated here for the second time in Acts: "Repent, then, and turn to God, so that your sins may be wiped out, that times of refreshing may come from the Lord, and that he may send the Christ, who has been appointed for you — even Jesus. He must remain in heaven until the time comes for God to restore everything as he promised long ago through his holy prophets" (3:19-21).

Just as with people Jesus encountered during his personal ministry, these people thought of themselves as God's "chosen people." They were confident of their relationship with God because of their genetic link to father Abraham (cf. John 8:33ff). Peter's call for repentance was a direct challenge to them. His argument about Jesus clearly entailed the conclusion that, in the rejection of Jesus as their Messiah, the Jews were refusing heaven's fulfillment of the covenant made with their forefathers.

A similar situation exists today in the United States where so many of us are "church members." Our tendency is to think that because we are on somebody's church membership list and go to church regularly we are saved. Salvation is much more personal a matter than that. What do you believe about Jesus? What is your relationship with him? Are you living in daily repentance and surrender?

Repentance is the turning of one's whole being from selfishness and rebellion against God to a life of submission to him. It must have been startling for these pious people to hear someone tell them they needed to repent — just as it startles us.

For those who would come to Christ in authentic repentance, Peter promised three things: sins would be "wiped out," "times of refreshing" would come to them, and God would "send the Christ who has been appointed for you." The first of these is forgiveness or removal of sin from one's record (cf. Psa. 51:1,9; Isa. 43:25). Although some take the "times of refreshing" to be a reference to the future state of believers at Christ's Second Coming, it seems more natural to understand it as the work of God that accompanies the wiping away of sin; it is the refreshment and renewal of our spirits by the invigorating presence of the Holy Spirit in a saved person's life (Titus 3:5; cf. Gal. 5:22-23). Finally, he pointed to the future time when Jesus, who is now in heaven, returns to "restore everything" to the perfection God originally envisioned for it (cf. 2 Pet. 3:13).

"What positive motivations for repentance! Our slate has been wiped clean. Our parched lives are refreshed in the present by seasons of the Spirit's outpouring. Our future perfection is beyond imagination." [Larkin, *Acts*, p. 69.]

Day 5
"I'm a Good Church Member"

Read John 8:31-47 for a similar case where people trusted their affiliation to save them.

1. What special promises did God make to Abraham and his descendants?

2. In what sense were the Jews made a "chosen people"? How did they come to understand that status?

3. What is the basis of acceptability with God? Cf. Acts 10:35.

4. Was Peter's call to repentance a repudiation of the Law and the Prophets? Explain.

5. Have you ever known someone to trust his church membership to save him? How do you respond to such an attitude?

Week Seven

Acts 4:1-37 (III C to III D in Outline)

Too many things were happening too quickly at Jerusalem for them to go unnoticed by the city's religious leaders. With 3,000 having been converted to this new movement on the most recent Pentecost Day and in light of the miracles and ongoing claims being made about Jesus of Nazareth, conflict was inevitable. Imagine the consternation that would come today if a dozen Mormon missionaries came onto the campus of a Christian College and converted hundreds of people in a matter of days. The analogy is appropriate, for Christianity was viewed as no less an aberration in first-century Judaism than Mormonism is held to be today by orthodox Christians.

C. The Beginning of Opposition to the Infant Faith. 4:1-31.

1. The arrest of Peter and John. 4:1-4.

The crowd attracted by the miracle and subsequent sermon aroused the attention of priests working at various tasks in the temple compound. In particular, "the priests and the captain of the temple guard and the Sadducees came up to Peter and John" and took them into custody. The captain of the temple was himself a priest, ranking second only to the High Priest. It was his duty to keep order in the temple area by means of the private police force under him. Because of the danger of a riot when a large group came together, he would have been concerned to break up the crowd for practical reasons.

The Sadducees, on the other hand, had a more theological concern. They were concerned about the

Day 1
Courage Before Opposition

Read the Beatitudes from Matthew 5:1-12, giving special attention to the final three verses.

1. Describe the source and nature of the opposition generated here.
2. Why were the Sadducees particularly concerned about the apostles' teaching?
3. How did Peter and John reply to the Sanhedrin order?
4. What forms of opposition does the church face today? From what source(s)?
5. What strategy should the church adopt before this opposition?

two apostles' "proclaiming in Jesus the resurrection of the dead." Because of their attitude toward the doctrine of bodily resurrection, they were willing to use their control of the priesthood to pressure them into silence. Because it was now evening, they locked up Peter and John and made no attempt to pursue the matter until the next day.

In a passing note, Luke informs his readers that the number of believers now totaled about 5,000 men (*ton andron* = adult males as opposed to females and children). The talk about Jesus had continued since Pentecost, and more and more were standing with him.

2. A defense before the Sanhedrin. 4:5-12.

The next day, the two Christian evangelists were brought before the Sanhedrin. This was the "Supreme Court" of Judaism. Seated in their customary semicircle with the two apostles seated opposite them, the council that had once interrogated Jesus demanded to know the "power" or "name" by which they had made the lame man whole. Please note that the question they put to them was not "Did a real miracle occur?" but "By what means did it happen?" As Peter was "filled by the Holy Spirit," he responded to the question (cf. Luke 21:14-15).

The healed man had either been summoned to the Sanhedrin hearing as a potential witness or had come on his own to see the outcome of this event that had started with him. Peter called attention to him and said: "It is by the name of Jesus Christ of Nazareth, whom you crucified but whom God raised from the dead, that this man stands before you healed" (4:10). In biblical literature, the "name" of an individual stands for the total personality and power of that person. For the man to have been healed "by the name of Jesus Christ" was for him to have been healed *on Jesus' authority* and *by Jesus' power*.

Day 2
"In the Name of Jesus"

Read John 16:17-24 for promises Jesus made about his name.

1. What does the phrase "in the name of x" mean?
2. What does this imply about doing things "in the name of Jesus"?
3. What are some of the specific things you do in his name?
4. Explain the meaning of Colossians 3:17.
5. How does this information about the "name" of Jesus relate to Exodus 20:7?

By this point in his response, Peter was no longer in a defensive posture before the Sanhedrin. Although he was the one on trial, he indicted them with having crucified the man who had brought about such a mighty miracle of healing. Beyond that, he pointed to the even greater miracle of Jesus' own resurrection from the dead. How the council members must have squirmed at hearing that. Only a few weeks had passed since they struck their bargain with Judas that resulted in the death of the man from Nazareth. They thought their problems with him had ended. Now there was a greater commotion over him than ever.

Peter quoted a messianic Psalm (118:22) and applied it to Jesus. He accused the Jewish high council of neglecting the most important stone in their role as architects and builders in Israel; the stone they rejected had become the "capstone" of God's building program. Verse 12 constitutes one of the most emphatic declarations anywhere in the Bible: There is no one in all the world who can save mankind but Jesus.

3. Peter and John released. 4:13-22.

The Sanhedrin was taken aback at the challenging response Peter and John had made to its inquiry. Although the apostles had no formal training under the rabbis, they had handled themselves well in their presence and had not been intimidated.

Dismissing the defendants while they conferred among themselves, the court members admitted to their perplexity. The lame man was well; the tomb of Jesus was empty. The best they could figure out to do was to release the apostles, after slapping their hands. They could not refute their deeds or statements; they could only ask that they stop doing such things in Jerusalem. What an admission from the very body that had earlier condemned Jesus to death!

Called in and charged by the council, Peter and John showed their continued and growing boldness. They said plainly that they were working under a greater authority than that of the Sanhedrin. They had been charged by God to bear witness to the things they had seen and heard — especially the resurrection.

Grasping the significance of this response, the predominantly Sadducee court members intensified their pressure with threats of the consequences that would follow if such preaching was not stopped. For the time being, however, there was no choice but to release Peter and John.

Day 3
A Second Pentecost

Read Romans 8:12-27 about the activity of the Holy Spirit.

1. What event in this text is sometimes called "a second Pentecost"? Why?
2. What had the disciples been praying for when this happened?
3. What is the relationship of the Holy Spirit to successful Christian living? Moral courage? Evangelism?
4. How might the Holy Spirit relate to the prayer requests you are making today?
5. What is the primary condition of experiencing the power of the Holy Spirit in one's life? Are you satisfying that condition?

4. A prayer for boldness by the believers. 4:23-31.

Upon their release, the two apostles returned to the larger company of believers. They recounted their arrest, the trial, and the threats. Far from being intimidated by these things, however, the group saw them as fulfillments of prophecy. Did not Psalm 2:1-2 predict that authorities would set themselves against the Messiah? Among both Jews and Gentiles, that very thing had come to pass.

As they began to pray to the Father about their situation, the disciples did not ask for relief or deliverance. They prayed instead for courage to continue their work with boldness: "Now, Lord, consider their threats and enable your servants to speak your word with great boldness." Further, they prayed for continued verification of their message with signs of the sort that had already been witnessed: "Stretch out your hand to heal and perform miraculous signs and wonders through the name of your holy servant Jesus."

When they finished their prayer, the place where they were shook as it might have in an earthquake. There was a renewed awareness of the presence and power of the Holy Spirit among all of them, and the result was that they spoke the gospel in Jerusalem with boldness and power. "The experience [of the room shaking and the disciples being filled with the Holy Spirit] has been called 'a second Pentecost'; and such indeed it was. Instead, however, of the sound like a wind and the tongues of fire there was a trembling of the ground, to symbolize a divine presence and power. Instead of the ability to speak foreign languages, courage was given to testify for Christ before their own countrymen. Christians need to be 'filled with the Holy Spirit' again and again. The supreme condition is surrender to Christ and a wholehearted desire to do his will in spite of peril and opposition and hatred. The result will be new courage and power in service, and not infrequently it will come when believers are assembled in some 'upper room' where they have met to read the Scriptures, to sing, and to unite their hearts in prayer." [Erdman, *Acts*, p. 53.]

Christians should never be surprised when our faith generates opposition. More often than not, opposition may come as in this case from insecure religious leaders who fear that their position as authority figures or leaders is being threatened.

"The ruling of the Sanhedrin was a gift of God! Startling? Perhaps. But look at it this way: the prohibition against speaking and teaching in the name of Jesus solidified the apostles and the church in courageous witness in a way that could never have happened without opposition. Peter and John had to decide whether to be obedient to God or to the Sanhedrin. Now they could understand existentially what Jesus had meant when He had challenged them to seek first the kingdom of God and put Him first before family, friends, recognition, or popularity. I know of no truly bold person who has not experienced the sharp razor's edge of that decision. When we know who we are and what we are to do because of prolonged time in prayer, we can play to the right

Day 4
The Community of Love

Read Ephesians 4:1-16 for Paul's ideal of a Christian community.

1. What effect did opposition have on the Jerusalem church?

2. What effects do criticism, tension, and opposition tend to have on families? Churches?

3. Is your church a "community of love"? Explain.

4. How does the life of your church testify to *unselfishness* among its members?

5. What affirming thing can you do today for some believer in need?

audience. Pressure comes in our lives when we equivocate and try to please everyone. Our insecurity often makes life a popularity contest and we must win people's approval at all costs. The cost is always exorbitant." [Lloyd J. Ogilvie, *Acts*, Communicator's Commentary Series (Dallas: Word, 1983) p. 105.]

D. Unity and Love among the Believers. 4:32-37.

Opposition served to drive the infant church at Jerusalem closer to God, and the Lord gave the believers great boldness before their enemies. The same opposition also served to unite its members in a bond of love and commitment. Luke informs us: "All the believers were one in heart and mind." Specifically, they were unselfish with their personal possessions. They shared whatever they had with one another. They met each other's needs. What a remarkable alternative community they showed themselves to be — over against the acquiring, hoarding, selfish spirit that dominated the unsaved world around them. It is no wonder that the preaching of the apostles in this context was done "with great power" — where "power" should be understood as a reference to effectiveness, not miraculous deeds. [Cf. Larkin, *Acts*, p. 82.]

Luke cites a particular instance of how those early Christians shared their goods with each other. A believer named Joseph sold a tract of land and gave the entire amount of money received for it to the apostles for distribution among needy members of the body.

Joseph is better known to people who read Scripture by the nickname given him by the apostles, Barnabas. As he does with so many Hebrew terms and practices, Luke translates the nickname for his fellow-Gentiles and explains that the name means

Day 5
A Barnabas Ministry

Read Acts 11:19-30 to see examples of Barnabas' ministry.

1. What does the nickname Barnabas mean?
2. Why did the apostles give him this nickname?
3. Name someone you have known who had a special gift for encouraging others.
4. If you formed a "Barnabas Ministry" for

"Son of Encouragement." The Semitic phrase "son of" identifies the quality or trait of character that distinguishes a person. Thus we are told that this generous man — "a Levite from Cyprus" who had relatives in Jerusalem (cf. Acts 12:12; Col. 4:10) — had the gift of encouraging and building up others.

Barnabas' ministry of encouraging others is demonstrated in Acts at Antioch of Syria (11:23), with Saul (11:25-26), and at a critical juncture in the life of John Mark (11:25-26). Larkin calls Barnabas "a 'bridge person,' bringing diverse parties together so that the cause of Christ advances and both older and newer believers are encouraged." [*Acts*, pp. 83-84.] His ministry of encouragement never has too many volunteers.

your church today, what would be its first challenging opportunity?

5. Pray for God to give you the opportunity to be someone's Barnabas today.

Week Eight

Acts 5:1-16 (III E to III F in Outline)

Day 1
Good Deeds and
False Motives

Read Matthew 6:1-18 about the temptation to do "acts of righteousness" to be seen by men.

1. Review the teaching of Jesus from Matt. 6:1-18.
2. Have you ever been tempted to do a good thing from a false motive? Explain.
3. What did Paul say about this issue at 1 Corinthians 13:1-3?
4. Why do you think Ananias and Sapphira attempted their fraud?
5. What do you do to keep your motives pure?

E. The Sad Episode with Ananias and Sapphira. 5:1-11.

Not every member of the original body of believers at Jerusalem was pure in motive and action. As the first Christians lived out their unity in generous sharing of their goods with one another — already cited twice by Luke in his narrative (2:44-45; 4:32-37) — their Spirit-generated virtue also created an opportunity for Satanic temptation. After Barnabas sold a piece of land, brought the gross amount received, and "put it at the apostles' feet," a husband and wife in the group were tempted to imitate him for the sake of drawing attention to themselves. This incident could have set back the progress of the church, but the superintending presence of God was able to turn even this ugly event into a means of stimulating additional zeal and growth.

1. Their conspiracy. 5:1-2.

Ananias [An-ə-nī´-əs] and Sapphira [Sə-fī´-rə] set about to perpetrate a deliberate act of deception and fraud. The beautiful and generous act of Barnabas stirred something unholy in them. As they observed the notoriety that must have come with his gift, they were apparently moved to want some of the spotlight and adoration for themselves. Not with a desire to help the poor as their primary motivation but with a craving for attention, Ananias and Sapphira sold a piece of land they owned. They conspired to withhold part of the money received but to present the balance as if it had been the full amount received. They made their fateful decision, and Ananias turned the money over to the apostles.

The setting for this event should be a warning to believers of every generation. It is not wrong to do a noteworthy and public thing, but it is wrong to do anything for the sake of calling attention to oneself. Letting one's light shine for the sake of giving glory is one thing; shining a light on oneself in the name of honoring God is something else again. While it would be wrong to withhold one's giftedness or resources from God, it would be equally wrong to use either to inflate one's ego. Jesus warned: "Be careful not to do your 'acts of righteousness' before men, to be seen by them. If you do, you will have no reward from your Father in heaven" (Matt. 6:1ff).

2. Their punishment. 5:3-10.

No sooner had Ananias offered his gift than he was unmasked. While some have supposed that Ananias's nervous or haughty spirit betrayed him, it seems more likely that a Spirit-empowered apostle was allowed to know the secrets of his heart. Peter confronted him and demanded that he account for the lie he had told. "Ananias, how is it that Satan has so filled your heart that you have lied to the Holy Spirit and have kept for yourself some of the money you received for the land?" All sin is ultimately against God (cf. Gen. 39:9b). Yet there was a sense in which this sin was particularly offensive in that it was done in the name of Christian charity. It was a false and treacherous calling of the name of God over an action that was deliberately unholy.

The charge that Satan had "filled" Ananias's heart to do this thing does not mean that he was caused to do something against his will. Whenever someone sins willfully (cf. Heb. 10:26; Exod. 21:14), the magnitude of the sin is compounded; he has allowed Satan to fill his heart and has yielded himself to the enemy of our souls. Neither should this statement

**Day 2
Lying to God**

Read Hebrews 4:12-13 about God's knowledge of human behavior.

1. Why did Peter accuse Ananias of lying "to God"?
2. In what sense is every human sin an act against God?
3. What does the term *omniscience* claim for God? Explain its meaning in your own words.
4. Why would anyone ever believe he could pull a fast one on God?
5. In what ways do you think people still try to lie to God?

be taken to mean that Ananias (and Sapphira) had never been truly converted to Christ, never really saved. That saved persons may still sin is evident from the fact that New Testament letters are filled with exhortations against doing so (Eph. 4:25ff; 1 John 2:1-2). For Christians to continue sinning serves to "grieve the Holy Spirit of God" (Eph. 4:30) and will eventually lead to spiritual death (1 John 5:16-17).

Verse four makes it clear that the selling of goods by some of the believers at Jerusalem was a voluntary thing. Ananias was not commanded to sell the land. If he had chosen to sell the land without giving any of its proceeds to the church, there would have been no sin involved. "Didn't it belong to you before it was sold?" asked Peter. "And after it was sold, wasn't the money at your disposal?" The evil here was in the attempted deception through a lie.

When Ananias heard Peter's rebuke, he fell dead. There was no mercy shown nor was there a call to repentance, for his deed was willful and arrogant. Certain young men wrapped his body in a shroud and took it out for burial. No provision was made for the traditional mourning rites that accompanied a death in Jewish culture of that time and place.

When Sapphira came to Peter some three hours afterward, she was unaware of what had happened with her husband. Perhaps part of their conspiracy had been the desire to extend and magnify the attention their gift would bring them by coming before the church's leaders at separate times. When Peter saw her, he asked whether the things he had been told earlier by her husband were in fact true. When she verified the story, she was challenged in the same direct manner Ananias had been. "How could you agree to test the Spirit of the Lord?" he demanded. The expression "test the Spirit" indicates what a brazen and premeditated sin this was. Two people

Day 3
Deadly Sin

Read 1 John 5:13-17 about "sin that leads to death."

1. Sin seldom brings immediate physical death. Can you think of some biblical episodes where it did?

2. What is the meaning of Romans 6:23? Cf. Revelation 20:14.

3. What is the "sin that leads to death" in 1 John 5? Cf. 1 John 1:9.

4. How may one interrupt the "death cycle" that sin sets in motion?

5. Why were Ananias and Sapphira given no opportunity of repentance?

had deliberately attempted to "put one over on" the Lord and to challenge his infinite knowledge of human behaviors and motivations. Sin cannot go undetected with God — even when men are deceived.

As with her husband before her, Sapphira "fell down at [Peter's] feet and died." She was buried in the same swift and unceremonious way her husband had been.

A sin is occasionally dealt with in the swift and strong manner of this one. More often, however, the perpetrators of evil deeds may go undetected for a long time or receive only minor punishment for the most horrible of deeds. Why this sin brought such startling severity is not difficult to understand. In its earliest and most formative days, God had to protect the church from hypocrites and willful sinners. If these two people had been allowed to get by with their deception, rise to a position of respect and/or leadership within the church, and infect others with the leaven of their impure motivations, the sound-ness of the body of Christ at Jerusalem could have been irrevocably compromised.

3. The reaction to this event. 5:11.

The effect of this sorry episode was hardly a nega-tive one. For one thing, "great fear seized the whole church." This is the first time in the text of Acts that Luke uses the word "church" (Gk. *ekklesia*). By doing so, he implicitly offers his own explanation for the severity of punishment brought against Ananias and Sapphira. Since the *ekklesia* is a "citizen assembly," it is important for its purity to be upheld; to sin against the body of people called by God to be his own is a terrible thing. Making an example of these two surely caused all the other members of the Jerusalem church to take heed to their actions and motives. Even non-Christians were affected by what had happened, for "all who heard about these events" were also filled with fear.

Day 4
Graceful Recoveries

Read of God's ability to turn something evil into a victory at Genesis 45:1-13.

1. How did God turn the potential harm of this episode into a triumph?
2. Why do you think a "growth spurt" for the church followed this episode?
3. Have you ever seen a potential tragedy in your own spiritual life turned into a victory by God's power? Explain.
4. What does the word

sovereignty claim for God? How does it relate to this matter of bringing triumphs out of tragedies?

5. State the meaning of Rom. 8:28 in your own words.

"The message of this for Christian and non-Christian alike is self-evident. Christians must realize that the selfless, transparent fellowship of the church must never be violated by selfish hypocrisy. Further, it is proper to employ discipline to guard the church's integrity, unity and purity. For the non-Christian, this account is a warning: Think twice before joining this holy fellowship. Are you willing to pay the price — fully renouncing wicked ways and full-heartedly embracing Christ and other believers in his body, the church?" [Larkin, *Acts*, pp. 87-88.]

This story is fully consistent with Luke's emphasis in his Gospel on the harm done when money becomes an obsession in someone's life. Many of the parables in his Gospel deal with money: the Parable of the Debtors (7:41ff), the Parable of the Good Samaritan (10:29ff), the Parable of the Rich Fool (12:16ff), the Parable of the Unjust Steward (16:1ff), and the Parable of the Pounds (19:11ff). In addition, there are stories about the rich man and Lazarus (16:19ff), the rich young ruler (18:18ff), and a rich man whom God called a fool because he thought his security could come from well-filled barns (12:15ff). Barnabas' wealth did not destroy him, for he was not in love with his land and money; he was able to use his prosperity to give God glory through generous sharing. In the case of a married couple without integrity, however, we see demonstrated again that "the love of money is a root of all kinds of evil" (1 Tim. 6:10). Although the name Ananias means "Yahweh is gracious," this man showed that he had not learned graciousness toward others; although Sapphira means "beautiful," this woman exhibited the ugliness of one who would conspire to deceive and dishonor God.

F. Additional Signs and Additional Conversions. 5:12-16.

One might expect to hear that the event just chronicled sent the growth of the Jerusalem church into a tailspin. The opposite proved to be the case. Using Solomon's Colonnade as a regular place to congregate (cf. 3:11), the believers continued to gather and grow. Yet their growth was among those seeking the Lord with sincerity of heart rather than among hangers-on who attached themselves to an interesting new movement.

Luke informs us that the apostles "performed many miraculous signs and wonders among the people." Verse 16 gives some details by explaining that the word of God's presence and activity at the hands of the apostles was spreading rapidly. Not only in Jerusalem but "from the towns around Jerusalem," people brought sick and demon-possessed friends of theirs to the apostles. "All of them were healed," Luke observes.

Verse 14 describes the overall result of this outburst of divine activity: "more and more men and women believed in the Lord and were added to their number." But how does that statement square with the statement at verse 13 that "no one dared join them, even though they were highly regarded by the people"? These two claims are perfectly intelligible when viewed in light of the Ananias and Sapphira episode. Given what had happened to those would-be deceivers, no one who was less than fully persuaded about Jesus and willing to follow him in sincerity of heart dared to attach himself to the church lest a similar fate befall him for his insincerity. Among those who saw the hand of God in what had happened and were willing to give themselves without reservation both to him and to his people, conversions continued to multiply at a phenomenal rate.

Luke is painting a consistent picture for us of the

Day 5
Building Community

Read Ephesians 4:17-28 about how God creates community among his saved people.

1. What does the term *community* imply about the church?
2. In what ways did God build community among the members of the first church at Jerusalem?
3. What factors work against community in today's church?
4. How do you see community being established among the members of your church?
5. Pray for God to use you as a catalyst for creating community among Christians.

earliest church. People who were in love with Jesus learned to love one another. They evidenced their love by the very practical action of sharing their goods with one another. Yet God's activity of building true community among believers could have been compromised and defeated by people who acted from false, self-seeking motives.

This story reminds us to be introspective about our relationships with one another. Is our love for Jesus generating an increasing love for other believers? Do we use our gifts and resources to assist one another? Does Satan ever tempt us to be self-serving with our actions? Are we able to keep our motivation Christ-centered rather than self-centered?

Week Nine

Acts 5:17-42 (III G in Outline)

Satan is a spoiler and has never been content to leave any good thing unchallenged. With the church at Jerusalem growing rapidly, it was to be expected that he would generate opposition. Peter and John had already been brought before the Sanhedrin in chapter 4. That episode had ended with threats but no actual persecution of the apostles. The confrontation Luke tells of next would not end so pleasantly, but it would also serve to stimulate rather than stifle the young church.

G. The Conflict with Judaism Intensifies. 5:17-42.

1. Imprisonment, release, and examination. 5:17-32.

Since their earlier encounter with Peter and John following the healing of a lame man, the High Priest and his fellow Sadducees had kept close watch on their activities. Enraged that their threat had been ignored and jealous over the popularity the apostles were gaining with the people of Jerusalem, they had the temple police arrest all twelve of the apostles to make good the earlier threat of dire consequences and to put an end to their troublesome preaching — particularly the matter of "proclaiming in Jesus the resurrection of the dead."

Heaven thwarted the High Priest's plan by sending an angel to open the prison doors and free the apostles during their very first night in captivity. The Twelve were not told to flee Jerusalem but to resume their work there: "Go, stand in the temple courts, and tell the people the full message of this new life."

Day 1
Jealousy

Read about godly jealousy at 2 Corinthians 11:1-6.

1. What is "godly jealousy"?
2. When is jealousy an unholy and ungodly thing?
3. Why were members of the Sanhedrin *jealous* of the apostles?
4. What sort of jealousy was this?
5. Is any unholy form of jealousy a threat to your spiritual life? Explain.

Early the following morning, "at daybreak" in fact, they were back at their business of preaching Jesus and the covenant life he alone can make possible.

Not realizing the apostles were free and teaching the people, the High Priest convened a meeting of the full Sanhedrin on the day following their arrest. He then sent for the Twelve to be brought in for trial. "But on arriving at the jail, the officers did not find them there." The temple police returned to the Sanhedrin and reported what they had discovered. They went into some detail to make it clear, however, that the loss of the prisoners was not their fault. They said: "We found the jail securely locked, with the guards standing at the doors; but when we opened them, we found no one inside."

As the commander of the temple police and the chief priests were trying to figure out what had become of the apostles, word came that they were circulating openly in the temple grounds and preaching. "Look! The men you put in jail are standing in the temple courts teaching the people." The captain took a delegation of officers with him and summoned the apostles to go with them into the chambers of the Sanhedrin. He was appropriately cautious, however, and did not use force or do anything that could precipitate a riot. He wisely discerned that they were held in high esteem by the people listening to their teaching and feared for himself and his men if the crowd should resist their attempt to arrest the Twelve.

Day 2
Standing Firm

Read Ephesians 6:10-20 about strength and standing firm for Christ.

1. What message did the Sanhedrin have for the apostles?

When they appeared before the Sanhedrin, the apostles were reminded of the strict orders that had been given to Peter and John about preaching Jesus. "We gave you strict orders not to teach in this name," the High Priest reminded them. "Yet you have filled Jerusalem with your teaching and are determined to make us guilty of this man's blood." They were *alarmed* that people all over Jerusalem had now been exposed to their teaching about Jesus and the resurrection. Even more, they were *outraged* that the apostles' teaching had had the effect of somehow blaming the Sanhedrin for having Jesus put to death.

While the general rule would have men under arrest nervous in facing a court with authority over them, the situation in this case seems to have been quite the reverse. It was the body of Jewish rulers that appears clearly on the defensive before the apostles.

Peter and the other men with him did not deny the charge. Rather, they eventually repeated and expanded it. But the first issue on Peter's agenda was to respond to the claim that an order from the Sanhedrin to cease their preaching should have ended the matter. "We must obey God rather than men!" he asserted boldly. "Thus he places on one side the chief council of the Jews, and on the other God and the followers of Christ. Here is not only a defiance of his judges; here again is a bold declaration that the Christian church is independent of the Jewish state." [Erdman, *Acts*, p. 61.]

With his accuser-judges reeling from his disclaimer of their accountability to them, Peter pressed the case for their share of the responsibility for the death of Jesus. "The God of our fathers raised Jesus from the dead — whom you had killed by hanging him on a tree. God exalted him to his own right hand as Prince and Savior that he might give repentance and forgiveness of sins to Israel. We are witnesses of these things, and so is the Holy Spirit, whom God has given to those who obey him."

Thus did the apostles make clear that their obligation and intention was to keep on preaching Jesus, his resurrection, and the Sanhedrin's complicity in his unjust death. Nor could the Jewish officials have missed Peter's emphasis on the need for repentance and forgiveness of sins for all in Israel — including

2. How did the apostles reply to the court's mandate?

3. What factors do you see combining to produce this sort of boldness in the apostles?

4. Are you aware of contemporary situations where Christians have been required to silence their witness to Jesus? How should they respond?

5. Would it be possible to confuse *poor judgment* or *overly aggressive tactics* with boldness? How may the two be distinguished?

Israel's leaders. Both in its discomfiting call for repentance and in its generous offer of pardon, the gospel really is for everyone.

2. The counsel of Gamaliel concerning the apostles. 5:33-39.

The uncompromising posture of the Twelve threw the council into a furor. Luke writes: "When they heard this, they were furious and wanted to put them to death." It takes little imagination to believe that the mood of the group on that day was little (if any!) short of the rage it would later vent against Stephen (cf. 7:54ff). On the latter occasion, however, there would be no voice of moderation raised to prevent a murder. Here the intercession came from a most unlikely source. One of the Sanhedrin's own members ventured to make a statement on behalf of the apostles.

The man who calmed the excited group was Gamaliel [Gə-mā´-lē-əl], otherwise known in Jewish literature as "Gamaliel the Elder." He was a minority member of the Sanhedrin and the respected Pharisee who led the famous School of Hillel. Saul of Tarsus was trained in the Torah under his guidance (cf. 22:3). What motivated his action? It may have stemmed from partisan politics within the Sanhedrin. While the Sadducees were particularly offended by the doctrine of the resurrection of the dead, Pharisees affirmed it — although their idea of the resurrection life was hardly that of Jesus and the apostles. On the other hand, Gamaliel's action in this setting may have come from his sense of moral responsibility. Or perhaps he somehow sensed that these men standing before him and his peers were not to be taken lightly in their claim that God was with them.

Gamaliel had the Twelve removed from the chamber so he could address his peers on the high court of Judaism. He began by reminding the council members of other movements before Christianity that had come

---

Day 3
The Voice of Reason

Read 1 Peter 3:1-7 for a biblical case where believers are called on to prove their faith with faithfulness over time.

1. What do you know about *Gamaliel* from other biblical or research tools?

2. What was the essence of his counsel to his Sanhedrin peers in this case?

3. What *wisdom* do you see in such counsel?

4. Do you see *limitations* to Gamaliel's approach? Explain.

5. Under what circumstances can you see yourself giving someone this advice about a difficult situation?

to the fore within their ancient religion. Specifically, he called them to remember Theudas and Judas of Galilee. Theudas was an otherwise unknown insurgent who should not be confused with a man of the same name who is mentioned by Josephus and who led an uprising some years after the events of this text. Judas of Galilee was a Jewish rebel who opposed the paying of tribute to the Romans and fomented a revolt against the empire in A.D. 6.

Why had the ill-fated movements of Theudas and Judas collapsed in failure? Their efforts were "of human origin," reasoned Gamaliel, and failed because God was not the author of their efforts. On the other hand, he continued, something that really was "of God" would surely succeed and efforts to stand against it would be a defiance of the Holy One. "Therefore, in the present case I advise you: Leave these men alone! Let them go!" said Gamaliel. "For if their purpose or activity is of human origin, it will fail. But if it is from God, you will not be able to stop these men; you will only find yourselves fighting against God."

As Charles R. Erdman points out: "This counsel was not perfect; it was not wholly courageous; it did not propose an effort to weigh evidence and to discover truth; but it was far from the mad intolerance which had swayed the Jewish court. It rebuked the impatience which so often is the essence of persecution and bigotry. It allowed time to test the right of the cause. Such advice is often needed; it is always infinitely better than a resort to violence, or than the suggestion that might makes right." [*Acts*, p. 62.] At the very least, Gamaliel counseled the group to adopt a *laissez faire* attitude for the time being and to watch for developments that would make the status of the apostles clear as to whether their actions were of God or not.

3. The apostles' boldness following their release. 5:40-42.

The Sanhedrin was calmed a bit by Gamaliel's

Day 4
Suffering for Jesus
Read 1 Peter 1:3-12 about suffering trials for one's faith.

1. What disposition did the Sanhedrin make of the apostles after the hearing?
2. How did the apostles react to the flogging they received?
3. Why do you think they were not intimidated by the threats and beating they received?
4. What embarrassment, intimidation, or threat have you ever experienced because of your faith?
5. Why does God allow people to suffer when they are doing right?

plea and abandoned the notion of putting the Twelve to death. But the consensus of the group was that some sort of punishment was required. Thus they had the men "flogged," presumably with the 39-stroke limit which was customary as a penalty for certain offenses under the Jewish law (cf. Deut. 25:3). They would not become party to another murder so soon after the death of Jesus, yet neither would they allow the apostles to leave their presence without attempting to intimidate them by a show of force.

In view of Jesus' warnings to the apostles that they would have to suffer for his sake and be subjected to the same indignities he had experienced, they looked upon their beating as an honor. "The apostles left the Sanhedrin, rejoicing because they had been counted worthy of suffering disgrace for the Name" (i.e., for the sake of Jesus, cf. Matt. 5:11). One of them would later write: "In this you greatly rejoice, though now for a little while you may have to suffer grief in all kinds of trials. These have come so that your faith — of greater worth than gold, which perishes even though refined by fire — may be proved genuine and may result in praise, glory and honor when Jesus Christ is revealed" (1 Pet. 1:6-7). Then, following their release, the apostles immediately resumed their daily routine of public (i.e., "in the temple courts") and private (i.e., "from house to house") proclamation of the joyous message about Jesus.

Our God is sovereign over all people and in all situations. If *appearance* said that the apostles were somehow at the mercy of the Sanhedrin, *reality* replied to affirm that the Sanhedrin was at the mercy of God. It could not stop the purposes of God that centered on the preaching of the gospel, and one of its own members could be used by the Lord to spare its messengers from the threat of death. Even in the face of opposition, his church would continue to grow and thrive.

Day 5
Holy Boldness

Read Psalm 138 and notice David's comment about being bold and stouthearted.

1. "What the comfortable church of modern times needs is a good dose of persecution!" How do you react to such a statement?
2. How does opposition sometimes make people bolder in their faith?
3. Apart from persecution, what factors tend to make Christians bold and courageous in their faith?
4. Can you recall a situation in which you believe you acted *boldly* as a believer? Explain.
5. Pray for God to enable you to be bold when your faith is challenged or offered any form of threatening compromise.

Week Ten

Acts 6:1-7 (III H to III I in Outline)

A far greater threat to a church than persecutions from some external source is tension from within. Think, for example, of Paul's experience two decades after this one in Acts with the situation of the church at Corinth. With all the problems that congregation faced — immorality among some of its members, doctrinal misunderstandings about the resurrection of the dead, and abuse of the Lord's Supper — the *first* issue he addressed in writing to that church was its potential for division (1 Cor. 1:10ff; cf. 3:1ff).

The brief threat to the Jerusalem church from the sin of Ananias and Sapphira had passed. It had even led to a period of renewed zeal and devotion on the part of the entire body of believers. But the problem that surfaces in 6:1ff was of far greater magnitude than the conspiracy of deceit involving only two members. It involved a potential division of the entire congregation into a body of Grecian Jews separated from a body of Hebraic Jews.

At the very least, the issue that surfaced here could have been used by Satan to distract the apostles from their primary duties of prayer and teaching. At its greatest potential for harm, the devil could have used it to turn a large and growing church's membership into two or more competing, warring factions.

H. Solving an Internal Problem in the Jerusalem Church. 6:1-6.

As the church continued to grow, there were now several thousand Christians in Jerusalem. Many continued to congregate in the temple grounds, and

Day 1
Caring for Widows

Read Deuteronomy 24:19-22 about Yahweh's concern for widows.

1. What are some of the Bible's provisions about caring for widows?
2. Why is God so concerned about this group of people?
3. How does your church serve the needs of widows?
4. Do you know of a widow with limited family members? Special needs?
5. What can you do to assist that person — perhaps anonymously?

many more were meeting in homes. One of the ministries the collective body appears to have undertaken from the start of its existence was a regular administration of money and/or goods to widows within its membership.

Care for widows and orphans — the most defenseless and helpless persons in an ancient culture — has been a distinguishing mark of the religion of the true God under both the old and new covenants. "Defend the cause of the fatherless, plead the case of the widow" (Isa. 1:17). "Religion that God our Father accepts as pure and faultless is this: to look after orphans in their distress and to keep oneself from being polluted by the world" (Jas. 1:27).

This compassionate work ran into difficulty when "the Grecian Jews among them complained against the Hebraic Jews because their widows were being overlooked in the daily distribution of food." A "Grecian Jew" was a Greek-speaking Jew whose adult life had been lived in the *diaspora* (i.e., scattered) situation that had been created by various events of displacement of Hebrew people from their homeland. These people had maintained their religious and ethnic identity through the synagogues in their own cities. Some of these widows may have been visitors to Jerusalem with their families for the Jewish festival of Pentecost who had become Christians and were extending their stay for the sake of being grounded more deeply in their new faith and life (cf. 2:9-11). More were probably widows whose husbands had lived outside Palestine and who had come to the Holy City to live out their final days, die, and be buried. A "Hebraic Jew" was an Aramaic-speaking Jew of Palestine.

There was an old and prejudicial division between these two groups. Because of their cultural heritage and language, the Hebraic Jews thought themselves superior to the Grecian Jews. Each group

Day 2
Settling Disputes

Read what Jesus said about settling matters of dispute at Matthew 5:21-26.

1. Do you think the Grecian Jews were being neglected? Deliberately?
2. Explain the background from which the suspicion of neglect could easily arise in the Jerusalem church.
3. What steps did the apostles take to clear things up? What responsibility did they give to the church? How did the church show good faith?
4. Are you aware of (or involved in) a situation of suspicion, misunderstanding, or alienation among Christians? If so, characterize it succinctly.

was suspicious of the other. All these prejudices and fears came to a focus in the complaint registered here. The Greek-speaking Jews believed favoritism was being shown the Aramaic-speaking women receiving food from the church.

This honest presentation of a first-century crisis helps us in a couple of ways. First, we sometimes hear or express a longing for the unity and peace of the first century in our churches. The first-century church was not perfect, and it was not always a model of unity and peace. There were tense times among those early Christians. They were saved human beings having to learn the meaning of their salvation and unity in Christ — just as we are. Second, just as the Grecian and Hebraic Jews brought their old attitudes and prejudices into the church with them, so have some of us brought racial, cultural, and denominational prejudices with us. We must be honest when we confront those old attitudes in our new life and allow the Lord to deal with them.

Today the potential divisions may be along the lines of foreign missions versus local ministry programs, caring for needy persons in the church versus caring for needy people in the larger community, traditional versus contemporary worship styles, or intellectual versus relational approaches to teaching the gospel. In his discussion of this tendency, Lloyd Ogilvie has said: "I have called these differences the tyranny of the either/or. It is bringing to the gospel our previous conditioning and wanting it all our way in affirmation of previous experience or loyalties. We often miss the potent formula of authentic Christianity: the both/and." [*Acts*, p. 135.]

The apostles acted immediately and decisively to head off the threat of division. Since their ministry was the joint task of prayer and preaching, they would not abandon that calling to personally see to

5. Is there any contribution you can make to resolving the matter? If so, are you willing to do it?

Day 3
Church Unity

Read 1 Corinthians 1:4-17 about the urgency of unity in the church.

1. How was the unity of the church threatened by this situation?
2. In what ways was this situation of grumbling in the church a greater threat than the sin of Ananias?
3. Why is unity so critical to the life of a church?
4. Have you ever witnessed a church polarization or division? How was it resolved?

5. What steps can a church's leadership take to promote the oneness of a body of diverse people?

**Day 4
Church Leadership**

Read Titus 1:5-16 for information about church leadership.

1. As the initial leaders of the Jerusalem church, what positive steps did the apostles take to deal with this crisis?

2. What does this episode tell you about *top-down* versus *bottom-up* leadership? Were the seven deacons appointed by the apostles or chosen by the church?

3. What three basic criteria were the new leaders to have? How generic are these to church leadership?

4. How do you understand the role of an elder? Deacon?

5. What personal duties and/or aspirations do you have about church leadership?

the daily provision for widows. They called the disciples together and had them select seven qualified men to put over that work. "Brothers, choose seven men from among you who are known to be full of the Spirit and wisdom," they said. "We will turn this responsibility over to them, and we will give our attention to prayer and the ministry of the word."

Church leaders should learn from the wisdom exhibited here. The responsible *delegation* of tasks in the church is the best way to get more good work done. Good leadership is seldom exercised by leaving a prior duty of vision-casting, teaching, and administration to try to carry through on every detail of the church's ministry. But even the act of delegating itself should be done through *consensus* rather than fiat. The apostles studied the problem, laid a proposed solution before the church, and allowed the church to take ownership of the solution by both approving the solution and then selecting the persons who would implement it. This is a far better approach than merely asking the church to ratify a decision already reached.

As to the qualifications expected of the seven, there were essentially three. Although the NIV reading tends to run the first two together, *The Message* correctly separates them: "So, friends, choose seven men from among you whom everyone trusts, men full of the Holy Spirit and good sense, and we'll assign them this task." First, they were to be persons "whom everyone trusts." The people who lead church ministries and represent the body in its work must have a good reputation. Second, they were to be "men full of the Holy Spirit." This simply affirms that people who carry responsibility in a church's ministry must give evidence of the Spirit's presence and fruitfulness (cf. Gal. 5:22-23). Third, they were to be "men full of . . . good sense." Men of this caliber could be trusted by everyone to see to the equitable handling of the funds used to help widows and thus relieve the apostles from distraction.

The seven men selected by the group's consent all have Greek names. This suggests that the Aramaic-speaking believers demonstrated their purity of motive in this matter by turning the ministry over to their Greek-speaking brothers. By this, they both showed good faith and preserved the unity of the church. Jerusalem did not need an either/or church of Greek-speakers on one corner and a congregation of Aramaic-speakers opposite it. The same can be said of the issues that often threaten the unity of churches today. Ogilvie's suggestion that Christianity offers a both/and solution to such tensions is certainly borne out in this instance.

Once the church had approved the apostles' suggestion and presented the seven men they had selected to them, the Twelve "prayed and laid their hands on them." The men were thereby commissioned to their task. Although the noun "deacon" is not used of these men, the verb form of the word is used to describe their work.

The Greek term *diakonos* appears 29 times in the New Testament. Our problem defining it in today's churches grows out of the fact that it is used so broadly. It refers to someone who serves at table (Matt. 22:13), holds a position in government (Rom. 13:4), servants of God (2 Cor. 6:4), a servant of Christ (Col. 1:7), male servants of the church (Col. 1:25), and female servants of the church (Rom. 16:1). If one adds the verb form of the word (*diakoneo*), a clearer — although still-broader — picture emerges. Jesus served his disciples (Luke 22:27b) and told us to lead in his kingdom by serving others (Luke 22:26). Everyone should serve with the gift God has given him or her (1 Pet. 4:10).

Fundamentally, then, anyone who serves, supports, or ministers in service to God is a deacon. It is

Day 5
Deacons

Read 1 Timothy 3:8-13 about the qualifications of deacons.

1. Distinguish *title* and *function* relative to the work of a deacon.
2. React to this statement: "Healthy churches are filled with deacons."
3. How may churches hamper their effectiveness by the failure to delegate responsibility?
4. Why do many churches appear to have difficulty with delegation?
5. Who are the deacons in your church? How can you identify them?

not a role for a limited number of God's people; it is the common role all Christians fill at one time or another and likely in a variety of ways.

There are a few places in the New Testament, however, where the service or ministry pointed to by the word *deacon* seems clearly to indicate what we would say is an "office" in the church. Paul addressed a letter to the church at Philippi "together with the overseers and deacons" (Phil. 1:1). First Timothy 3:8-13 gives character criteria for a church's deacons.

Interestingly, however, the same title is applied to the woman Phoebe in Romans 16:1, and the "office" she filled may be specified at 1 Timothy 3:11. The New International Version translates: "In the same way, their *wives* . . ." But a footnote to the NIV offers: "In the same way, *deaconesses* . . ." The original text simply has the word for "women" (Gk. *gynaikas*) at verse 11, and whether the "women" are women in general, wives of male deacons, or female deacons is impossible to know for certain.

As an official position, a deacon is best understood as any person in the church who is entrusted with a specific task by the congregation. Some tasks may be long-term and others of short duration. Thus Sunday School teachers or Small-Group Leaders are that church's deacons/deaconesses-ministers-servants for teaching the Bible in small settings, men and women who make bank deposits, monitor accounts, and/or write checks are its financial ministers-deacons, etc. People serving on committees, directing worship, coordinating summer camps — all these people are filling the "office" (i.e., functional leadership) of deacon. They are to be measured for their tasks by the criteria given at Acts 6:3 and 1 Timothy 3:8ff.

Because of the confusion over the *titular* — rather than *functional* — office of deacon, many churches prefer to use the term ministry leader or some equivalent for those functional coordinators of a church's work. Several years ago, we adopted this method at the church where I serve. Thus our letterhead doesn't carry a list of deacons for the simple reason that it is both incredibly long and in constant flux as tasks are assigned and completed.

I. Another Period of Evangelistic Progress. 6:7.

Following the successful resolution of the problem involving welfare provisions for its widows, the Jerusalem church renewed its commitment to spreading the gospel. Luke's progress report at this point is especially interesting in view of the impact on the Jewish order that is noted.

More and more people heard and responded to the gospel. Noteworthy among this ever-growing number was "a large number of priests." Some have estimated that there were 18,000 priests and Levites in Palestine at this time, 8,000 of whom were priests. The fact that significant inroads were being made into the ranks of the priesthood indicates something about the effectiveness of Christian evangelism. It also points to the sincerity that characterized many of the ordinary priests whose attitude toward the gospel was vastly different from that of the "chief priests" who were concerned to protect the vested interests of the establishment.

Week Eleven

Acts 6:8–8:3 (III J to III K in Outline)

Day 1
Ministry to One's Own

Read 1 Corinthians 9:19-23 about culturally appropriate ministry.

1. Why was Stephen particularly effective as a teacher of Greek-speaking Jews?

2. How does cultural understanding contribute to effective communication of the gospel?

3. Is this the same as *racism* and *cultural exclusivism*? Distinguish clearly.

4. How might the church learn from this case study about our own evangelism?

5. Are there particular ethnic groups, professions, or other cultures where you have meaningful connections? How are you using them to communicate the gospel?

Among the seven deacons appointed in the Jerusalem church (6:5), there were two men of special prominence. Chapter 7 tells the story of Stephen, and chapter 8 relates the work of Philip.

J. The Martyrdom of Stephen. 6:8–8:1a.

1. Opposition to Stephen's ministry and his arrest. 6:8-15.

Stephen was not only a man capable of administering relief to widows, he was also an adept student-teacher of the Word of God. He was blessed with "God's grace and power" to the degree that he could both teach persuasively and perform miraculous signs in confirmation of what he said.

Because he was a Grecian Jew himself, Stephen focused his energy on Greek-speaking Jews with a similar background. Several of the scores of synagogues in and around Jerusalem at the time were populated with people with a *diaspora* background. He went to those synagogues, presented Jesus as the Messiah, and debated with people who opposed his message. So successful was this ministry (i.e., people who opposed him "could not stand up against his wisdom or the Spirit by whom he spoke") that it aroused particularly fierce opposition from one of those synagogues.

Stephen came to be opposed by the "Synagogue of the Freedmen (as it was called) — Jews of Cyrene [Sī-rē´-nē] and Alexandria as well as the provinces of Cilicia [Sə-lĭ´-shə] and Asia." The effective power of his ministry and the apparent conversion of some of the men from this synagogue to the new Christ-movement soon became the background for a smear campaign against him. Certain leaders in the group "secretly persuaded some men" to charge Stephen with blaspheming both Moses and God. The whispering campaign eventually led to a formal charge being lodged against him with the Sanhedrin. This was the complaint against him: "This fellow never stops speaking against this holy place and against the law. For we have heard him say that this Jesus of Nazareth will destroy this place and change the customs Moses handed down to us."

This sort of dirty tactic is still common in politics and religion. When serious discussion and search for the truth are abandoned, personal attacks aimed at the messenger are started. And the great likelihood is that in the Synagogue of the Freedmen, none other than the brilliant, young, Greek-speaking Pharisee Saul of Tarsus led the campaign against Stephen.

The false charges against Stephen ultimately reduce to two: (1) that he blasphemed God by speaking disparagingly against the Jewish temple and (2) that he blasphemed Moses by opposing the Law given through him. The former charge probably related to his citation of certain prophecies Jesus made either about his own body (cf. John 2:19-21) or about the destruction of the Jerusalem temple (cf. Matt. 24:1ff); the latter centered on a change in the "customs Moses handed down" to the Jews and probably stemmed from remarks he would have made about Jesus' death on the cross having made all other sacrifices unnecessary. The first charge would appeal to the Sadducees who controlled the priesthood and temple; the second would agitate the Pharisees who were zealously devoted to preserving the Law and the traditions they had evolved around it.

As he stood in the well of the Sanhedrin chamber to answer these charges, every eye was glued on Stephen.

Day 2
Slander

Read James 3:1-12 about the harm that can be done by out-of-control tongues.

1. What sort of "smear campaign" was mounted against Stephen by his opponents?
2. What things taught by Stephen were at the root of the slanderous charges? How were those teachings twisted by his opponents?
3. Have you ever witnessed a smear campaign against someone? What was its effect? Were you influenced by it? Were you able to do anything to counteract it?
4. Define *slander* in your own words.
5. Why is slander such a mean-spirited evil?

Luke records that his accusers and judges "saw that his face was like the face of an angel." This could mean that his face glowed in a way similar to that of Jesus at his transfiguration; it may be simply a reference to the calm and serene spirit exhibited on his face as he stood in the presence of his accusers.

2. *His defense before the Sanhedrin. 7:1-53.*

With the High Priest presiding over the trial, Stephen would have been required to respond to the serious accusations that had been brought against him. The deacon-evangelist's defense was not of his own person or behavior but of God's activity in the history of his Jewish kinsmen. With Old Testament history as his platform, he preached the gospel of Jesus Christ to the Sanhedrin.

Stephen traced the history of Israel from the call of Abraham to the building of Solomon's temple. From this factual survey, he showed that the Jews had followed a consistent pattern of persecuting the prophets and rejecting God's word when it was delivered to them. He finally ended his speech with a stinging accusation to the effect that the Jews of his own time were guilty of the same sin of hardening their hearts against God. Specifically, he charged that in their rejection of Jesus as their Messiah, the Jews had committed the greatest of all sins in the nation's history.

The climax to his sermon came in these words: "You stiff-necked people, with uncircumcised hearts and ears! You are just like your fathers: You always resist the Holy Spirit! Was there ever a prophet your fathers did not persecute? They even killed those who predicted the coming of the Righteous One. And now you have betrayed and murdered him — you who have received the law that was put into effect through angels but have not obeyed it."

**Day 3
A Philosophy of
History**

Read Ecclesiastes 1:1-11 for a sad man's view of history as meaningless.

1. Why was Solomon so pessimistic about history in Eccl. 1?
2. Stephen reviewed Jewish history and saw it as *purposeful.* What had been Yahweh's purpose in their history?
3. What constant pattern of reaction to God's work in history by his own Hebrew race did Stephen see and point out?
4. What is the value of this sort of factual account of God's work in history?
5. What was the effect of this overview of Jewish history on the Sanhedrin?

3. His death at the hands of the angry mob. 7:54–8:1a.

The speech Stephen made left his hearers with only two choices. They could either repent of their sin of rejecting Jesus or kill Stephen. They did not repent.

The Sanhedrin members were "furious and gnashed their teeth at him." One can almost see the contorted facial expressions and the clenched jaws. Over against that sight, however, Stephen showed neither anxiety nor anger. With an amazing calmness and serenity, he fixed his gaze heavenward. The Lord graciously showed himself to Stephen in a vision as the evangelist "looked up to heaven and saw the glory of God, and Jesus standing at the right hand of God."

The fate of Stephen was sealed when he spoke aloud to the angry mob to tell them of what he had seen in the vision: "I see heaven open and the Son of Man standing at the right hand of God." This confession of Jesus as the Son of Man who, along with Yahweh, is worthy of worship was more than they could bear. To them, it was clearly blasphemous (cf. Mark 14:61-64) and proved that Stephen deserved to die. The Sanhedrin members "covered their ears and, yelling at the top of their voices, they all rushed at him, dragged him out of the city and began to stone him."

According to Jewish practice, the victim about to be stoned would be taken to a cliff, have his hands tied behind him, and then be pushed over. The fall would sometimes bring death. When it did not, large stones would be rolled or thrown from the cliff onto the person. After he was thrown down and as his accusers prepared to crush him with rocks from above, Stephen prayed.

If Jewish custom about stonings was followed here — and it is by no means sure that it was! — Stephen would have been asked one last time to confess his sin as the stoning began. To the contrary, his

Day 4
Mob Mentality

Read Luke 23:13-25 to see Jesus falling victim to a mob mentality.

1. What ignited the wrath of the Sanhedrin against Stephen?
2. Have you ever witnessed a scene of mob violence? Seen one on TV news? Describe the phenomenon.
3. Why are mobs so dangerous? What tends to happen even to "innocent bystanders" around mob scenes?
4. What happened to Stephen as a result of the mob's attack? How might it have ended differently?
5. What was Stephen's reaction to his fate?

prayers further affirmed his innocence of any crime and showed a Christlike spirit toward his enemies. First, he prayed, "Lord Jesus, receive my spirit." Attaching the title "Lord" to the name of Jesus, Stephen confessed the deity of the Son of Man before the angry mob. Second, he said, "Lord, do not hold this sin against them." Consciously or not, he echoed the very words the Savior had used as he was dying on the cross (Luke 23:34). So praying, Stephen "fell asleep" — thus becoming the first martyr of the Christian church.

Consistent with his marvelous ability as a writer to set the stage for what is yet to come, Luke adds this concluding note to the story of Stephen's martyrdom: "And Saul was there, giving approval to his death." That Saul is the only person singled out and named in the murderous mob likely indicates that he played an important role in bringing about Stephen's death and certainly prepares us for the role he will shortly play in Acts as the great advocate of Jesus Christ. "Luke is laying the groundwork for the great victory God will win through Saul's conversion and subsequent missionary service." [Larkin, *Acts*, p.123.]

"The saying is true: the blood of the martyrs is the seed of the church. This is never more true than with the blood of the first martyr. Stephen, whose natural crown of human ability was crowned with gifts of the Lord's Spirit, then His crown of thorns, and finally the crown of glory, had lived a relatively short life. But he accomplished his purpose. Stephen was the turning point, and eventually the cause of the gnawing questions of Saul of Tarsus that only the Lord could answer." [Ogilvie, *Acts*, p.149.]

K. The Scattering of the Believers under Persecution. 8:1b-3.

The death of Stephen lit the fires of a widespread persecution of the church in the Holy City. "On that day a great persecution broke out against the church at Jerusalem, and all except the apostles were scattered throughout Judea and Samaria."

The statement that the apostles did not leave Jerusalem may be accounted for in either of two ways. Perhaps they felt compelled to stay in the city to try to hold the young church together; at considerable risk to themselves, then, they continued to teach and minister in Jerusalem. But their ability to remain in the city may trace to the fact that the persecution following Stephen's death was targeted toward Greek-speaking Jews like him rather than toward Aramaic-speaking Jews like the Twelve.

In passing, one should take note of the statement Luke makes about the burial of Stephen: "Godly men buried Stephen and mourned deeply for him." In view of the fact that Jewish custom prohibited public mourning on behalf of anyone who died as a blasphemer, it was a courageous act for some of Stephen's Christian brothers to go to the place of stoning, retrieve his body, and give it a respectful burial. Their courage may well have put them among the first to be sought out and targeted for punishment by Saul and his gang of religious thugs.

Whatever the precise extent of the persecution, it served to move the gospel message outside the city where the church had been born into the surrounding territory of Judea and even into the adjoining region of Samaria. The beginning of fulfillment for Acts 1:8 took place under most unusual and unexpected circumstances. One wonders how long the church would have remained confined to Jerusalem if severe opposition had not forced its members to flee the city for their very lives. As the Christians were scattered to other places, they took their faith in Jesus with them. They continued to speak of him, tell the story of his saving death and resurrection, and invite people to follow him as Lord and Christ.

Day 5
Persecution of the Church

Read John 15:18-25 to find a prediction from Jesus that his followers would be persecuted.

1. What happened to the Jerusalem church after Stephen's death?
2. Who led the anti-Christian propaganda and persecution? What irony do you see in this?
3. What tends to happen when the church is persecuted? What happened in this case?
4. Do you know of situations in the world today where Christians are suffering for their faith?
5. Pray for the *boldness* of modern-day Christians facing persecution.

The one certainty given us about the persecution begun with Stephen's death is that its ringleader was Saul of Tarsus. He was viciously determined to "destroy the church" and set about his task by "going from house to house" and dragging off both "men and women" to prison.

As modern Christians read this account, we should not be unmindful of the fact that some of our brothers and sisters in the Lord Jesus are being persecuted today. In China, for example, Christians have been harassed, jailed, and killed in the Communist purges that have periodically swept through that nation. Yet a huge underground church continues to grow — due, at least in part, to the faithful witness borne by those who have suffered for their faith.

We are members of a vast community of faith that extends across continents and across the centuries. God is not unjust to allow some to suffer or even die for their faith. Indeed, such persons are to be counted fortunate in being able to bear witness to their love for Christ in the face of threats and punishments. "Blessed are those who are persecuted because of righteousness, for theirs is the kingdom of heaven" (Matt. 5:10).

Week Twelve

Acts 8:4-25 (IV A to IV B in Outline)

IV. The Ministry of Philip. 8:4-40.

The preaching ministry of Philip deserves distinct attention as students move through the Acts narrative. The first seven chapters of Acts relate activity that is confined to Jerusalem. It is certainly critical activity, for it tells of the ascension of Jesus, the descent of the Holy Spirit, the establishment of the church, and some of the early trials that believers had to face. These seven chapters likely cover a period of four or five years.

Important as that data is to us, it tells of an exclusively Jewish church operating in a thoroughly Jewish environment. But the gospel is for all people. Chapters 8 through 12 trace the spread of the church through Judea into Samaria and on into Gentile territory. They describe the spread of the gospel over a ten-year period from the beginning of persecution in Jerusalem to the death of King Herod. These five chapters of Acts set the stage for Paul's incredible missionary tours that fill the remaining chapters of the book.

Philip's preaching came about after he fled Jerusalem for Samaria, crossed the rigid line of racial prejudice that had long separated Jews from Samaritans, and witnessed what some have called "the Samaritan Pentecost." Heaven affirmed Philip's work with an outpouring of signs and with a great ingathering of souls. From Samaria, the same evangelist was called to share Christ with a man from Ethiopia who also became a believer.

Day 1
The Samaritans

Read 2 Kings 17:24-41 to learn about the origin of the Samaritans.

1. Summarize the background of the Samaritans.
2. What was the relationship between Samaritans and Jews in the first century?
3. What steps did Jesus take toward breaking down the barriers with Samaritans?
4. Imagine you are Philip. What feelings come over you as you begin to preach among the Samaritans?
5. How did the Holy Spirit affirm Philip's actions?

A. Preaching Christ in Samaria. 8:4-8.

When the Northern Kingdom fell to the Assyrians in 721 B.C., many Jews were slaughtered and many more were taken away from their homeland as slaves. Many of the latter continued to live in Gentile areas and were part of the Greek-speaking diaspora already referred to in Acts. The few Jews who were left in Palestine intermarried with Assyrians who came in to occupy land taken as the spoils of war. The offspring of these interracial marriages came to be called "Samaritans" — named for the central region of Palestine where they eventually congregated as Jews began returning to their homeland and contesting them for the land. A bitter hatred developed between the two groups (cf. John 4:9). Jews regarded Samaritans as unclean half-breeds; Samaritans viewed Jews as arrogant enemies to their existence in the land.

1. Proclaiming the Christ. 8:4-5.

Philip had been one of the seven men responsible for administering relief among the widows of the Jerusalem church. But his talents were not limited to administration, and he was clearly a gifted evangelist. But why did he choose to go to Samaria? Perhaps Philip knew Jesus' personal history of preaching among the Samaritans and chose to go to Samaria for that reason (John 4:4ff). Perhaps he was influenced by Jesus' positive statements about Samaritans in his teachings (Luke 10:30-37; 17:11-19). Or perhaps the Holy Spirit directed him there by revelation. Whatever the motivation, the results were wondrous. Defying the racial prejudice that traditionally kept Jews and Samaritans apart, Philip "went down to a city of Samaria and proclaimed the Christ there."

2. Confirming the word with signs. 8:6-8.

Philip's preaching was accompanied by an outpouring of "miraculous signs" the Holy Spirit gave in confirmation of his message. Samaritan religion was a mixture of Jewish Scripture-tradition with Assyrian superstition-occultism (cf. Simon the sorcerer). Thus the Lord empowered Philip to display a great many impressive and genuine miracles that would distinguish the one in whose name he did the miracles from the tricks and fakery with which the Samaritans were so familiar. The authentic powers Philip exercised made such an impression that the people of the city "paid close attention to what he said." After all, genuine miracles are never ends in themselves but a means to the greater end of authenticating the servants of God and the saving message of God.

Not only were there magicians and sorcerers at work in Samaria, Satan himself was further exploiting the ignorance and superstition of the people there. "Evil spirits" possessed many and made their lives miserable. Thus the miracles wrought at Philip's hands were set over against deceptive human magic, demonic spirits, and physical disease: "With shrieks, evil spirits came out of many, and many paralytics and cripples were healed. So there was great joy in that city."

B. The Conversion of Simon the Sorcerer. 8:9-25.

The episode with Simon the sorcerer is fascinating not only for its sadness but for its strong attestation of the work of the Holy Spirit among the early Christians. The story is certainly sad because of the weakness in Simon that caused him to try to purchase the Holy Spirit for his own manipulative and greedy purposes. Thus did his name (i.e., simony) become permanently associated with the abuse of religious practices and offices for personal gain. Yet we should not overlook an important apologetic feature of this episode. If there had been any magic, trickery, or sleight of hand involved in the miracles performed by

**Day 2
Superstition**

Read Deuteronomy 18:9-14 for God's attitude toward occult superstition.

1. What was Simon's history when he met Philip?
2. What did he learn from watching Philip's activity?
3. To what degree is superstition still entrenched in our culture?
4. What superstitious practices did you once observe? When and how did you break free of them?
5. What is the spiritual danger of horoscopes, tarot cards, and the like?

Philip, Peter, and John, it certainly would have been discovered by someone who was expert at such things. That the shady magician recognized the things happening at the hands of the Christian teachers as something qualitatively different from anything he could duplicate should not be overlooked.

1. A brief description of Simon and his past. 8:9-11.

The first Christian century was not unlike our own time in that its people were spiritually uprooted by the failures of religion and therefore vulnerable to the "isms" of astrology, cults, and even witchcraft. Simon had long exploited this situation in Samaria. He appears to have offered himself as either divine in his own person or, at the very least, an incarnate divine power. "He boasted that he was someone great," Luke informs us. Specifically, the people of his city said of him: "This man is the divine power known as the Great Power." His following was not confined to the poor and illiterate. As in our own time, "both high and low" were numbered among his enthralled disciples.

2. His conversion and association with Philip. 8:12-13.

There is an initial irony that the man who once caused the Samaritans to marvel at his alleged powers followed Philip around and was constantly "astonished by the great signs and miracles he saw." Indeed, Simon "believed" the message Philip preached and was — along with many others in the city — baptized in Jesus' name.

In view of what Luke will subsequently tell us about Simon's behavior, we are forced to wonder at this point about the genuineness of his conversion. Was he "converted" at all? Was he simply caught up in an event? Did he have in mind from the beginning to attach himself to Philip in order to become an insider to the powers he saw in him? We should remember that faith comes in a variety of forms.

Day 3
Pseudo-Conversions

Read 1 John 1:5–2:6 about Christian experience with sin even after true conversion.

1. Do you think Simon's conversion was genuine? Explain.
2. What is the fundamental difference between a true and false conversion claim?
3. How can you be sure your own conversion was authentic?
4. What sin did Simon commit in Peter's presence? What was the apostle's reaction?
5. Do people with authentic conversion experiences still sin? How does their reaction to sin differ from the person whose conversion was false?

One who is forced to admit that something is true because of overwhelming evidence may claim to "believe" without being deeply affected by such faith. "Even the demons believe [there is but one God] — and shudder" (Jas. 2:19), yet they are still demons and damned.

Simon's faith was probably never more than an intellectual assurance that he was witnessing genuine divine power. It was not the deep, saving faith that accompanies the new birth and leads to new life in Christ. Neither his shallow faith of assent nor his baptism could make Simon right with God. Right words and right acts are empty without genuine trust in the saving power of God as exercised solely through the name of Jesus of Nazareth. When the gospel net is cast among humankind, both good and bad fish are caught. It will be the Lord's task in final Judgment to separate the two (cf. Matt. 13:47-50).

3. Peter and John visit Samaria. 8:14-24.

When word reached the apostles in Jerusalem (cf. 8:1a) that people in Samaria had "accepted the word of God," the decision was made to send two of their number there. The purpose of the delegation seems less to examine the reports and/or converts for legitimacy as to affirm the unity of the church. It was a marvelous affirmation of the oneness of the spiritual body of Christ that Jewish apostles from Jerusalem made the visit to Samaria in order to affirm as Christian brothers and sisters people who had long been alienated by racial prejudice.

When they arrived at Samaria, the visiting apostles "prayed for them that they might receive the Holy Spirit." Although some hold that the Holy Spirit was withheld from the Samaritans absolutely until the apostles prayed for them [Larkin, *Acts*, p. 128], it is more likely that the text simply reflects the fact that the Holy Spirit was given in a variety of ways in Acts. At conversion and baptism, the Spirit

Day 4
Racial Prejudice

Read James 2:1-12 about showing favoritism toward certain people.

1. What problems might Philip's ministry have created among the early Jewish Christians?
2. What initiative to prevent these problems did the apostles take? The Holy Spirit?
3. What forms of racial prejudice still hinder the progress of the gospel?
4. What issues of racial prejudice have you had to face in your personal life?

101

5. Suggest some things your church could do to improve relationships among ethnic groups in your immediate environment.

was conferred as heaven's gift to the penitent believer (cf. Acts 2:38); in certain cases, a measure of the Holy Spirit that carried with it miraculous powers was also given. "This gift does not here denote the usual influence of the Spirit which results in repentance and faith and holiness, but the extraordinary and miraculous 'gifts' which were frequently bestowed upon believers, particularly in the early days of the apostolic church. These signs had the specific design of attesting the truth, and as here in Samaria, they were evidences of the new life which resulted from faith in Christ. Even the apostles had no power to confer these gifts; but the fact that they prayed for their bestowal shows that the apostles recognized the fact that Samaritans had actually become Christians, and that the apostles gave their sanction to the new step which Philip had taken in preaching the gospel to those who were not Jews." [Erdman, *Acts*, p. 81.]

When Simon saw people receiving supernatural powers in association with the laying on of the apostles' hands, "he offered them money and said, 'Give me also this ability so that everyone on whom I lay my hands may receive the Holy Spirit.'" Apparently unable to divorce himself from his unscrupulous past, Simon wanted to purchase the ability he saw Peter and John exercising. He would have his social position as "the Great Power" restored and could make a fortune selling his favor to others!

Peter's stern response to Simon called him to repent of what he had done — but also acknowledged the unlikeliness of repentance. God can and will forgive any sin repented of with sincerity, but Peter discerned both that Simon's heart was "not right before God" and that the sorcerer was "full of bitterness and captive to sin." Simon responded to Peter by asking him to pray that no terrible fate come upon him because of what he had just done.

Day 5
Simony

Read Numbers 22:21-41 for an ancient form version of simony.

1. What is *simony*?
2. How did the name of Simon come to be associated with this awful sin?
3. Why was this sin so common in the Middle Ages? What effect did the practice have on the career of Martin Luther?
4. Do you recall or see modern traces of this detestable practice?
5. How should the church confront simony? Guard against it?

Whether this was true penitence or merely the hope of being spared punishment is not clear from the text. At the very least, the once-popular and once-powerful Simon had been discredited before the believers of Samaria so that he could not be put back in position to further exploit people.

"In our day some nominal Christians have syncretized their faith with cultural religious ways. They may be Christopagans in Two-Thirds World traditional societies or practitioners of Western spirituality accommodating consciously or unconsciously to postmodern New Age thinking. Like Simon, they must realize the seriousness of their condition. Those who think they have 'the best of both worlds' must repent, or in the age to come they will experience the worst of all possible worlds." [Larkin, *Acts*, p. 131.]

There is an old tradition to the effect that Simon became a bitter enemy of Peter for years following this event. According to that tradition, he founded a sect called the Simonians, accepted the worship of those he gathered around him at Rome, and attempted to duplicate the miracle of Christ's resurrection. He had his followers bury him alive for three days. When they opened the grave, he was dead.

4. Peter and John return to Jerusalem via many preaching stops in villages of the Samaritans. 8:25.

As Peter and John made their way back to Jerusalem, they stopped along the way in "many Samaritan villages" to preach the gospel. This showed their personal affirmation of Philip's strategy of preaching to the Samaritans in still another way. It was also a step in broadening Peter's personal horizons about the gospel prior to his call to preach Jesus to a Gentile named Cornelius.

People who love Jesus also love one another — regardless of race, language, culture, or other distinctions that otherwise would have kept them separated from and perhaps even hostile toward one another.

Week Thirteen

Acts 8:26-40 (IV C to IV D in Outline)

Day 1
Varieties of Ministry

Read Romans 12:1-8 about the different gifts God distributes to believers.

1. Using the list of gifts in Rom. 12, identify the ones Philip possessed and used.
2. Does every Christian have every spiritual gift? Explain.
3. How does one discover his or her area(s) of spiritual giftedness?
4. What is your primary spiritual gift? How are you using it?
5. How should these gifts be ranked? Which deserve greater appreciation?

There is good reason to be fascinated by the man Philip. Every time we meet him in the Acts narrative, he is serving God faithfully and in a different setting. He was clearly a bright and multi-talented man. There is a distinct section of Luke's history of the early church devoted to his career.

Philip first emerges as one of the seven deacons in charge of assistance to the widows of the Jerusalem church; he was chosen for that post because he was "known to be full of the Spirit and wisdom" by the church's larger membership (6:3). Next he is preaching effectively to large crowds in a city of Samaria (8:5ff). In the section of text at hand, he leaves the crowds to teach a single confused soul (8:26ff). Then, about 20 years after this episode, we will meet him a final time at his home in Caesarea where he and his four virgin daughters who had the gift of prophecy receive Paul and his entourage traveling toward Jerusalem (21:8-9).

Although he is one man serving God in a variety of ways, Philip's career reminds us all that there are many different ways to communicate the gospel to the world. Some serve in ministries of compassion. Some can preach to thousands, while others are better at sharing their faith with a single person at a time. And still others minister by enabling servants of God along the way or by creating and maintaining the solid influence of a Christian home. Let no one envy another's gift or consider his or her own ministry insignificant by comparison to that given some other believer.

C. Philip and a Man from Ethiopia. 8:26-39.

1. The two are brought together. 8:26-29.

With no reason at all to think that Philip had exhausted his usefulness in Samaria, an angel from the Lord told Philip to make his way toward the hilly region of southern Judea. With a ready and obedient heart, Philip left on his new assignment. He had no illusions that the new church he had founded could not survive without his guidance or that he was henceforth suited only for big-city, big-church ministry. As he traveled, he had what to everyone else must have seemed to be a mere "chance encounter" with a traveler on the Jerusalem-to-Gaza road.

The few facts we have about the man Philip met and led to Christ that day inform us that he was "an Ethiopian eunuch, an important official in charge of all the treasury of Candace, queen of the Ethiopians. This man had gone to Jerusalem to worship, and on his way home was sitting in his chariot reading the book of Isaiah the prophet."

This Ethiopian is a significant widening of the circle for preaching the gospel in Acts. We have now gone from Jews to Samaritans to an Ethiopian who is somehow linked to Judaism; only the final step remains of communicating the message of Christ to a full-fledged Gentile (i.e., pagan). Was this man an Ethiopian who had proselyted to Judaism sometime earlier? Was he an Ethiopian among the larger class that Luke calls "God-fearers" (i.e., Gentiles who worshiped the God of the Jews, affiliated themselves loosely with a Jewish synagogue, but stopped short of proselyting, cf. 10:2; 13:16,26)? We cannot be sure, but the latter seems more likely.

On the assumption that the man's description as a "eunuch" is physically specific rather than — as some have suggested — merely a synonym for government official or bureaucrat, the Law of Moses would not have allowed him to "enter the assembly

Day 2
Chance Encounters

Read about another "chance encounter" at Luke 24:13-35.

1. The Bible speaks of those who "have entertained angels without knowing it." Explain.
2. Do you recall an episode that you later believed to be a visit from an angel?
3. Can you recount a "chance encounter" that somehow changed the course of your life?
4. How are believers supposed to redeem the chance encounters of our lives to the Lord?
5. Pray for God to use you to say or do just the right thing in someone's life today.

of the Lord" (Deut. 23:1). He was Secretary of the Treasury to Ethiopia's queen, thus a man of position and responsibility. [Note: "Candace" [Kăn-dā′-sē] is not a personal name. It is a title that belongs to an Ethiopian dynasty of matriarchs in charge of civil administration for their nation. Males in service to such women were typically castrated.] Both his education and wealth, along with his piety, are indicated in the facts that he possessed a scroll of the Old Testament prophets and was reading from it as he rode along in his chariot.

Ethiopia was considered the farthest edge of the civilized world by many in the first century. Both iron and gold were mined there, and it was a center of trade for both. Contrary to what a modern reader might import into ancient texts from his own culture, the dark-skinned Africans of Ethiopia were regarded as exotic persons and held considerable fascination for both Romans and Jews.

When the paths of the Jewish-Christian evangelist and the God-fearing Ethiopian crossed, the Holy Spirit told Philip, "Go to that chariot and stay near it." A man who had always wanted to know the God of Israel but who had been kept from any formal association with "the assembly of the Lord" was about to learn of one who had himself suffered rejection and humiliation. In hearing the gospel of Jesus Christ, he would discover not only someone who understood his own sense of being an outcast but who had eventually taken away all barriers between men and God by his death for sinners.

2. Philip preaches Christ from an Old Testament text. 8:30-35.

Eagerly obedient to the prompting of the Spirit, Philip *"ran"* up to the chariot" in which the Ethiopian was riding. Since reading aloud was the normal practice in ancient times, Philip recognized what the man was reading. It was the Old Testament prophet Isaiah.

Day 3
Divine Proddings

Read Romans 8:1-17 about life in the Spirit.

1. What two divine promptings brought Philip to the Ethiopian in this narrative?
2. Do you believe God nudges his saints today? Explain.
3. What cautions need to be given here? Do Christians ever have impulses that need to be resisted?
4. How does one distinguish a "divine prodding" from a "satanic urge"?
5. How does the Holy Spirit guide the lives of believers today?

Specifically, the Ethiopian was reading aloud from the Septuagint at Isaiah 53:7-8. There is no more ideal text in the entire Old Testament from which to present the saving message of the crucified Christ.

Isaiah 53 is one of the so-called "servant songs" in the most messianic book among the major prophets. In the progression of the songs, Yahweh's servant is initially the nation of Israel (Isa. 44:1), then a holy remnant within the nation (Isa. 49:8ff), and finally a single individual whom the Lord raises up to save his people (Isa. 52:13ff). In the early preaching of the Christian church, Isaiah 53 was a favorite text from which to explain the ministry of Jesus of Nazareth. Indeed, what better text could there be than one which tells of a man "despised and rejected" (v. 3), who was "pierced for our transgressions" (v. 5a), and suffered the "punishment that brought us peace" (v. 5c)? What clearer anticipation is there of his redemptive role than in this prediction of one who would be put to death though altogether innocent (v. 9), only to be raised to life again (vv. 10-11)?

When Philip heard him reading this text, he asked the Ethiopian, "Do you understand what you are reading?" There is clearly a note of anguish and frustration in his answer. "How can I, unless someone explains it to me?" came the response. He invited Philip to join him in his chariot to discuss the matter. The man of wealth, prominence, and piety had traveled from Ethiopia to Jerusalem to worship God — and was going home with a sense of emptiness. He knew at least some of the Old Testament anticipations of the Messiah but had no idea what to make of them. Was Isaiah talking about his own prophetic work in the lines he was reading? Were his words about the Messiah? If the latter, who was the Messiah? When would he appear? "Tell me, please," he pleaded with Philip, "who is the prophet talking about, himself or some other?"

**Day 4
God's Suffering
Servant**

Read Isaiah 53 about the Suffering Servant of the Lord.

1. What central truths about Jesus are highlighted in Isa. 53?
2. Trace the development of the Servant of the Lord in Isaiah.
3. Which verses from this chapter was the Ethiopian reading when Philip joined him?
4. Imagining that you are Philip, explain how you use these verses to tell the good news about Jesus.
5. Find at least three other NT sermons or texts that build on Isaiah 53.

That was all the opening Philip needed. He began from the Isaiah passage and "told him the good news about Jesus."

3. The baptism of the Ethiopian. 8:36-39.

As the two men rode, continued to read, and talked about Jesus as the fulfillment of Scripture, the heart of the Ethiopian was filled to overflowing with excitement. His question had been answered. He was confident that he knew the prophet's meaning now. And he was anxious to make a commitment to the one in whom he had come to believe. So, as they came near a body of water, he said, "Look, here is water. Why shouldn't I be baptized?"

Philip had been telling the Ethiopian about Jesus. So where did the man get the idea that baptism was something he should consider? Perhaps Philip had given a summary of Jesus' ministry that included an account of Jesus' baptism by John; the eunuch's knowledge of Judaism would have led him to associate baptism with proselyting (i.e., conversion), and he may have offered himself as a proselyte to Jesus by suggesting baptism. Perhaps Philip had explored not only Isaiah 53 but its fuller setting in the servant songs and had come to Isaiah 54:9-10 about the "waters of Noah" that suggested something about baptism; Peter would later associate the flood of waters that destroyed many but saved Noah and his family with Christian baptism (1 Pet. 3:21). Or perhaps Philip had explained to the man that baptism was the normative rite by which people confessed their acceptance of Christ publicly; this had been true both in Jesus' public ministry and since the founding of the church under apostolic guidance (cf. 2:37-38).

The Ethiopian had admired and learned of the Jewish faith in Ethiopia. Perhaps he had offered himself as a proselyte only to be refused the baptism and circumcision rituals that all proselytes had to go through because of his status as a eunuch. If this is true, his question "Why shouldn't I be baptized?" probably reflects more sadness and apprehension than theological insight. If he had been rejected from formal membership in the Jewish community because he was a eunuch, would he also be rejected from the community of Christians for the same reason? Would rejection become the standard response this pious and seeking man would receive when he sought to move toward Yahweh?

Philip showed no hesitation whatever about baptizing the Ethiopian eunuch. Perhaps the strong affirmation of his earlier ministry among Samaritans had been used of God to prepare his heart for accepting this dark-skinned man of Africa as his new brother in Christ. The Holy Spirit had affirmed his work with signs and wonders, and the apostles had added their consent through the visit and ministry of Peter.

The "baptismal confession" of v. 37 does not appear in any manuscript of Acts prior to the sixth century, although Irenaeus (*Against Heresies* 3. 12. 8.) quotes it in the second century. The NIV and other translations that respect the best textual evidence for the New Testament therefore do not include the statement in the text. The statement was probably inserted by a copyist who knew a common form of confession that had come to be generally accepted among Christians. It therefore reflects an acceptable but not mandatory form of verbal confession that has been tied to baptism from the earliest days of the church.

The baptism done, "the Spirit of the Lord suddenly took Philip away." This language gives the impression of a supernatural transport of Philip from the scene. Many scholars understand it just that way, although it may mean nothing more than an immediate end to the relationship between these two men after the baptismal event. Whatever the circum-

Day 5
Rejoicing in Christ

Remembering that he wrote this epistle from prison, read Philippians 2:28, 3:1, and 4:4.

1. List some justifications the Ethiopian would have had for rejoicing as this story ended.
2. Do any of the Ethiopian's justifications for joy apply to you?
3. Do you think people see you as a joyous Christian? Explain.
4. How does a Christian's joy enable him or her to bear witness to Jesus before unbelievers?
5. How might a believer's lack of joy hinder his or her witness to Jesus?

stances of Philip's departure, the Ethiopian was neither unduly perplexed nor confused by his departure. Indeed, the eunuch "went on his way rejoicing."

A report in Eusebius (*Church History* 2.2. 13-14) says that this Ethiopian returned home and became an evangelist to his own people. There is even a tradition that his queen became a Christian. Whether this is true or not, we have no way of knowing. What our own experience teaches us about leading others to Christ, however, is at least this consistent with the Ethiopian's story: only those who have found joy in Christ are likely to draw others to him.

D. A Final Comment on Philip's Activity. 8:40.

The final piece of information about Philip in this text tells us of his continuing travels on behalf of the gospel. After his departure from the Ethiopian, he was next in a seacoast town about 30 miles away, Azotus. He continued his work of "preaching the gospel in all the towns until he reached Caesarea."

Caesarea was Philip's home town. Luke places him there and mentions him only once more in Acts, when Paul and his companions pass through Caesarea on the apostle's final trip to Jerusalem (21:8).

Week Fourteen

Acts 9:1-31 (V in Outline)

V. The Conversion of Saul of Tarsus. 9:1-31.

The importance of the conversion of Saul of Tarsus from enemy to advocate is hard to overemphasize — not only in the narrative of Acts but in the larger history of the Christian faith. That the story is told three times in Acts (9, 22, 26) is a clear indication of its importance to the Spirit-guided Luke.

Saul was a Jew who held Roman citizenship by virtue of being a man of Tarsus in Asia Minor. He was reared in the strict traditions of Pharisaic Judaism and observed what he would later call "legalistic righteousness" with passion (Phil. 3:5-6). He received a first-class education under Rabbi Gamaliel (22:3; cf. 5:34ff). Our introduction to Saul in Acts was in connection with the death of Stephen. Saul had participated in stoning him and immediately became the driving force behind a major persecution that followed (8:1-3).

That someone so hostile to Christ could be won to him and become his most ardent advocate in the Roman Empire is emphatic testimony to the truth of the Christian religion. If a risen Christ did not appear to Saul and win his heart, how else can his turnaround be explained? Furthermore, Saul's conversion offers hope that we should never give up on even the most unlikely prospects for faith.

Day 1
Suited for Service

Read Exodus 2:1-25 about the first 80 years of Moses' life.

1. How did the backgrounds of these men prepare them for special roles in the divine drama: Joseph? Moses? Daniel?
2. Explain how Saul's unusual background prepared him for a unique mission.
3. Did Paul consciously sanctify his background to his ministry? Cf. 1 Corinthians 9:19-23.
4. Name someone you know today whose life experience has made her or him especially effective in some Christian ministry.
5. What in your personal background has enabled you to offer a special service to the Lord?

Read the account of Paul's conversion at Acts 26:4-23.

1. Why do dramatic stories of conversion have such effect on audiences?

2. Can you identify a NT story of conversion that was gradual and deliberate rather than dramatic?

3. Is one type of conversion experience to be preferred over another? Explain.

4. What was the nature of your experience of conversion?

5. How does one know that his or her conversion is genuine?

A. Events on the Road to Damascus. 9:1-7.

1. The purpose of the journey. 9:1-2.

Consistent with our earliest sighting of Saul in Acts, he "was still breathing out murderous threats against the Lord's disciples." But he was no longer content with harassing believers in Jerusalem. He sought and obtained authorization from the high priest to pursue heretical (i.e., Jesus-affirming) Jews of the *diaspora* in the synagogues of Damascus, 140 miles northeast of Jerusalem. His plan was to bring them back to Jerusalem to stand trial before the Sanhedrin for their apostasy. But something happened on that journey which was to change everything for him.

2. The journey interrupted by the Lord. 9:3-7.

As Saul neared Damascus at the end of his week-long trip, a brilliant light surrounded him, he and his companions were terrified, and he heard a voice saying, "Saul, Saul, why do you persecute me?" When Saul asked the voice to identify itself, he addressed it as "Lord." Although we use this term almost exclusively as a title for deity, common usage of Saul's day used it as a respectful address that corresponds to our "Sir."

The emphatic answer, "I am Jesus, whom you are persecuting," signifies at least two things. First, it told Saul how wrong he had been to discount the witness of Stephen and other Christians he had persecuted about the resurrection of Jesus. No one could doubt Saul's sincerity. Yet his sincere and zealous faith had simply been dead wrong. Jesus *was* alive, and he was revealing himself to Saul! Second, it let both Saul and us know how closely Jesus identifies with his church. How had Saul persecuted Jesus? He had hounded and tormented Stephen and many other believers. Jesus had taken each of those actions as a personal assault against himself (cf. Matt. 25:40,45). The glorified Christ ordered Saul to get up, continue into the city, and wait for further instructions about the meaning of what had been started by this confrontation.

Luke lets us know in passing that the Damascus Road events were specific to Saul, though witnessed in part by his traveling party. His companions "heard the sound but did not see anyone." That is, they apparently saw a flash of light and heard thunderous noise. They did not, however, see the risen, glorious Christ in the light or discern the intelligible words he spoke to Saul. This vision and its contents were for the purpose of calling to repentance and qualifying for apostleship only one person, not the entire company that happened to be on the road with him.

B. Saul's Three-Day Wait at Damascus. 9:8-9.

Saul had been physically thrown to the ground by the dramatic (and perhaps physical) force of what had just happened. The man who stood up was very different from the one who had been thrown down. He had been so cocksure, adamant, and arrogant before hitting the ground; on his feet again, he was broken, teachable, and searching. How like certain life experiences others have had before and since!

Because he had been blinded by the light, the men with him "led him by the hand into Damascus." Again, one is struck by the symbolism in this event. The man who had been leading others so confidently was now depending on the leadership of another. Indeed, he would soon abandon himself completely to Jesus and eventually say this about his experience of conversion: "Whatever was to my profit I now consider loss for the sake of Christ. What is more, I consider everything a loss compared to the surpassing greatness of knowing Christ Jesus my Lord, for whose sake I have lost all things" (Phil. 3:7-8a).

The sighted Saul had been blind; the blinded Saul would soon see all things clearly. What terrible wrestlings there must have been in the mind and heart of this man during his three days of waiting in Damascus. Still blind and refusing anything to eat or drink, he must have rehearsed Stephen's speech endlessly and thought about various statements of faith from men and women he had dragged into prison. Could he have been on the wrong side in this struggle? Had he been fighting God? There is no more horrible thought to a man of honest mind and pious intent.

Day 3
Reluctant Servants

Read the classic story of a reluctant servant from Jonah 1:1-17.

1. Imagine you are Ananias, and explain why you are not enthusiastic about going to Saul.
2. What other biblical characters can you name who were given tasks you would not envy for yourself?
3. What assignments are hardest to fill in your congregation? Why?
4. How would you recommend creating a greater pool of volunteers for Christian ministry?
5. What would Ananias say to a hesitant volunteer in a contemporary church?

C. Ananias Instructs and Baptizes Saul. 9:10-19a.

Almost lost to most readers in the Saul story is the imbedded account of the one who would be called to bear personal witness to him about the gospel. Lest Saul or we take the Damascus Road experience to have been a merely subjective event, God sent a teacher to ground what had happened in a confirming word of instruction. Yet Ananias had good reason to hesitate about going to the notorious tormentor of Christians whose reputation had preceded him to Damascus.

1. Ananias' hesitation about going to Saul. 9:10-14.

With Saul's dark night of blasphemy and persecution ready to yield to a dawn of faith and proclamation, someone was needed to act as God's instrument for opening his eyes to the light of heaven's sun/Son. So an otherwise obscure disciple named Ananias was approached in a vision and told to go to Saul. He was to be not only the one through whom the Lord would fulfill his promise of further information (i.e., "you will be told what you must do," v. 6b) but the vehicle of confirmation to Saul of the authenticity of his experiences to date (i.e., he had seen a vision in which a man named Ananias restored his eyesight, v. 12).

Ananias voiced an understandable reluctance about seeking out the man who had come to

Damascus to seek out just such persons as himself. Saul had not been able to bring his letters of authority to seek out and arrest for trial Jewish disciples of Christ to that city before word of his intention arrived.

2. An explanation of the situation by the Lord. 9:15-16.

Ananias was moved to act beyond his fears by an assurance from the Lord of the great work Saul was ordained to do in Jesus' name — work that would be accomplished in the context of suffering for that holy name. Saul was to be heaven's "chosen instrument" for carrying the name of Jesus to both Jews and Gentiles. Specifically, he would speak of Christ "before the people and their kings and before the people of Israel." This makes Luke's purpose in relating the story of Saul's conversion in the sequence of Acts events that runs as follows: Christ's ascent, Spirit's descent, church in Jerusalem, gospel to Samaria, conversion of an Ethiopian eunuch, conversion of Saul, conversion of Cornelius, and evangelistic success in the Roman Empire.

The critical event necessary to move the gospel successfully from the geographical and ethnic boundaries of the Hebrew homeland to the "ends of the earth" was the calling of Saul of Tarsus. His Hebrew knowledge of Scripture and tradition would be combined with his cosmopolitan experience of the university city Tarsus under the tutelage of the Holy Spirit to make him the most effective missionary in the history of the church. As Moses had been ideally suited to the call Yahweh made on his life to lead Israel out of Egypt, Saul was the person ideally suited to Christ's call for evangelistic vision and outreach for the first-century church.

3. Ananias' message and Saul's response. 9:17-19a.

Thus assured by the Lord, Ananias went to Saul, identified himself unmistakably by relating the Damascus Road vision, restored his eyesight, and blessed him to receive the Holy Spirit. At that, Saul "got up and was baptized" — hesitating not at all to identify himself with Jesus and the movement bearing his name. Of interest in all this, however, is that Ananias apparently did not relate to Saul all that the Lord had told him about either his status as a "chosen instrument" or "how much he must suffer" for Christ. Some things are better learned step by step rather than all at once.

Day 4
Skepticism about a
Brother

Read Romans 14:1-23 about judging other believers.

1. Why were Christians at Jerusalem hesitant about accepting Saul?

2. How would you have reacted to the report of Saul's conversion?

3. Have you ever seen a church treat someone as Saul was treated? What was the effect?

4. Does a church have the right to expect the "fruit of repentance" from a convert? Relate this idea to Saul's experience.

5. What sorts of issues were at stake in Romans 14? Have you ever seen judgments of similar nature passed on other believers? If so, with what outcome?

D. Saul Preaches at Damascus and Arouses Jewish Opposition. 9:19b-25.

1. His proclamation concerning Jesus. 9:19b-22.

Immediately after his baptism, Saul moved quickly to begin preaching what he now knew to be the truth that "Jesus is the Christ." Imagine the stir it caused in both the Christian and Jewish communities for the very man who had come to Damascus to rebut the Christian message by force to be found moving from synagogue to synagogue affirming that message.

[Special Note: From Galatians 1:16-17 we learn that after only a brief period of preaching in Damascus Saul "went immediately into Arabia and later returned to Damascus." The desert solitude of Arabia surely served as a time of reflection and further revelation from the Lord to prepare him for his great mission ahead. At the end of that period, he returned to Damascus where the events of our text — without mention of the Arabian interim — continue.]

With his sharp intellect, knowledge of Scripture, and fulness of the Spirit combined and focused on preaching the gospel, this was the result: Saul "grew more and more powerful and baffled the Jews living in Damascus by proving that Jesus is the Christ."

2. His escape from a plot against his life. 9:23-25.

With Saul's increasing boldness and effectiveness, the Damascus pot quickly came to a boil and he had to flee the city for his life. An elaborate plot was hatched to arrest and kill him (cf. 2 Cor. 11:32-33), and he escaped only when some of "his followers" (i.e., people converted under his teaching) unceremoniously lowered him over the city wall in a basket.

E. Saul's Return to Jerusalem. 9:26-30.

1. Skepticism among the disciples. 9:26.

When he made his way back to Jerusalem from Damascus, he faced a predictably cool greeting — which may nevertheless have taken Saul off guard — from Christians. They refused to believe he had been truly turned to faith in Christ. He faced the same sort of skepticism others have had to deal with after a prison term or pregnancy outside marriage. Forgiven people were reluctant to affirm forgiveness for those whose sins were more widely known.

2. The gracious act of Barnabas. 9:27.

The good man Barnabas who was widely known and respected by believers throughout the city (cf. 4:36) took Saul under his wing, vouched for him, and secured his acceptance by the larger group.

3. More bold preaching and more Jewish opposition. 9:28-29a.

Eager to teach and defend the gospel among his former colleagues in Judaism, Saul immediately began to preach boldly. Perhaps out of a sense of special duty to the "Grecian Jews" (i.e., persons such as Stephen and those he was winning to Christ before Saul cut short his career), much of his ministry focused on them.

4. Another plot against him and his escape. 9:29b-30.

But the Hellenists would have nothing of the message of this traitor (as they would have viewed him). Instead, they turned on him and sought to kill him. The "brothers" who had initially been skeptical of

**Day 5
Befriending Outsiders**

Read Acts 15:36-41 to find another case of Barnabas befriending an outsider.

1. How did Paul gain acceptance among the Jerusalem Christians?
2. What irony do you see in the Acts 15 episode?
3. What motivates someone to do what Barnabas did?
4. What groups need special attention and friendship in your church? Why?
5. How will you be a Barnabas to someone this week?

Saul now escorted him out of Jerusalem to Caesarea and then on to Tarsus.

F. A Further Lucan Observation about the General Status of the Church. 9:31.

This verse likely covers a period of three to five years. Community building continued among the churches of Judea, Galilee, and Samaria. The people who loved Jesus learned more about loving one another in an atmosphere of peace, general edification, and evangelistic outreach. For the persecutions that would eventually come, such times of strengthening would be necessary.

Week Fifteen

Acts 9:32-43 (VI A to VI B in Outline)

VI. An Enlargement of the Ministry of Peter. 9:32–11:18.

The stage is almost fully set now for the final great step of the first-century church in accepting the Savior's Great Commission to preach repentance and forgiveness of sins in his name "to *all nations*, beginning at Jerusalem" (Luke 24:47). Some seven to ten years after the establishment of the church at Jerusalem, the gospel has now been preached not only in surrounding Judea but among the Samaritans and to an Ethiopian. The conversion of the key person who has been chosen to spearhead the Gentile mission (i.e., Saul of Tarsus) has been told, and his relationship with Barnabas — who will be his partner in beginning and defending the evangelization of Gentiles — has been explained. With all these items in place, why does Luke "digress" from his story line to tell the stories of two miracles by Peter during a time of peace and growth in the church? (cf. 9:31).

Good narrators always keep their central characters in bold relief, weave them into the story periodically to validate them, and repeatedly affirm their importance to those who are trying to follow the story. Since Peter has been a leader among the apostles from the beginning and is to be the person who will initially open the door of faith to Gentiles, Luke brings him center stage again at the present juncture in his narrative to legitimate what is about to happen. The impression cannot be left that there are

Day 1
Keys of the Kingdom
Read Matthew 16:13-20 for Peter's confession and Jesus' response.

1. What was Peter's special role among the apostles?
2. What is meant by "keys of the kingdom"? What was Peter's task with them?
3. Did Peter ultimately have more authority than the other apostles? Cf. Matthew 18:18.
4. Why was it critical for Peter rather than Paul to bring the first Gentile converts to the Lord?
5. How did Peter help keep the church unified after the controversy broke out over Gentile converts?

119

two churches — one Jewish and one Gentile. So the apostle who first used the "keys of the kingdom of heaven" (Matt. 16:19; cf. 18:18) on Pentecost will be used by the Spirit of God to bring the Good News to a Gentile at Caesarea. Once that momentous transition has occurred and has been validated for the larger body of believers, Peter will resume his primary mission as Apostle to the Jews and Paul will take up his role as Apostle to the Gentiles.

In what appears to be a mini-version of Paul's later missionary journeys, Luke shows Peter on a preaching circuit that takes him to Lydda to Joppa to Caesarea. In the former places, he reestablishes himself in the narrative as an agent of divine truth and power; in the latter, he crosses the final racial and cultural divide with that same truth and power.

Day 2
What Is a "Miracle"?

Read John 10:22-42 for the significance Jesus attached to miracles.

1. Give your own definition for the term *miracle*.
2. What are the essential features of a genuine miracle?
3. Distinguish *miracles* from *blessings*.
4. Do you find the discussion of terminology about miracles helpful? Explain.
5. When you pray for God's activity, are you able to leave his method of response to his sovereignty? Explain.

A. The Healing of Aeneas at Lydda. 9:32-35.

As the church grew during a time of great spiritual prosperity, Peter "traveled about the country" to evangelize the unconverted and to strengthen believers. He came to Lydda [Lĭ´-də], some 25 miles northwest of Jerusalem, to "visit the saints" there. In this predominantly Jewish town situated in a racially mixed territory, he encountered a man named Aeneas [A-nē´-əs].

Aeneas was the victim of a condition that had left his lower body paralyzed. He "had been bedridden for eight years" at the time of his encounter with Peter. In a dramatic deed of compassion coupled with power, Peter said, "Aeneas, Jesus Christ heals you. Get up and take care of your mat." The result was that the formerly paralyzed man "immediately" got up and was free of any disability.

The word "immediately" distinguishes a genuine miracle from other wondrous things we are inclined to (mistakenly) call miracles. It is not a miracle, for example, when a person with cancer undergoes surgery and chemotherapy for two years and is still free of cancer ten years later. A believer in whose life this happens certainly will have prayed for God to heal him and will give thanks for the "good gift" of health that results (cf. Jas. 1:17). He may even tell his friends, "It's a miracle that I am here and doing well!" And so for others who recover from heart surgery, severe burns, or grinding automobile accidents. Technically, however, a miracle is an immediate (i.e., not through surgery, medication, or rehabilitation; in an instant rather than over time) and complete (i.e., not by gradual stages; from blindness to vision or from paralysis to soundness of limb) action of God in relation to some human situation. Again, it is not a miracle when a storm passes during a 36-hour ordeal of high winds and rain, leaving one's house relatively unscathed; it is a miracle when someone stands in a boat and says, "Peace! Be still!" and creates an immediate calmness in the forces of nature.

The point of this distinction is not to discourage either prayer for divine intervention or giving God praise for healing, surviving a storm, or recovering from a terrible accident. Rather, it is to encourage greater clarity of thought and precision of expression when we speak of God's activities. Eve's creation from one of Adam's ribs was a *miracle*; the coming of their children by conception, gestation, and childbirth were *blessings from God*. A similar distinction in our own life experiences might be helpful to some who teeter on the brink of unbelief at times of crisis because "God isn't doing anything." God occasionally acts by a miracle, but he constantly gives blessings and assistance in response to human need.

The impact of the miracle on Aeneas the Christian was an opportunity for the evangelization of witnesses who were not Christians. People in Lydda and the surrounding coastal plain region (i.e., Sharon) saw Aeneas completely and immediately

Day 3
Miracles and Faith

Read Acts 14:8-20 to see how a miracle could generate a negative result.

1. Larkin (Acts, p.151) writes: "In the end, saving faith must not rest on the impression the miracle has made but on the truth of the message to which it points." What is your reaction?
2. Why did miracles not always generate faith among witnesses to Jesus' ministry?
3. Why did the miracle at Acts 14:8ff produce a negative result?

4. What does the term *superstition* mean?

5. In either ancient or modern times, how do *miracles* and *superstitions* relate to one another? How may one keep from confusing them?

whole and "turned to the Lord." Their conversion did not result directly from the miracle, of course, but from their response of faith to the message Peter preached among them. The miracle had served as an authentication of the messenger at whose hands it was performed and of the message he was preaching among the people.

B. The Raising of Tabitha at Joppa. 9:36-43.

1. A description of this good lady. 9:36.

Joppa, Jerusalem's ancient seaport and modern Jaffa, was approximately eleven miles to the northwest of Lydda. "A disciple named Tabitha (which, when translated, is Dorcas)" lived in that city who was known for good works. In particular, she ministered with great compassion by "helping the poor." Luke's Gospel gives particular notice to women, the poor, and widows. It is therefore not surprising that he should select from among many miraculous deeds in Peter's ministry one that involved a woman whose particular passion was to help widows. By way of anticipation, one should not overlook the fact that one of the distinguishing traits Luke will note about the first Gentile to become a follower of Christ is that "he gave generously to help those in need" (10:2b).

Many churches and Christian aid societies have taken the name of Dorcas to their ministries. That her name should be so identified with compassion to the poor across the centuries is no small tribute to her. "In Dorcas Luke gives us a model of Christian charity to the marginalized in society. Then orphans and widows were the most economically vulnerable (Luke 20:47). No government safety net was there to catch them. And today too, Christians must bring as much [well-being born of full health] as possible to those on the margins." [Larkin, *Acts*, p. 152.] Other than the information given here, we know nothing further about her.

2. Her death and a summons to Peter. 9:37-38.

Dorcas became ill and died, and grief-stricken friends and beneficiaries of her goodness began making preparation for her burial. Since the Jews did not embalm their dead, burial preparations moved very quickly. Interment typically took place on the day of a person's death or on the day following. So "her body was washed and placed in an upstairs room," apparently to await burial on the next day. Simultaneously, the mourners sent two men to Peter at Lydda with the request, "Please come at once."

Did the disciples at Joppa send for Peter in the hope that he would raise Dorcas from the dead? Did they send for him simply out of their regard for her and in hopes that Peter would join them in paying respectful tribute to her? Or was their urgent plea simply an expression of their sense of loss and bewilderment over the good woman's death? Any one or all of these are possible under the circumstances.

3. Her return to life and the response to this miracle. 9:39-43.

Peter responded immediately and affirmatively to the request for his presence. He joined the men who had come for him, made the quick trip from Lydda to Joppa, and was immediately taken to the upstairs room where Dorcas's body was when he arrived. There must have been quite a commotion around him as "all the widows stood around him, crying and showing him the robes and other clothing that Dorcas had made while she was still with them."

Peter emptied the room of all the mourners who had greeted him there with their wailing, and "then he got down on his knees and prayed." He was totally dependent on the will of God in this situation and did nothing to make a display of his intention or work. Then, addressing the corpse by her Aramaic name (i.e., Tabitha; Dorcas is Greek), he commanded, "Get up."

**Day 4
Compassion Ministries**

Read Matthew 25:31-46 to affirm the importance of compassion ministries to a Christian life.

1. Why was Dorcas so dearly loved at Joppa?
2. Why do you think this woman has been used so often as a model of Christian charity?
3. What are the greatest needs of our time that churches should address through compassion ministries?
4. How effectively does your church accept the challenge to help the weak and marginalized?
5. Are there personal challenges you sense in this component of your Christian life?

In response to Peter's word, Dorcas opened her eyes, saw Peter, and sat up. "Surprise! Death will not have the final say. There is a power loose which is able to break the last recalcitrant region (I Cor. 15:26). In this new community, widows will not be left to perish. Tabitha is restored to them by Peter's bold word and act of solidarity. The name of Jesus Christ bears the same life-and-death-giving power as the creator of the whole universe. All the boundaries of life, the highest heavens, the breath of life obey his command. Yet the story says that name belongs to widows and others who have no hope nor power except this name." [Willimon, *Acts*, p. 85.]

The excitement level must have been outrageous when Peter helped Dorcas to her feet, opened the door of the room where they had been alone, and "called the believers and the widows and presented her to them alive." Resurrection power had come to Joppa. The same power that had reportedly raised Jesus Christ from the dead had been witnessed among the citizens of that city in bringing Dorcas back to life. We are therefore not surprised to find out that this ultimate divine act of raising the dead "became known all over Joppa" and became the preaching foundation from which "many people believed in the Lord."

Because of the evangelistic success that followed on this episode, Peter chose to remain in Joppa "for some time." He preached the gospel and watched as God called men and women unto Christ for salvation.

Day 5
Patient and Gradual
Preparation

Read Ephesians 2:11-22 about God's purpose to unite Jews and Gentiles in one body.

1. Why was it unacceptable to the Lord to have

The final line of this section of text at first seems incidental and nothing more than a throwaway line, telling us that Peter stayed at Joppa "with a tanner named Simon." But is this merely an insignificant detail? The occupation of tanner dealt with the curing of animal hides. This meant that such a person stayed ritually unclean before the Lord in Judaism and excluded from the worshiping community. Whether Peter's acceptance of lodging from an "unclean" host triggered his subsequent visions about unclean animals and thus helped set the stage for his role in taking the gospel to a Gentile cannot be said with certainty, for the text makes no affirmation to that effect. On the other hand, why would Luke mention the fact at all if it was totally unrelated to the events about to happen in Acts 10 and 11?

What Peter was about to do at Caesarea would be a far more astonishing thing than either healing Aeneas from paralysis or raising Dorcas to life again. He would end the "time of peace" the church had enjoyed by throwing it into a controversy about Gentile membership. In doing so, he would be following the lead of the Holy Spirit in turning the church into a worldwide movement.

a Jewish church and a Gentile church?

2. Why were Jews and Gentiles not both evangelized from the start?

3. Dramatic change requires a combination of *boldness* and *patience*. Do you agree? Which is more important?

4. What evidence can you see in Acts of God's patient and gradual preparation for the mission to Gentiles?

5. Are there areas in your Christian life where you are trying to force something that needs more patient, gentle preparation? In your church?

Week Sixteen

Acts 10:1-48 (VI C in Outline)

Day 1
Borderland of
the Kingdom

Read Mark 12:28-34 about a man "not far from the kingdom of God."

1. What did Jesus mean in describing the man at Mark 12:34?
2. Do you think it would be correct to describe preconversion Cornelius the same way? Explain.
3. Who are the "border-land people" of the kingdom of God today?
4. How can these people be reached for Christ?
5. Is there such a person you can help reach? How will you proceed?

It is customary to refer to the man whose story we are about to read as the "first Gentile convert to Christ." More precisely, Cornelius is the first Gentile whose conversion to Christ is recorded for us. Other Gentiles may have been led to salvation by believers who were scattered from Jerusalem after Stephen's death (8:1). If so, their baptisms and subsequent participation in the life of a local church had not happened in the spotlight glare that accompanied a Roman officer's conversion under the preaching influence of an apostle. Therefore the case involving Cornelius became the precedent for all Gentile conversions that were to follow. Much depended on what happened here and how it was reacted to by the Jewish church.

Amazingly, we are probably close to ten years out from the Pentecost Day on which the church was established. It has taken that long for heaven to set in place the persons (e.g., Philip, Paul) and half-steps (e.g., Samaria, the Ethiopian) necessary to secure the acceptance of non-Jews into the church and to launch an effective work of evangelism into the larger world of the Roman Empire. The importance of this episode to the Acts narrative is evident from the fact that it is the longest single narrative in the entire volume, running 66 verses from the start of Acts 10 through the defense of his actions by Peter in Acts 11.

C. The Conversion of Cornelius. 10:1-48.

Caesarea was a Roman garrison town, the Roman provincial capital for Judea. It was therefore the residence of the proconsul for the region. Because of its heavy military fortification, Paul will be sent there later in the Acts narrative for security reasons (23:12ff). Its life revolved around the men and money brought to it by the presence of so large a military outpost. Although it had all the raucous life one would associate with a garrison town, it was also the home of a particularly pious man who was a God-fearer (i.e., a non-Jew who attached himself to the synagogue, gave allegiance to the Decalogue, but had not proselyted to Judaism) and eager to know more about the God of Israel.

1. Background events which set the stage for a Gentile conversion. 10:1-16.

Earlier in Acts we have seen the precedent of interrelated visions bringing persons together. Saul had a vision about a man named Ananias coming to him (9:11-12); Ananias had a vision about God's choice to send him to Saul with the gospel (9:10-16). This interesting phenomenon was used in the present case to bring a seeking Gentile into contact with a messenger of the gospel who could answer his questions about redemption.

The first vision (10:1-8) was given to a man named Cornelius. He was a "centurion" (i.e., over a group of approximately 100 men, roughly the equivalent of a captain in the U.S. Army) in the Italian Regiment. Reliable men of this rank formed the solid center of the Roman army. Centurions were typically sensible, reliable soldiers who had shown leadership ability in the field. This particular centurion, along with "all his family" (Gk., "household," a term that includes not only his blood kin but also his personal servants, cf. 10:7) were known to the local Jewish community as "devout and God-fearing." Specifically, "he gave generously to those in need and prayed to God regularly."

In the vision given him, Cornelius "distinctly saw an angel of God" who called his name. His response

Day 2
Prepared Hearts

Read Romans 10:1-21 about hearts that resist the Word of God.

1. Do you agree that Cornelius's heart was well-prepared for the gospel? Explain.
2. What common situations of life help prepare people to hear the gospel?
3. How can Christians better recognize hearts that are eager to receive the gospel?
4. What methods of teaching do you think are most effective in reaching such persons?
5. How do you keep your own heart tender and ready to respond to the Word of God?

"What is it, Lord?" reminds us of Saul's response on the Damascus Road (9:5); it is a typical use of "Lord" as polite address rather than a title for deity. The angel told him that his prayers and generosity to the poor had "come up as a memorial offering before God." This comment neither teaches salvation by human good works nor that Cornelius himself was regarded as saved at this point (cf. 11:14). Rather, it indicates that God honors the person who has a good and honest heart who has given himself to do all he understands to date of the divine will. Such a person will be eager to hear and receive whatever else there is of the Word of God that pertains to his need.

That there was still more that Cornelius needed to know of God's will is implied in the angel's instruction to him: "Now send men to Joppa to bring back a man named Simon who is called Peter." With the vision over, the Roman officer called two trusted personal servants and a God-fearing soldier who was a personal assistant, told them of the vision, and sent them on their way to bring Peter to Caesarea. Their one-way trip from Caesarea to Joppa would have taken them 30 miles to the south.

A second vision (10:9-16) took place around noontime the next day. It was given not to Cornelius but to Peter. Situated on the flat rooftop of his host's house, Peter was observing the noon hour of prayer that pious Jews traditionally kept. He became hungry and went into a trance. In this state of mind, he saw a vision of "heaven opened and something like a large sheet being let down to earth by its four corners."

The sheet-container Peter saw in his vision contained a variety of unclean animals, ranging from four-footed animals to reptiles to winged creatures. "Get up, Peter," a voice commanded him. "Kill and eat." As a man of kosher background and habit, the apostle protested that he had "never eaten anything impure or unclean." But the same voice that had given him the original command responded, "Do not call anything impure that God has made clean." This exchange was repeated three times.

2. Messengers from Cornelius are sent to bring Peter. 10:17-23a.

Peter was convinced that his vision was a communication from God, but he was far from sure about its meaning. At just that point of reflection on the vision's significance, the messengers from Cornelius arrived at the house of Simon the tanner and asked for Peter. The Holy Spirit communicated this message to Peter: "Simon, three men are looking for you. So get up and go downstairs. Do not hesitate to go with them, for I have sent them."

Peter responded without hesitation to go down and identify himself to the three men. Imagine his shock at greeting three Gentiles! They greeted Peter, told him something about their "righteous and God-fearing" master, and related the vision he had been given just short of 24 hours earlier. Before his own vision on the housetop, Peter almost surely would have refused their request. After all, he did not associate with "impure" and "unclean" Gentiles. But after the things he had just seen and heard, how could he label any human being with those terms? The messenger of Christ's gospel is not to shrink back from contact with people of any nation or race, color or tongue. So Peter "invited the men into the house to be his guests," thus choosing to entertain his first Gentile houseguests ever.

3. Peter goes to the home of Cornelius. 10:23b-33.

As Peter left for Caesarea the next morning, "some of the brothers from Joppa went along." Whether at Peter's request or on their own initiative, it was a wise and providential thing that they did

Day 3
Comfort Zones

Read a parable about people refusing to leave their comfort zones at Luke 14:15-24.

1. What is a "comfort zone"?
2. What comfort zones in Peter's life were challenged in these events?
3. How was Peter able to make the adjustments called for by these challenging situations?
4. How has Christ challenged your comfort zones?
5. How have you dealt with his challenges?

accompany him. He would soon need witnesses to confirm the events at Caesarea to many of the brothers who would challenge his actions.

Upon Peter's arrival at Cornelius's house, the Roman officer "was expecting them and had called together his relatives and close friends" in addition to his immediate family and household servants. The greeting between the two principal characters was awkward, to say the least. Perhaps in awe from the vision of two days ago and perhaps reacting out of his pagan background of superstition, Cornelius fell at the apostle's feet and appears to have been ready to worship him. But Peter would have none of it and rebuked him rather sharply. "Stand up!" he ordered and proceeded to assure Cornelius that he was nothing more than a human being.

If he had seemed stern and imposing in the first thing he taught Cornelius (i.e., human beings are not to be worshiped), Peter followed that by telling both his host and the "large gathering of people" he had assembled what he had just learned himself. "God has shown me that I should not call any man impure or unclean," he told them. Only someone who has had to repent of racial prejudice in the face of the very person(s) that spirit has insulted and demeaned could understand Peter's warranted embarrassment at that moment. The entire trip from Joppa to Caesarea had undoubtedly been a time for turning over in his mind the vision of the sheet filled with animals — and perhaps a sleepless night before as well. And he had not missed its force or application.

4. The gospel is preached to Gentiles for the first time. 10:34-43.

If there was ever a well-prepared audience for the gospel message, this was it. Cornelius and the people under his immediate influence had long ago taken a major step of repentance in rejecting the polytheism and institutionalized immorality of Greco-Roman

Day 4
Teachable Hearts

Read John 16:5-16 to hear Jesus tell his disciples that their grasp of the truth would come gradually.

1. Acts 10:43 quotes Peter about the OT prophets and their prediction that "everyone" calling on the Messiah would be saved. Had Peter always seen this truth in Scripture?
2. What caused Peter to see something in Scripture that had escaped him earlier?
3. Have you ever had an experience similar to Peter's? If so, on what issue?
4. What sorts of things tend to open human beings to new insights into old texts or topics?
5. Pray for God to keep your heart teachable and responsive to his word.

religion. They had moved toward the true God to seek the knowledge of his will by associating themselves with the Law and the Prophets via the Jewish synagogue. They were God-fearing, committed to helping the needy in God's name, and prayed to God regularly. Who can doubt that the burden of their prayers was a fuller knowledge of the will of God for themselves?

Peter began his sermon with a second (cf. v. 28b) assurance to his hearers that he now understood that "God does not show favoritism but *accepts men from every nation* who fear him and do what is right." As Paul would later put it: "[T]he gospel . . . is the power of God for the salvation of everyone who believes: first for the Jew, then for the Gentile" (Rom. 1:16).

Since their reverence and piety had proved his audience ready for the gospel yet still left them unsaved without the knowledge of Christ, Peter moved quickly to articulate the message Cornelius, his family, and his invited guests needed to hear. Although Jesus was born a Jew and announced the kingdom of God to the "people of Israel," he is now to be preached as "Lord of *all*."

Peter's brief summary of the life of Christ came around to a central truth about his ministry that he knew would connect with his hearers. He explained "how he went around doing good and healing all who were under the power of the devil, because God was with him." He then moved quickly to the ultimate Christian affirmation about Jesus: "They killed him by hanging him on a tree, but God raised him from the dead on the third day and caused him to be seen." Among those who had in fact seen him alive was Peter. Now, in response to Jesus' post-resurrection commission, the gospel was being preached to the whole world. "All the prophets testify about him that *everyone who believes in him* receives forgiveness of sin through his name."

Day 5
The Gentile Pentecost

Read Acts 2:1-13 for a reminder about events of the original Pentecost activities of the Holy Spirit.

1. Why is Acts 10 called "The Gentile Pentecost"?
2. Why did there need to be such an event involving Gentiles? For the Gentiles? For the Jews?
3. What was the essence of Peter's message that day?
4. How closely did his sermon resemble the one he preached in Acts 2?
5. What is the significance of the baptism of Cornelius and his household to the larger story of Acts?

5. The Holy Spirit poured out upon the Gentiles. 10:44-46a.

At the point in his sermon where the gospel of salvation in Jesus' name had been declared, the Holy Spirit moved directly and dramatically. In what is often dubbed "The Gentile Pentecost," the Spirit fell on Peter's hearers, caused them to praise God by speaking in tongues, and "astonished" the brothers who had come from Joppa with Peter.

6. Peter commands baptism in water for the Gentiles. 10:46b-48.

Since the Holy Spirit had supernaturally affirmed Peter's new understanding about the acceptability of Gentiles and Jews alike through Christ, the apostle boldly called on Cornelius and his friends to attest their faith in the universal Lord of humankind through water baptism. In the New Testament, there is no such thing as an "unbaptized Christian." The very term would be as offensive to a biblically literate ear as an "unmarried wife" or "unwarm fire." Water baptism is not at the heart of the gospel message; that message is about the death, burial, and resurrection of Jesus. Water baptism is, however, the normative response of a penitent person who believes the gospel; under the watery symbol of the death, burial, and resurrection of Jesus, he confesses and claims heaven's free gift of eternal life (Rom. 6:1-4).

Following the excitement of this event, the Gentile Christians "asked Peter to stay with them for a few days" for the sake of instructing them in their new faith. What a time it must have been as the church's first exercise in community-building between two ethnic groups that had been so deeply divided for so very long. It was a time that verified the gospel truth that people who love Jesus can learn to love all others who belong to him.

Week Seventeen

Acts 11:1-30 (VI D to VII C in Outline)

Progress is seldom made without resistance and controversy. The *status quo* of "things as they have always been" is the consistent enemy of repentance, spiritual progress, and the pursuit of God. This was certainly the case with the conversion of a Gentile (i.e., Cornelius) and the potential implications of that event for the future of the church.

Would the early Christians regard this as a precedent-setting episode? Would the predominantly Jewish church begin a program of outreach to Gentiles? Would they see broad implications for Jew-Gentile relationships? The answer to all these questions is the same: No, not without resistance and controversy. Peter would have to defend what he had done at Caesarea when he returned to Jerusalem (11:1ff). A church would have to be established at Antioch that could serve as the base for Gentile evangelism (11:19ff). A church-wide gathering would have to be held to debate the appropriateness of taking the gospel to Gentiles (15:1ff). Even so, the problem would persist over time as people attempted to bind the Law of Moses and Jewish traditions on Gentile believers (cf. Galatians).

D. Peter's Report of Gentile Conversions before the Jerusalem Church. 11:1-18.

1. Criticism from an element of the church. 11:1-3.

After the baptism of Cornelius and his household, Peter and his associates stayed at Caesarea to instruct the new believers in the gospel "for a few days" (10:48). Then, by the time they could return to Jerusalem, news of what had happened had outrun them to the city. So

Day 1
Controversy

Read what Jesus said about controversy over his own ministry at Luke 12:49-53.

1. Why did Jesus' ministry cause resistance and controversy?
2. What was the nature of the controversy over the conversion of Cornelius?
3. What social controversies have you witnessed in your lifetime? What church controversies?
4. What distinguishes a *principled controversy* from a *needless controversy*?
5. Are you aware of controversy in your church or about your church? Is it "principled" or "needless" in nature?

Day 2
When to Defend Yourself

Read Romans 12:9-21 about how Christians treat their critics and enemies.

1. What did Jesus mean at Matthew 5:38-42?
2. Why did Peter defend himself in this situation?
3. Why did Paul defend himself in 2 Corinthians 10?
4. When should you defend yourself or a brother before criticism?
5. When should a believer "just walk away" from criticism?

startling a turn of events could not have been kept quiet, even if Peter had attempted to conceal it.

When Peter arrived at Jerusalem, he had to defend his actions. "The circumcised believers criticized him and said, 'You went into the house of uncircumcised men and ate with them.'" The force of their criticism seems to have been less that he preached the gospel to Gentiles than that he "ate with" Gentiles. The expression in this context would signify much more than sharing food with Cornelius and his family. The criticism from Jerusalem was that Peter had blurred the long-established distinction between circumcision and uncircumcision, the Chosen People and Outsiders. The charge was that he had set aside the superiority and privilege his critics understood they had as Jews.

2. His explanation and defense of the episode. 11:4-17.

Peter formulated an immediate and vigorous defense of his actions. He offered a colorful narrative of his experience on the roof in Joppa, Cornelius's vision that told him to send for Peter, and what happened when he arrived at Caesarea. With regard to Caesarea, he offered the testimony of the "six [Jewish] brothers" (11:12b) who had accompanied him from Joppa.

Based on his narrative, Peter made a compelling argument in support of the inclusion of the Gentiles in Christ. He did not make himself the focus of the argument. He hinged everything on divine activity. It had been the Holy Spirit who told Peter to have "no hesitation" about going with Cornelius's messengers. Then, upon his arrival at Caesarea and as he was starting to speak, "the Holy Spirit came on them as he had come on us at the beginning."

It is interesting that Peter told his questioners that his own mind had immediately linked the coming of the Holy Spirit on Cornelius with a promise from the personal ministry of the Lord

Jesus. Jesus had told the apostles, "John indeed baptized with water, but you will be baptized with the Holy Spirit" (cf. Mark 1:8). Peter had inferred that what he had seen with his own eyes showed that this promise included Gentiles as well as Jews. Thus he had reached the following conclusion: "So if God gave them the same gift as he gave us when we believed in the Lord Jesus Christ, who was I to think I could oppose God!"

3. A positive reaction to his defense. 11:18.

When he finished his explanation and argument, the Jewish brothers who had originally challenged him "had no further objections" to make and "praised God" for the report. They affirmed Peter's conclusion that God had called the Gentiles unto himself by the gospel of Christ. There would be other persons to protest accepting non-Jews into the church on equal footing with Jews, but these had been convinced and silenced.

VII. The Gospel Comes to Antioch. 11:19-30.

Luke was a skilled writer who held to his purpose of writing an "orderly account" (Luke 1:3) of the ministry of Christ and the establishment of the church that grew out of that ministry. Here he supplies the next "orderly" step that allowed the gospel to move from Jerusalem through Judea and Samaria into the larger Roman Empire. After telling how Philip carried the gospel to Samaritans and Peter took it to Gentiles, he now tells the circumstances of the establishment of the strategic Gentile church that would become the base of operation for Paul's missionary journeys throughout the empire.

At this point in Acts, Luke shifts away from Jerusalem as the center of activity and leadership among the earliest Christians to Antioch of Syria. At

Day 3
A Strategic City

Read Psalm 122 about the importance of Jerusalem to a biblical writer.

1. How can a "strategic city" be important to a missionary effort? Cf. Acts 19:10.
2. Why was Antioch a strategic city in spreading the gospel?
3. How is Antioch like your city? How different?
4. What is the strategic importance of your church to your city? Your city to a surrounding area?

5. What significance does Antioch have to the second half of Acts?

the same time, he also shifts the focus from Peter and the other apostles to Paul and his missionary associates.

Antioch of Syria, frequently identified in ancient literature as Antioch on the Orontes [O-rŏn´-tēs], was located some 300 miles north of Jerusalem and almost 20 miles east of the Mediterranean Sea. It stood at the strategic place where the Orontes River breaks through the junction of the Lebanon and Taurus mountain ranges and flows to the Mediterranean. The city was founded by the Seleucid general Seleucus I Nicator [Sə-lyoō´-kəs Nī-kā´-tŏr] around 300 B.C.

When the events Luke tells about took place, Antioch was a thriving city of more than half a million souls. After only Rome and Alexandria, it was the third-largest city of the Roman Empire. It was a melting pot of Western and Eastern cultures, with the Jewish population somewhere around 70,000. Although widely known for its art and literature, it was also identified with immorality on a grand scale; the pleasure park of Daphne, which contained the Temple of Apollo, was nearby and hosted an incredibly large enterprise in cult prostitution. "In Christian history, apart from Jerusalem, no other city of the Roman Empire played as large a part in the early life and fortunes of the church as Antioch of Syria. It was the birthplace of foreign missions (31:2) and the home base for Paul's outreach to the eastern half of the empire. It was the place where those of 'the way' (9:2) were first called 'Christians' (11:26) and where the question as to the necessity for Gentile converts to submit to the rite of circumcision first arose (15:1-2; cf. Gal. 2:11-21). It had among its teachers such illustrious persons as Barnabas, Paul, and Peter (cf. Gal. 2:11-13) in the first century; Ignatius [Ig-nā´-shəs] and Theophilus in the second; and Lucian, Theodore, Chrysostom [Krĭs´-əs-təm], and Theodoret [Thē-ŏ´-də-rət] (as well as a host of others, including Nestorius) at the end of the third and throughout the fourth centuries."

[Richard N. Longnecker, "The Acts of the Apostles," *Expositor's Bible Commentary*, Vol. 9 (Grand Rapids: Zondervan Publishing Co., 1981), p. 399.]

A. Circumstances of the Church's Establishment at Antioch. 11:19-21.

Important as the move to Antioch is for his narrative, Luke summarizes the establishment of the church in that great city in a few words. By repeating the "formula" of Acts 8:4, Luke clearly intends for us to understand that he is picking up another strand of the same story of the spread of the gospel that he had told from that starting point.

In connection with the persecution that started on the heels of Stephen's martyrdom, some believers were scattered as far away from Jerusalem as Phoenicia [Phə-nē´-shə], Cyprus, and Antioch. These persons had confined their preaching of the gospel "only to Jews" in those places. Consistent with God's purpose to break down the barriers separating Jews from Gentiles, however, he moved certain men "from Cyprus and Cyrene" (cf. 13:1) to cross the racial barrier. So these teachers "went to Antioch and began to speak to Greeks also, telling them the good news about the Lord Jesus." While this shows that Peter's experience at Cornelius's house had not itself precipitated a missionary outreach to the Gentiles, it also shows that God was working through other persons and situations to achieve his purpose. Even though we do not even know the names of these barrier-crossing believers, Luke informs us "the Lord's hand was with them, and a great number of people believed and turned to the Lord."

From Paul's later writings, we know that the "great number" of believers included both Jews and Gentiles (Gal. 2:12). This means that the church at Antioch was different from any other we know about from this period (c. A.D. 45). It was a racially

Day 4
Unity in Christ

Read about the importance of Gentile-Jew unity at Ephesians 2:11-22.

1. Name some factors dividing Gentiles from Jews in the first century.
2. Trace the strategy of God's deliberate plan for the unity of the church in Acts.
3. What insights does the Acts plan give you about working toward racial harmony?
4. In light of the Acts strategy, evaluate this statement: "People just naturally want to be with their own kind."
5. What divisions other than racial-ethnic threaten the church today?

mixed body of Jews and Gentiles that had discovered their unity with one another through a shared allegiance to Jesus of Nazareth.

B. Barnabas and Saul at Antioch. 11:22-26.

1. Barnabas sent by church at Jerusalem. 11:22-24.

When word of the new congregation of believers and its unique composition reached Jerusalem, that church immediately sent Barnabas there. He was apparently sent both to affirm what was happening and to provide stable leadership at this early, critical juncture at Antioch. That he was from Cyprus (4:36a; cf. 11:20) and had the gift of encouragement (4:36b) made him the ideal choice for such a mission. His work at Antioch resulted in even greater evangelistic outreach.

2. Secures the assistance of Saul. 11:25-26a.

Seeing the success of the work at Antioch and realizing the need for more teaching and leadership, it occurred to Barnabas that Saul of Tarsus would be appropriate to the task. Barnabas had sponsored Saul at Jerusalem when believers there had been initially suspicious of his conversion (cf. 9:27), so the two men knew each other as friends as well as brothers. Presumably, Barnabas knew from Saul of God's intention to make him a witness to Christ among the Gentiles (cf. 26:17-18). We do not know what Saul had been doing between the time of his return to Tarsus earlier (9:30) and now. Perhaps he had been attempting to evangelize the racially mixed city of his birth, and word of that ministry had reached Barnabas.

The two men worked together at Antioch for "a whole year" and "taught great numbers of people." Time would show the brilliant and uniquely equipped Saul outstripping Barnabas in evangelistic success. Barnabas likely knew it would happen before he sought him to be his partner at Antioch.

His concern was for the success of the gospel, and there is no evidence that he was ever bothered by taking a secondary role.

3. Their work together at Antioch. 11:26b.

Larkin says Antioch was "famous for its humor, especially the coining of jesting nicknames." [*Acts*, p. 175.] Whether meant as an insult or as a mere descriptive term, the people of Antioch soon dubbed the disciples "Christians" (i.e., Christ-loyalists, Christ-followers). The term has since become the common way to designate those who affirm Jesus as their Savior and Lord.

C. Famine Relief to Judea through Barnabas and Saul. 11:27-30.

One of the most dramatic affirmations of the unity of the larger body of Christ came about when a prophet named Agabus [Ag´-ə-bəs] visited Antioch from Jerusalem. The Spirit enabled him to predict that "a severe famine would spread over the entire Roman world." Luke's parenthetical note informs us that this did in fact occur during the reign of Claudius, who was emperor during the years A.D. 41-54. Several non-biblical writers document the conditions of bad harvests and resulting famine conditions under Claudius. One that was particularly severe in Palestine is referred to in Josephus (*Antiquities* 20. 51-53.) and hit the area around A.D. 45-47.

Like their Jewish brothers before them (4:32-36), these Gentile believers understood that their faith obliged them to act on what they learned. So, when they learned of the impending famine, they set about to get assistance to the Christians in Judea. They sent their gift by Barnabas and Saul (cf. Gal. 2:2a), thus expressing in a practical way their compassion and their commitment to the oneness of the church.

Day 5
Love One Another

Read 1 John 4:7-21 about loving one's Christian brothers and sisters.

1. How did the Antioch church show its love for Jewish Christians?
2. What did this action say about the believers at Antioch?
3. Imagine that you are a Christian at Jerusalem when Barnabas and Saul arrive with famine relief from Antioch. What effect does it have on you? What do you say to others about it?
4. Have you ever seen loving help heal a division between two individuals or groups?
5. Do you know of a situation where loving assistance might bring some people closer together?

Week Eighteen

Acts 12:1-24 (VIII in Outline)

Day 1
"To the Jews First . . ."

Read Romans 9:1-33 and sense Paul's passion for his fellow-Israelites.

1. Why was Israel made God's "chosen people"?
2. How did Israel understand its special status?
3. What sort of equality was established between Jews and Gentiles after the death of Jesus?
4. Did the equality of Gentiles with Jews imply the rejection of Israel? Explain.
5. Why is the notion of Israelite rejection called a "hateful heresy" in the notes? How does this heresy relate to anti-semitism?

One of the hateful heresies that has beset the Christian church from earliest times has been the notion that God's acceptance of the Gentiles is somehow a repudiation of the Jews. Luke will have none of it. It is legitimate for the gospel to be preached to Samaritans and Gentiles, but it is also still God's power to save the Jews as well (cf. Rom. 1:16). Therefore, poised to complete his careful narrative about the gospel moving from Jerusalem to Judea to Samaria to the larger Roman Empire, Luke pauses to relate two additional anecdotes of God's powerful intervention on behalf of the church at Jerusalem.

The natural bridge to these stories is the account of the visit to Jerusalem by Barnabas and Saul that has been reported at the end of chapter 11. The famine relief was likely carried to Jerusalem in A.D. 46. The events Luke is about to relate would have taken place during the two years previous, so they would have still been current topics of discussion among the believers.

VIII. Perils for the Saints from Herod. 12:1-24.

A. Herod's Violence against the Church. 12:1-5.

The Herodian dynasty figures prominently in the New Testament. About the only thing that is consistent about its central figures is the hatred of the Jewish people for the entire family of puppet rulers.

They ruled only because of shrewd political maneuvering under the Romans and were always despised as foreigners by the Jews because of their Idumean descent. Antipater [An-tĭ´-pə-tər], an Idumean who founded the dynasty, was made the ruler of Judea by Julius Caesar in 47 B.C.

Of the several Herods who must be distinguished, the one of this episode is Herod Agrippa I. Born in 10 B.C., he was the grandson of the infamous Herod the Great. Agrippa had grown up in Rome. With access to the imperial court, he lived the undisciplined and extravagant life of a playboy. He had to flee Rome for Idumea in A.D. 23 because of an impossible debt he had amassed. Yet he was intelligent and charming enough that he stayed on the good side of most of the emperors.

Emperor Caligula gave him a northern region of Palestine — the tetrarchies of his uncle Herod Philip and Lysanius [Lĭ-sā´-nē-əs] (cf. Luke 3:1) — and the title "king" in A.D. 37. He received the territory of another uncle two years later when Herod Antipas, the murderer of John the Baptist, was banished by the emperor. Then, when Caligula died in A.D. 41, Agrippa's good fortune was made complete. Caligula was succeeded by Claudius, a friend to Agrippa since their youth in Rome. Claudius gave him Judea and Samaria and thereby made Agrippa I the ruler of a territory as large as that of his grandfather, Herod the Great. He ruled over it for only three years, however, for he died in A.D. 44. [Note: See chart of the Herod family on p. 148.]

1. James murdered. 12:1-2.

Herod Agrippa I did everything in his power to ingratiate himself to the Jewish masses who hated his family. He enhanced the prestige of Jerusalem and began to rebuild its northern wall and fortifications. He supported the priesthood and dealt with troublesome minorities swiftly and severely.

Day 2
Herod Agrippa I

Read about the infamous grandfather of Herod Agrippa I at Matthew 2:1-18.

1. What reputation does the Herodian dynasty have in history? Why?
2. What do we know about Agrippa's background? His rise to power?
3. Why did Agrippa initiate a persecution against the church?
4. How did he react to Peter's escape from prison?
5. What does his reaction tell you about his character?

Day 3
Playing to the Crowd

Read Exodus 23:1-9 about the responsibility to exhibit justice and fairness.

1. In what sense did Herod Agrippa I "play

141

to the crowd" in this situation?

2. What does his behavior prove about his sense of justice?

3. Give a modern example of some public figure who has acted unjustly by catering to public demands. How was justice denied in the situation?

4. When are you most tempted to "play to the crowd" in your life?

5. How can parents help their children develop the strength of character necessary to resist pressure to do wrong?

When Agrippa learned of the difficulty being created for the Jewish authorities by the growth of the Christian community, he "arrested some who belonged to the church, intending to persecute them." Exactly what he intended to do or how extensive he planned for the persecution to be, we do not know. In all likelihood, he was formulating his plans as he went — consulting with his key advisors among the Sadducees. The initial dramatic outcome of his activity was the murder of the apostle James. That James was "put to death with the sword" may indicate that he was executed on a charge of apostasy from the Jewish faith (cf. Deut. 13:12ff). Although Stephen was the first Christian to suffer martyrdom, James thus became the first apostle to die for the sake of Christ.

2. Peter arrested. 12:3-5.

Having found a way to curry favor from his Jewish constituents, Agrippa was emboldened to follow the murder of James with the arrest of Peter. Because Peter was arrested during Passover Week (i.e., "the Feast of Unleavened Bread"), cruel and self-serving Herod was simply biding his time about a trial for Peter until the holy days had passed. He put him under strict guard in prison, with "four squads of four soldiers each" charged to keep him from escaping. Clearly there was nothing about Peter or the actions of the Jerusalem church to make anyone fear an escape. This was showmanship to appease Agrippa's audience of Jewish authorities who were so hostile to the Christian movement.

The Jerusalem church reacted predictably to all this. Already shocked by the death of one of its apostle-leaders, the horrifying prospect of losing Peter sent that community into earnest prayer for him. Heaven's response was a miraculous deliverance.

B. Peter's Rescue from Prison by a Miracle. 12:6-19.

1. His deliverance. 12:6-11.

Perhaps because this was such a serious crisis for the Jerusalem church, the account of Peter's deliverance is told in unusual detail. In the night before Herod intended to bring him to trial and near-certain execution, an angel of the Lord woke Peter up. Peter appears to have been sleeping soundly on what might well have been the last night of his life on earth. The angel had to coach him to put on his cloak and follow him. Peter was so groggy, in fact, that "he had no idea that what the angel was doing was really happening; he thought he was seeing a vision."

Peter had been chained to two soldiers, and those shackles fell from his wrists when the angel awakened him. He then passed two other soldiers standing guard between himself and the iron gate at the prison's main entrance. The gate opened "by itself," and the apostle and the angel leading him through a series of supernatural events passed through. About the time Peter came clear-headed from walking in the cool night air, the angel left him on his own. He realized what had happened to him and gave God the glory for his release from prison.

2. His report of it to certain of the saints. 12:12-17.

Where could Peter go to get off the streets and avoid being recognized and rearrested? It came to him that he should go to the home of "Mary the mother of John, also called Mark, where many people had gathered and were praying." That a servant girl was tending the gate indicates that Mary's house was large enough to accommodate a group of some size. It likely served as the meeting site for one of Jerusalem's many house churches where the Christians met regularly for prayer and fellowship (Acts 2:46b-47). Mary's son, John Mark, would later accompany Barnabas and Saul on part of the first missionary tour (Acts 13:5, 13), minister faithfully with both Paul (Col. 4:10) and Peter (1 Pet. 5:13), and write our Gospel of Mark.

Day 4
Surprised by God's Answer to Prayer

Read Psalm 86 to find a moving prayer from David.

1. What situation had moved the Jerusalem church to urgent prayer?
2. How did the Lord respond to their prayers?
3. Why do you think Peter chose to go to Mary's house upon his deliverance from prison?
4. What was the comic response of the Christians to Peter's arrival?
5. Can you recall a recent situation in which you were "surprised" that God answered your prayer so dramatically?

There is a comic note about Peter's arrival at the gate of the house. The servant girl, Rhoda, was so excited to see him that she ran inside to tell the others "without opening [the gate]" to him. While Peter stood outside — doubtless looking over his shoulders for soldiers who might be coming for him! — Rhoda was inside trying to convince the praying Christians that God had heard their pleas and freed the apostle. "You're out of your mind," they told her. When she would not be silent, they finally condescended to say she must have seen his angel at the gate.

Peter finally created enough commotion outside that some of the people came, opened the entrance, and saw for themselves that he had been delivered from jail. They were "astonished" — as all of us are occasionally when the very things we have been praying for come to pass. Peter then motioned for quiet and related the experiences he had just lived. Knowing that he was still not safe, he shortly left for "another place." This likely means that he left the city until things calmed down from the commotion that was certain to follow.

Before he departed for a safer place, however, Peter gave explicit instructions that the word of his release be communicated throughout the church in the city. He named James as one person to be notified; this was, of course, the half-brother of Jesus who was already emerging as one of the "pillars" of the Jerusalem church (cf. Gal. 2:9).

3. Herod's punishment of Peter's guards. 12:18-19.

Peter's absence the next morning precipitated a great tumult. After an investigation at the prison and a thorough-but-unsuccessful search for Peter, an embarrassed, angry, and pitiless Herod Agrippa I ordered the execution of the guards in whose custody the apostle had been.

C. The Miserable Death of Herod. 12:20-23.

After this embarrassing episode, Herod left Jerusalem for Caesarea. Caesarea was his administrative capital and the most fortified city in Palestine. It was there that Agrippa wielded his purest power. Jerusalem might embroil him in religious-civil disputes that left him frustrated, but Caesarea was where his word was final for everyone in the region.

Luke refers to an ongoing dispute between Herod Agrippa and the people of Tyre and Sidon, just to the north of Caesarea. He had effectively beaten the cities into submission and had them at his mercy. The means of his victory appears to have been an economic boycott, for Luke says they sued for peace "because they depended on the king's country for their food supply."

Josephus as well as Luke relates the story of Herod's miserable death. On a day when he was prepared to enjoy trampling the Tyrians and Sidonians into submission, Herod put on resplendent robes, made a speech to the crowd, and accepted the fawning cheers of his audience. The people shouted, "This is the voice of a god, not of a man." So vain and pretentious a man as Herod Agrippa I was not about to disclaim the veneration offered him.

Because of Herod's blasphemous arrogance, "an angel of the Lord struck him down, and he was eaten by worms and died." Ever the physician, Luke identifies the specific cause of death as intestinal roundworms. These parasites can grow a foot long or more, obstruct the intestines, and cause severe pain and vomiting. The death that comes by this means is neither swift nor merciful. Such was the fate of one who dared both to abuse his civil power

Day 5
Divine Judgment

Read Isaiah 42:1-9 to see that God will not allow his glory to be stolen by pretenders.

1. Under what circumstances did Herod Agrippa I become ill? How does Luke account for it?

2. What was his illness? What sort of death does it bring about?

3. In what ways does God judge people in this life?

4. Are all illnesses, accidents, and deaths divine judgments? Explain.

5. How will God's ultimate judgment be dispensed to humans?

to persecute a servant of God and to accept the praise of men as if he were divine.

D. Another Observation about the Growth of the Church. 12:24.

Luke closes this section as he has two previous ones (cf. Acts 6:7; 9:31) with a summary statement of the continued progress of the gospel. As he prepares to focus the remainder of Acts on Gentile mission, he leaves no doubt that "God was still at work on behalf of the Jerusalem church and its ministry and was still concerned for his ancient people Israel." [Longnecker, "Acts," p. 414.]

A Chronology of Acts of the Apostles

World History		Events of Acts
	A.D. **30**	Jesus crucified; church established
	31	
	32	(?) Stephen martyred at Jerusalem
	33	(?) Saul of Tarsus converted
	34	
	35	
Pontius Pilate removed from office	36	
Caligula becomes emperor	37	
	38	
	39	
	40	(?) Cornelius converted
Claudius becomes emperor;	41	Church founded at Antioch; James
Agrippa I rules Palestine	42	murdered and Peter imprisoned
Famine in Palestine	43	
	44	Church persecuted in Palestine
	45	
	46	Saul's "famine visit" to Jerusalem;
	47	First Missionary Tour (46–47)
	48	Gathering at Jerusalem; Second
Jews banished from Rome by Claudius	49	Missionary Tour (48–51/52)
	50	
Gallio becomes proconsul of Achaia (July)	51	
Felix made procurator of Judea	52	Third Missionary Tour (52–57)
	53	
Nero becomes emperor	54	
	55	
	56	
	57	Paul arrested at Jerusalem;
	58	imprisoned at Caesarea (57–59)
Festus made procurator of Judea	59	Paul appeals to Caesar; voyage to Rome
	60	Paul under house arrest at Rome (60–62)
	61	
	62	Paul released (spring)
	63	
Great fire at Rome (July); Nero begins	64	
major persecution of Christians	65	(?) Paul martyred at Rome
Jewish revolt begins in Palestine	66	
	67	(?) Peter martyred at Rome
	68	
	69	
Jerusalem destroyed by Roman army	70	

Rulers of Palestine from
Herod the Great to Jewish-Roman War

37 B.C. ———————————————————— 37 B.C

All Palestine ruled by **Herod the Great** as "King of the Jews"

4 B.C. ———————————————————— 4 B.C

Judea, Samaria,
and Idumea
under **Archelaus**
as ethnarch

Iturea
and
Trachonitis
under **Philip**
as tetrarch

Galilee and Perea

under

Herod Antipas

A.D. 6 ————————————

as tetrarch

Ruled by
a series of
Roman procurators

A.D. 34 ————————————
Roman procurators
in charge
A.D. 37 ————————————

A.D. 39 ————————————

A.D. 41 ————————

Ruled by **Herod Agrippa I** as puppet-king under Rome

A.D. 44 ———————————————————— A.D. 44

R o m a n   p r o c u r a t o r s

Under
Roman
procurators

A.D. 53 ————————————

A.D. 56 (or 61) - - - - - - - -

Herod Agrippa II
as king

Partially under
Herod Agrippa II

A.D. 66 ———————————————————— A.D. 66

Adapted from Bruce M. Metzger, *The New Testament: Its Background, Growth, and Content*
(Nashville: Abingdon Press, 1965), p. 29.

Week Nineteen

Acts 12:25–13:52 (IX A to IX C in Outline)

Chapters 13 and 14 exhibit the radical new approach to sharing Christ for which Luke has prepared his readers (i.e., preaching directly to Gentiles and allowing them to express their faith independently of Jewish law and lifestyle), show the success of gospel missions among the Gentiles (i.e., the missionary tour by Barnabas and Saul), and provide the relevant background for the church conference at Jerusalem in Acts 15 (i.e., dialogue about the appropriate method of mission work among Gentiles).

IX. The First Missionary Tour. 12:25–14:28.

A. Barnabas and Saul Set Apart for a Special Work. 12:25–13:3.

To this point in Acts, the preaching of Christ had been done in response to local opportunity or challenge and as a result of specific divine promptings. Fully fifteen years after the establishment of the church, there was still no "missionary strategy" for reaching the world with the gospel. Both the promptings toward and procedures for mission work in the Antioch church should challenge us as we read about them.

1. Their return from the relief mission to Judea. 12:25.

The church at Antioch had learned of a famine that would affect the Roman Empire through the prophet Agabus. They immediately "decided to provide help for the brothers living in Judea." This act of charity and solidarity had been executed through

Day 1
Missionary Passion

Read 1 Corinthians 1:18–2:5 about the power of the Christian message.

1. Why was the Antioch church compelled to begin a missions program?
2. Should it have started a missions program before completely evangelizing Antioch? Explain.
3. How do today's churches compare to Antioch in commitment to missionary work?
4. What is the key to creating a passion for missions in a church?
5. What personal passion do you feel for missions?

a relief visit to Jerusalem by Barnabas and Saul (11:27-30). With that task completed, the two messengers returned to Antioch. They brought John Mark, the nephew of Barnabas and the son of a wealthy Christian in Jerusalem in whose home a house church met (12:12).

Day 2
Missionary Principles

Read Romans 11:11-24 for one of the issues related to Antioch's missionary principles.

1. What qualities did Antioch have that made it a good sponsoring church for missionary work?
2. What qualities made Saul and Barnabas ideal missionary candidates?
3. What principles should guide a church in its selection of missionary personnel?
4. How effective is your church in supporting, encouraging, and empowering its missionary workers?
5. The Holy Spirit guided the selection and ordination of Saul and Barnabas. How does he guide our missionary efforts today?

2. The Holy Spirit makes the divine purpose known. 13:1-3.

As the Antioch church sought the will of God through worship and fasting, the Holy Spirit communicated a call to missionary work. The details of that communication — whether vision, word through a prophet, or some other method — are not given, only the essential message: "Set apart for me Barnabas and Saul for the work to which I have called them." So, with additional prayer and fasting, the church ordained them to the work and sent them off.

Were there not enough unevangelized people among Antioch's half-million souls to keep these evangelists busy? Did that church have to undertake missionary work away from home to have work to do? God himself put the burden of missions on the heart of the Antioch body. He still puts the same burden on churches that are seeking him through worship, fasting, and sensitivity to the Holy Spirit.

B. Preaching on Cyprus. 13:4-12.

It is doubtful that Barnabas and Saul left Antioch with a detailed travel itinerary in hand. On the second tour, Luke tells of on-the-spot guidance given by the Lord (cf. 16:6-9). The same sort of guidance was likely provided on this trip. Before returning to Antioch of Syria, the men covered approximately 1,200 miles preaching the Word of God to all who would hear. The traveling team included not only Barnabas and Saul but John Mark and perhaps even other unnamed brothers (cf. 13:13).

1. Their arrival and initial preaching in the synagogues. 13:4-5.

The group left Antioch via Antioch's seaport town, Seleucia, and first saw land again about 130 miles later on Cyprus. Barnabas was from there (4:36), and it was easily accessible by sea. Likely there were already several Christians on the island, and its population included a great many Jews. Landing on the eastern coast of the island at Salamis [Să´-lə-məs], the group sought out the Jewish synagogues in a predominantly Greek city and preached Christ.

2. Their encounter with a false prophet at Paphos. 13:6-12.

They traveled about 100 miles east to Paphos along the Roman road that traversed the island. There they experienced both the joy of sharing the gospel with a bright and honest man and the anguish of meeting opposition to their message.

Sergius Paulus was the Roman proconsul serving on Cyprus. He was an "intelligent man" who inquired of the missionary team on his island about the message being preached. We are left to wonder whether this was an official inquiry or a personal quest for the truth on his part. When he apparently showed some interest in the gospel, "a Jewish sorcerer and false prophet named [Elymas, El´-ĭ-məs] Bar-Jesus" comes into the picture. He was an attendant to the proconsul and was determined to keep him from coming to faith in Christ.

A "sorcerer" (cf. 8:9; 19:13) dealt in magic, fortune-telling, and drugs. They were officially condemned within Jewish law (Deut. 18:9-13) but appear to have thrived across the years. They were alternative spokespersons for those who rejected the Law of Moses or for people taken in by superstition. Although the general procedure for Christian teachers should be gentle instruction and patience with opposition (cf. 2 Tim. 2:24-25), the activity of Elymas

Day 3
Missionary Methods

Read a description of one of Paul's missionary experiences from 2 Corinthians 2:12–3:6.

1. From today's devotional reading, identify Paul's source of "competence" for missionary work. Explain.
2. Paul typically worked in cities and population centers. Why?
3. Why did Paul typically begin his evangelism by seeking out a Jewish synagogue?
4. What was the gist of Paul's first recorded sermon? How is it a pattern for missionary preaching?
5. Daniel T. Niles has written: "[Evangelism] is one beggar telling another beggar where to get food." Does this fit Paul? Does it fit you?

was so evil and perverse that Saul used the power of the Spirit to bring a curse upon him. "You are a child of the devil and an enemy of everything that is right!" said the apostle. "You are full of all kinds of deceit and trickery. Will you never stop perverting the right ways of the Lord?" Elymas was struck blind by the power of the Lord — albeit only temporarily (i.e., "for a time").

The confrontation between the pseudo-power of sorcery and the genuine power of the Holy Spirit became a testimony to Sergius Paulus about the message being preached by Barnabas and Saul. The Roman governor "believed," yet Luke makes it clear that the primary basis for his faith was not the miracle he has witnessed but the content of the message itself. Sergius Paulus "was amazed at the teaching about the Lord."

In the history of missions, the first named convert is the Roman procurator of Cyprus. This is particularly interesting in view of the charges made earlier against Jesus and later against his followers that he and they were hostile to Roman authority. To the contrary, Luke seems to be determined throughout Acts to show that fair-minded Roman officials always treated the Christian message and its messengers with fairness.

C. Their Ministry in Antioch of Pisidia. 13:13-52.

In passing, one should not miss two subtle turns at this point in the narrative. Henceforth, the name Paul replaces Saul in naming this apostle. These are Greek and Hebrew names that he bore throughout his life, but — since the focus of his ministry is now the larger Roman Empire — Luke consistently refers to "the apostle to the Gentiles" by his Greek name in the remainder of Acts. Also, from this place in the record forward, we no longer read of "Barnabas and

Saul" but "Paul and Barnabas." As he took the leadership position in this missionary ministry, Paul's name was put first in order of citation.

1. John Mark leaves the company at Perga. 13:13.

When Paul and his company left Cyprus and sailed to Perga, a town on the southern coast of Asia Minor in the small province of Pamphylia, Luke records that "John [Mark] left them to return to Jerusalem." Why did the missionary apprentice turn back at that point? A variety of conjectures has been offered, ranging from simple homesickness to the rigors of their missionary work to Paul's displacement of Barnabas as team leader. The strength of Paul's opposition to allowing John Mark to go along on his second missionary journey (15:37-39) leads one to think that something other than a strictly personal reason lay behind his departure. Longnecker ["Acts," p. 421] raises the possibility that he disagreed with Paul's willingness to approach the Gentiles directly and to take them into full fellowship in Christ. If this is so, his return to Jerusalem may have been the stimulus for the "Judaizers" in that church to protest Paul's mission and methods. Although this is only conjecture, it would establish a plausible link between his return to Jerusalem and the necessity of Paul's defense of his ministry after his first tour of missionary preaching.

2. Paul's sermon in the synagogue at Antioch. 13:14-41.

Paul and Barnabas moved on from Perga to Antioch of Pisidia. The city was a hundred miles north of Perga and accessible only by climbing the steep passes of the Taurus Mountains. Set on the high plateau of central Asia Minor, this Antioch — one of sixteen cities founded in the third century B.C. by Seleucus I Nicator and named for either his father or his son, both of whom were named Antiochus — was an important and large city that

**Day 4
Missionary Results**

Read the Parable of the Soils from Luke 8:1-15.

1. Why does the preaching of the gospel produce a variety of results?
2. What was the reaction to Paul's preaching at Pisidian Antioch?
3. To what degree is a presenter responsible for

the reaction to the gospel?

4. Even though Paul and Barnabas left Antioch, what was the state of mind of the church they left behind?

5. What circumstances get people's hearts ready for the gospel? How should these factors guide us in selecting sites for mission work?

had a Jewish population of some size. Upon reaching the city, Paul located the synagogue and attended a sabbath assembly. Perhaps his Jewish wardrobe with tassels, phylacteries, and shawl identified him to his countrymen as a Pharisee. At any rate, he was invited to offer any teaching he felt moved to share.

Paul took advantage of the opportunity offered him at the synagogue to preach a sermon about Jesus. Addressing the "Men of Israel" (i.e., Jews such as himself) and "you Gentiles who worship God" (i.e., perhaps both proselytes and God-fearers similar to Cornelius), he presented a survey of Jewish history similar to Stephen's and showed how that history came to fulfillment in Jesus of Nazareth. In Pisidian Antioch, Paul not only set the precedent he would follow in other cities of seeking out a synagogue as his point of missionary departure but also established the basic argument about Jesus that he would use in those settings. His first recorded sermon becomes the pattern for many more he will deliver.

The first part of his sermon (13:16-25) traced the redemptive work of God among the Jews from Abraham to David to John the Baptist. The point is clear that he wanted his hearers to see Jesus as the fulfillment of all the messianic promises made by Yahweh across the centuries. The second part (13:26-37) is a straightforward preaching of Jesus in a form that anticipates what Paul would later call the message of "first importance" (cf. 1 Cor. 15:3ff). It tells of the crucifixion, burial, resurrection, and post-resurrection appearances of Jesus. As proof that Jesus was the risen Christ and Savior, Paul offered both the testimony of living witnesses and the witness of Holy Scripture (Psa. 2:7; Isa. 55:3; Psa. 16:10).

Paul ended his sermon on this evangelistic note: "Therefore, my brothers, I want you to know that through Jesus the forgiveness of sins is proclaimed to you. Through him everyone who believes is justified from everything you could not be justified from by the law of Moses."

3. The interest created by the sermon. 13:42-43.

What impact did the sermon have on the people present at the synagogue that day? Some were curious enough about Jesus to invite Paul and Barnabas to return on the following sabbath to "speak further about these things." Others were more urgent and followed the men from the synagogue for additional immediate word about Jesus.

4. Jewish jealousy and a turn to the Gentiles. 13:44-52.

Eager to accept the invitation to speak at the synagogue a week later, Paul and Barnabas appeared — as did "almost the whole city" to hear what they had to say. Moved by jealousy, the Jewish leaders opposed Paul and "talked abusively against what Paul was saying" (i.e., Jesus and the message of redemption by his death and resurrection).

Paul announced his intention of turning to the Gentiles with his message and quoted an Old Testament text in support of his plan. The Gentiles heard this with joy, and many turned to Jesus for salvation. The word continued to spread with such effectiveness among the Gentiles that the rebuffed Jewish leaders used their connections in Antioch to stir up persecution for Paul and Barnabas and force them to leave the city.

Day 5
Missionary Opposition

Read 2 Corinthians 11:16-33 about Paul's sufferings for Christ.

1. What circumstance initiated persecution against Paul and Barnabas at Antioch of Pisidia?
2. Were the missionaries cowardly to leave? Explain.
3. What was the significance when "they shook the dust from their feet" as Paul and Barnabas left Antioch?
4. What situations of persecution against missionaries do you know about in our own time?
5. Pray for the safety and boldness of persons preaching the gospel in contexts of opposition.

Week Twenty

Acts 14:1-28 (IX D to IX F in Outline)

Day 1
Opportunities for
Outreach

Read Paul's comments about the people of Galatia at Galatians 4:8-20.

1. How did Roman roads help set the agenda for Paul's missionary tours?
2. What other features of the first-century world contributed to the spread of the gospel?
3. Do you believe there are unique features of our own time that could facilitate evangelistic outreach? Name a few.
4. What are believers doing to use the special tools and openings for the gospel in our world setting?
5. Does your church have any unique opportunities for local evangelism? If so, are they being used to the fullest?

Fortunately for Paul and his missionary work, the Romans were great road builders. Some of the ancient highways they put in place are still in use today. One of their important roads, the Via Sebaste, ran from Ephesus to the Euphrates River. It passed through Pisidian Antioch, with its southeast fork leading to Iconium. When Paul and Barnabas left Antioch, they traveled eighty miles along the Via Sebaste to Iconium and preached the gospel there.

D. The Work at Iconium. 14:1-7.

When Paul and his company arrived at Iconium, they were still in the large Roman province of Galatia — subdivided by the Romans into various political regions (e.g., Pisidia, Phrygia [Frĭ´-jē-ə], Lycaonia [Lī-kā-ō´-nē-ə]) for effective administration. Antioch, Iconium [I-kō´-nē-əm], Lystra, and Derbe all belonged to the area sometimes called South Galatia. Our Epistle to the Galatians (written c. 48, probably only six months or so after the close of this preaching tour) was a circular letter to be shared among the several churches of that area.

Iconium was a beautiful city. It had a moderate climate and was blessed with abundant water and rich vegetation. The city prospered in antiquity and survives still as the modern town of Konya. Consistent with his missionary pattern of selecting cities along his travel route for evangelization and church planting, Paul would not pass by this influential place without preaching the gospel.

Paul and Barnabas arrived in Iconium and immediately sought out a Jewish synagogue. This gave them immediate access to a group that knew the Law and Prophets. It was from this biblical background that they could effectively show Jesus of Nazareth to be the fulfillment of Scripture and the long-expected Messiah. Indeed, their synagogue preaching was so effective that "a great number of Jews and Gentiles (i.e., God-fearers attending synagogue services) believed."

As one might expect, this success in the synagogue angered the Jews who did not believe Paul's message. They used their influence with the city's majority population and "stirred up the Gentiles and poisoned their minds against" the Christian missionaries. As the opposition became more intense, Paul's preaching became bolder and the Holy Spirit provided strong confirmation of his words through "miraculous signs and wonders" (cf. Gal. 3:5).

Although the Apostle to the Gentiles "spent considerable time there," their ministry at Iconium was eventually abandoned. The proclamation of the Christian message seems to have become the "hot issue" for the entire city. Some of the population "sided with the Jews" against the missionaries; others sided "with the apostles." [Note: The plural term "apostles" (v. 4, cf. v. 14) has Luke referring to Barnabas as an apostle. The word simply means "one who has been sent on a mission" and likely views both Paul and Barnabas as apostles of the church in Syrian Antioch. Paul sometimes used the word in this broader sense to include gospel messengers other than The Twelve (cf. 2 Cor. 8:23, "representatives"; Gal. 1:19, James the brother of Jesus is an "apostle"; Phil. 2:25, "messenger").]

The opposition to the work of Paul and Barnabas intensified until a "plot" was hatched by a group of Jews and Gentiles to stone them. They somehow learned of the plot and decided that discretion was the better part of valor. It was better to continue their Galatian mission from another base than to die as martyrs at Iconium.

Day 2
Biblical Terminology

Read Ephesians 4:1-16 and note some of the terms used for Christian servants.

1. What issue surfaces in Acts 14 about Barnabas?
2. How do you understand Barnabas to have been an apostle"?
3. How rigid and precise are biblical terms of this sort? Illustrate your answer.
4. Show how each of these terms may be used correctly of persons today: apostle, prophet, evangelist, pastor, and teacher.
5. Do any of these terms fit you? Explain.

Day 3
The Universal Message

Read Jeremiah 31:31-34 about God's intention to make himself known to all people.

1. What was the cultural setting for the citizens of Lystra and Derbe?
2. What special difficulties did their situation create for Paul and Barnabas?
3. Would it have been better for Paul to have avoided these cities?
4. What cultural barriers do we allow to keep us from spreading the gospel on a worldwide scale? In our own communities?
5. Pray for God to open our eyes to the fact that people of all backgrounds, social settings, and cultures need Christ.

E. Their Work and Persecution at Lystra. 14:8-20a.

Lystra was in many ways quite different from Antioch and Iconium. Its population was mostly uneducated, crass, rustic, and uncouth. The people of the city came principally from a tiny Anatolian tribe and preserved their own tribal language (cf. "the Lycaonian language," v. 11). Everyone needs to hear the gospel of Jesus Christ — whether city-dweller or farmer, literate or illiterate, cultured or unsophisticated.

1. A miracle performed and an unfortunate response. 14:8-18.

Paul's second sermon in Acts is a remarkable parallel to Peter's second sermon (3:1ff). Both involve the healing of a man "lame from birth" and preaching in response to the crowd's reaction to the miracle. In this case, however, the situation was greatly complicated by the superstitious mindset of the people that caused them to read the event a particular way.

When Paul encountered the lame man at Lystra, it was in the context of a teaching episode. Paul was preaching, and the man was listening and appears to have been on his way to saving faith in Christ. The missionary discerned that the lame man believed what Paul had taught about Jesus as a miracle-worker and healer. Seeing that the man "had faith to be healed," Paul healed him instantly and completely. The crippled man "jumped up and began to walk" in response to the apostle's order.

When the crowd witnessed this miracle, they did not interpret it against the background of Jewish Scripture. Instead, they saw it through their superstitious eyes and interpreted it against their own traditions. Fifty years earlier than this event, the Roman writer Ovid retold an ancient legend about Zeus and

Hermes visiting that region disguised as mortals, seeking lodging among the residents, and being turned away repeatedly. A couple finally received them into their tiny cottage. To reward their kindness, the "gods" turned their humble house into a temple with marble columns and golden roof. They then destroyed the houses of the people who had been inhospitable toward them.

The Lystrans apparently knew that legend and immediately recalled it when they saw the two strangers in their midst perform a miracle. Paul and Barnabas would have been preaching in Greek, the common tongue of the Mediterranean world and the second language of the Lycaonians. But when the citizens of Lystra began talking excitedly about the meaning of what they had just witnessed, they used their own Lycaonian language. They shouted, "The gods have come down to us in human form!" They identified Barnabas with Zeus (Latin, Jupiter) and Paul with Hermes (Latin, Mercury). Because they did not know the language being spoken around them, the Christian missionaries had no idea that they had been equated with Greek deities for a miracle that had been performed in the name of Jesus of Nazareth!

The priest from the temple of Zeus brought sacrifices to offer to the Christian missionaries, and a large crowd of people was urging the process along. But when Paul and Barnabas figured out what was happening, their were horrified (i.e., "tore their clothes") and spoke to the crowd saying, "Men, why are you doing this? We too are only men, human like you." What a marked contrast to Herod Agrippa I and his willingness to be proclaimed a deity (12:21-23).

Taking this interruption of events as his opening to speak, Paul immediately began to preach. The brief summary of his sermon indicates that it had two points. First, the sermon opened with a repudiation of idolatry and superstition (i.e., "these worthless

159

things"). Second, it offered the true God who had come among men as Jesus Christ as an alternative to their myths and legends. The sermon was not rooted in Scripture — which Paul's hearers did not know — but in natural theology (cf. Rom. 1:18ff). Unlike some, Paul knew that every audience has to be addressed in terms of its own peculiar background and life situation. Even with firm protests and disclaimers, Paul and Barnabas "had difficulty keeping the crowd from sacrificing to them."

Day 4
Suffering for Christ

Read what Peter said about suffering for Christ at 1 Peter 3:8-22.

1. What particularly tragic thing happened to Paul at Lystra?
2. What references to this event does Paul make in his own writings?
3. Relate the circumstances of Paul's rescue from danger.
4. What form is suffering for Christ most likely to take in your life?
5. What would you be willing to endure as suffering for Jesus' sake?

2. Paul stoned by his enemies. 14:19.

Sometime after this distressing episode, certain Jewish opponents Paul and Barnabas had created at Antioch and Iconium followed them to Lystra. Working first among the Jews of the city and eventually among the wider populace, they succeeded in turning the people against Paul. They stoned him and "dragged him outside the city, thinking he was dead."

3. His deliverance from death. 14:20a.

Whether Paul died from the stoning or not is not clear. His recovery from it — whether a resurrection from the dead or a healing from fatal wounds — was clearly miraculous. A number of brave Christians from the city "gathered around him" (to pray), and Paul recovered and walked back into Lystra under his own power. He referred to this episode later in writing to Corinth (2 Cor. 11:25) and may have referred to it in his letter to the Galatians (cf. Gal. 6:17)

F. The Work in Derbe and a Retracing of their Route to Antioch in Syria. 14:20b-28.

1. Encouraging the young churches. 14:20b-23.

The day following, Paul and Barnabas left Lystra and traveled some sixty miles southeast to Derbe. In a brief account of the mission there, Luke says "a large number of disciples" were won to the Lord through their preaching. The evangelists apparently left soon after establishing the church at Derbe. They essentially retraced their travel path and made brief stops — because of the recent intense opposition to them — at Lystra, Iconium, and Pisidian Antioch. They warned the young churches of "many hardships" their faith would create for them as their opponents eventually turned on the churches they had established.

The principal point of this trip was to stabilize new converts and young churches. In spite of the opposition and hardships they might face, they were exhorted to "remain true to the faith." Again modeling good missionary practice, they ordained elders in the churches for the sake of their oversight and nurture.

2. Preaching as they travel. 14:24-25.

Moving southward, they passed successively through the regions of Phrygia and Pisidia into Pamphylia. The primary city of that region was Perga, and the group of missionaries preached there — something they apparently chose not to do upon their first visit to the city, perhaps due in part to the circumstances surrounding John Mark's decision to turn back at Perga (13:13). We are given no information as to the outcome of their work there. When they judged it complete, they left Perga and went eight miles further south to the port town of Attalia. From there they went by ship to Antioch of Syria.

3. A report to the church at Antioch on their work. 14:26-28.

Since the church in Syrian Antioch had been the point of origin and base of support for their mission, Paul and Barnabas made a report on their experiences over the space of approximately one year. One can almost sense the excitement of their report as they told "all that God had done through them and how he had opened the door of faith to the Gentiles."

Day 5
Self-Sustaining Churches

Read 1 Timothy 3 about the role of elders and deacons.

1. Why did Paul want the churches he founded to be self-supporting and self-sustaining?
2. Why was the appointment of elders in those churches important to his goal?
3. What insight should we gain from Paul's methods for our own missionary efforts?
4. What should supporting churches and missionaries do to help the churches they plant become self-sustaining?
5. How does your church's missions program encourage self-sustaining churches in mission settings?

Week Twenty-One

Acts 15:1-35 (X in Outline)

Day 1
Cultural Diversity

Read Isaiah 2:1-5 about God's purpose to embrace all nations in Christ.

1. Trace the spread of the gospel across cultures in the first twenty years of the church.
2. What challenges were created by first-century cultural diversity in the church?
3. In what ways were these tensions natural and nonsinister? How did they originate?
4. How is cultural diversity a problem for missionaries? For people in local churches?
5. What is your church doing to address this problem? What more can it do?

Cultural diversity in the early church was God's will, yet it was clearly a challenge to the church. How should Jews and Gentiles relate to each other? Should they have different congregations in the same city? Should there be an even broader recognition of two churches with different messages and lifestyles? What should the expectations of Christian brothers from very different cultural backgrounds be of each other? These issues were as difficult to resolve in the first century as today.

At the root of the problem was not a division between "good people" and "bad people" in the church. Although we have sometimes cast it this simplistically in studying this text, that is unfair. Godly people came to an impasse over matters growing out of their backgrounds and training. The Lord extended patience in working with them over time, yet he clearly challenged the wrongheaded thinking among them. Only when some set themselves to reject what God had shown them through his appointed leaders did their behavior endanger their own relationship with Christ.

X. The Gathering at Jerusalem. 15:1-35.

The church was founded at Jerusalem in A.D. 30 and at Antioch approximately ten years later; Paul and Barnabas went on their Antioch-sponsored missionary journey in A.D. 46-47. Thus the church had thousands of Jewish members before there were any Gentile Christians. The earliest Christian experience was decidedly Jewish with regard to kosher food, clothing styles, circumcision of infants, holiday celebrations, and the like. Cornelius, believers at Antioch, and other Gentile converts to Christ who were brought to faith by the preaching of Paul and Barnabas would not bring Jewish background and habits to their Christian lives. It takes very little imagination to visualize the tensions that emerged.

To put this issue in more contemporary focus, imagine modern-day missionaries from America's "Bible Belt" culture working in France, Africa, or Australia. It is altogether possible that they would have to struggle with the sincere and correct convictions they had developed from their cultural background about social drinking, worship styles, or standards of modesty in dress. The temptation would be to impose the conclusions and habits from their previous culture onto a different one, to confuse the message of salvation in Christ with a set of cultural principles, to reduce the gospel to legalism.

When this problem arose in the first century, it was faced directly by the leaders of the church at a conference held in Jerusalem. They voiced their points of view, treated each other with respect in arguing their respective cases, and listened for the voice of God to give them a resolution of the problem.

A. A Threat to Further Missionary Work among the Gentiles. 15:1-5.

1. Troublesome teachers from Judea visit Antioch. 15:1-2.

Almost twenty years into the life of the church now, word had reached Jerusalem about Gentile baptisms and the central role of the Antioch church in evangelizing non-Jews. There was enough concern about the implications of all this that some Pharisaic (cf. v. 5) teachers from Judea took it upon themselves to travel to Antioch with this message: "Unless

Day 2
Disputes in the Church
Read Titus 3:1-11 about avoiding quarrels in the church.

1. Explain the background of the views held by the believers who came to Antioch from Jerusalem.
2. Why was Paul willing to engage them in "sharp dispute"?

3. What was the real issue at stake in this debate?
4. Have you ever seen this issue at stake in a church dispute? Explain.
5. How could the Jerusalem conference be a model for handling church disputes?

you are circumcised, according to the custom taught by Moses, you cannot be saved."

One should understand that circumcision was viewed by these Jewish teachers as a pledge to keep the entirety of the Law of Moses. Thus did a group of pious, moral, and conscientious Jewish teachers — who had been taught all their lives that the Law of Moses embodies the requirements of holiness to Yahweh — take it upon themselves both to protect the integrity of biblical revelation and to make a sincere effort to elevate the spiritual lives of the new Gentile believers at Antioch. There is no indication that these men had a sinister motive of wanting to keep the Christians at Antioch from their Messiah. To the contrary, they wanted them to receive Jesus as the Messiah but assumed that could only be done via the same perspective that had allowed them to know him.

Regardless of the genuineness of conviction and motive in what these Jewish brothers were teaching, Paul and Barnabas could not allow them to work without challenge. There was a "sharp dispute and debate with them." The issue, after all, was not eating lamb versus pork or even circumcision versus uncircumcision. The matter at stake was really this: Is the gospel alone sufficient unto salvation, or must the gospel rest on the platform of the rules and lifestyle of the Law of Moses? This was so unsettling a dispute that the Antioch church delegated Paul and Barnabas to go to Jerusalem, meet with the apostles and elders of the Jerusalem church, and seek a resolution to the matter.

[Note: The first of his several epistles was likely written by Paul at this juncture. With the believers in the churches he and Barnabas had just established being challenged by this teaching, he wrote the churches of Galatia (i.e., Antioch of Pisidia, Iconium, Lystra, Derbe) a circular letter. He called the attempt to yoke Christians with the requirements of the Law of Moses "another gospel" (Gal. 1:7), defended his apostolic ministry and authority (Gal. 2:1ff), and pleaded that the Galatian churches not yield to the "yoke of slavery" the Judaizers wanted to impose (Gal. 5:1ff). Galatians was clearly written after Paul's famine visit to Jerusalem (Gal. 2:1; cf. Acts 11:27ff), yet it was almost certainly written before the conference of Acts 15 because Paul made no reference to its outcome in defending his position. Galatians is therefore presumed to have been written in A.D. 48.]

2. Paul and Barnabas go to Jerusalem over the question. 15:3-5.

Paul and Barnabas were escorted some distance on their overland journey by Christians from Antioch. More significantly, they stopped along their route with churches in Phoenicia and Samaria and reported on their recent evangelistic outreach among the Gentiles. Among these believers, their "news made all the brothers very glad."

Arriving at Jerusalem, the two men were received warmly, reported on what they had been doing since leaving the Holy City, and immediately faced a challenge from the Pharisaic Christians.

B. A Speech by Peter. 15:6-11.

The apostles and elders convened a meeting to discuss the issue brought to them by the Antioch delegation. If the initial contact between Paul's group and the Jerusalem leaders was a private conference (v. 4), this seems clearly to have been a discussion open to the public. The activity of the conference revolved around three speeches.

Peter spoke first and reminded everyone of his experience with Cornelius and his household. God had given the Holy Spirit to Cornelius — "just as he did to us." Furthermore, the Roman centurion's salvation was in no way predicated on circumcision or

**Day 3
The Jerusalem
Conference**

Read Psalm 133 about unity among brothers.

1. Who requested the conference at Jerusalem? Why?
2. What risks were involved in calling for the public discussion of a church problem?
3. Trace the progression of thought in the statements made at the conference.
4. How was the consensus at the conference communicated to others? Why was this important?
5. When might public discussions of church problems be useful today? When are they more likely to be harmful?

any other element of legal observance. "He made no distinction between us and them, for he purified their hearts by faith." After all, Peter continued, the Law had been unable to save the Jews — so why should the advocates of legalism be allowed to "test God by putting on the necks of the (Gentile) disciples a yoke that neither we nor our fathers have been able to bear?" To the contrary, salvation does not come by keeping law for either Jews or Gentiles. "We believe it is through the grace of our Lord Jesus that we are saved, just as they are" (cf. Gal. 2:16).

Day 4
What Salvation Demands

Read Galatians 3:1-14 to discover the essence of salvation.

1. What were the Pharisaic Christians teaching about the requirements of salvation for those who turned to Jesus?
2. What was James's judgment about problems created by that teaching?
3. Identify the demands of salvation published in the letter produced at the Jerusalem conference. Explain each.
4. How would you expect a Jew to respond to this letter upon first reading? A Gentile?
5. What relevance do these requirements have to contemporary Christians?

C. Barnabas and Paul Relate Their Experiences among the Gentiles. 15:12.

The second speech that day was made by Barnabas and Paul. They told about their experiences at Antioch and on the first missionary tour. They stressed the "miraculous signs and wonders God had done among the Gentiles through them." These were offered as proof of heaven's certification of what they were doing in offering salvation to the Gentiles through the simple gospel message they had preached.

D. The Speech of James. 15:13-21.

The final speech made at the Jerusalem conference was by James, the half-brother of Jesus. He had risen to great prominence among the Judean disciples by this point and rose to summarize what had come from the day's discussion. He affirmed the inclusion of the Gentiles within the scope of the gospel and cited Amos 9:11-12 to support his thesis. An Old Testament prophet had spoken of the time when the Messiah would arise from David's posterity and offer salvation to the Gentiles. James saw no biblical ground for imposing the Law of Moses on them and insisted instead that "we should not make it difficult for the Gentiles who are turning to God." Thus he reduced the hundreds of Levitical rules of ceremonial purity the Jews had known to a more fundamental call for holiness of life before the Lord and mankind. Gentiles were to abstain from foods sacrificed to idols lest they be implicated again with idolatry, avoid ingesting blood or meat that had not been drained of its blood (i.e., a law antedating the Law of Moses, cf. Gen. 9:4), and avoid sexual immorality.

E. A Letter Written to the Gentile Churches. 15:22-29.

The conclusion of the conference was summarized in a letter for distribution among Gentile believers. "The decision, suggested by James, and accepted by the council, included three points: (1) Liberty (cf. 15:19); the law of Moses need not be kept, and could not be a ground of salvation. This decision was the 'Magna Carta' of Christian liberty. (Gal. 2:15-21.) (2) Purity (ch. 15:20); liberty is not license, but a life of holiness, by faith in Christ. (Gal. 5:13-26.) (3) Charity; in matters of indifference let us not needlessly offend those who prefer to observe certain forms and ceremonies. (Gal. 6:2.)" [Erdman, *Acts*, p. 126.]

The letter not only put into permanent form the conclusion reached at Jerusalem but began with a rebuke of those who "went out from us without our authorization and disturbed you." It gave the Gentile believers a way of silencing those who were subverting their faith.

F. Reception of the Letter by the Church at Antioch. 15:30-35.

When the letter was read to the Christians in Antioch, its "encouraging message" produced great joy. A spirit of unity and peace replaced the agitation that had been present. Judas and Silas, prophets from the Jerusalem church who accompanied the letter to Antioch, sought to repair the harm that had

**Day 5
Liberty, Purity, and Charity**

Read Galatians 5 for Paul's comments on liberty, purity, and charity.

1. Do you agree that Erdman's summary represents the conference statement correctly? Explain.
2. What is the essence of Christian *liberty*?
3. Lest liberty be interpreted as license, the apostles and elders stressed *purity* as well. What does this demand entail?
4. In what specific matters would Jews need to be *charitable* with Gentiles? Gentiles with Jews?
5. Identify some contemporary tensions among Christians that could be resolved by applying these principles.

been done by their troublesome predecessors. They "said much to encourage and strengthen the brothers" and were eventually authorized to return to Jerusalem with a "blessing of peace" to the church there. For whatever reason, Silas decided against going back to Jerusalem — a decision that would shortly prove fortuitous for Paul (cf. 15:40).

With the unity-threatening crisis now handled at Antioch, the church resumed its ministry with renewed zeal. Paul and Barnabas were acknowledged leaders in the group as it continued to thrive in the Lord.

Week Twenty-Two

Acts 15:36–16:10 (XI A to XI B in Outline)

The future of Gentile missions had been in jeopardy before the great gathering in Jerusalem. The outcome of that conference, however, had solidified the church's commitment to sharing the good news about Jesus with people of all territories, races, and ethnic backgrounds. As the second missionary tour began, Paul was eager — especially in locations where churches had already been established — to share what had come of the discussions at Jerusalem. Luke writes: "As they traveled from town to town, they delivered the decisions reached by the apostles and elders in Jerusalem for the people to obey" (16:4).

Starting the second journey with the announced intention of revisiting the places where churches had been established on the first tour, Paul's openness to the leading of the Holy Spirit widened it considerably. The second missionary journey resulted in the spread of the gospel to Europe. Philippi, Thessalonica, and Corinth would become centers of influence for evangelization on a new continent.

XI. The Second Missionary Tour. 15:36–18:22.

We cannot be sure just how long Paul and Barnabas worked at Antioch following their return from the conference at Jerusalem. They remained long enough to do a considerable amount of teaching and encouragement in the Word of God (15:35). At some point, however, it occurred to Paul that he

Day 1
One Thing Leads to Another

Read Ecclesiastes 3 about the interconnectedness of life.

1. How did the Jerusalem conference solidify the church's commitment to Gentile missions?
2. How do you think things might have been different if the decision had gone with the Pharisaic believers?
3. In what ways do you think your life would be different if you were not a Christian?
4. How has being a member of your home church affected your life?
5. Identify a decision or commitment in your life that has shifted its direction in a significant way.

should revisit the young churches that had been planted a year or more ago.

A. The Proposal for the Second Tour. 15:36-39.

It was not Paul's intention to let the new converts he and Barnabas had made to "die on the vine" for a lack of teaching and encouragement. But it would be necessary to announce his intention to the believers at Antioch, gather his team of workers together, and formulate an itinerary. This turned out to be more eventful than he could have envisioned. The events Luke tells about in this regard reveal both the humanness of the Christian workers involved and the sovereign power of God to achieve his ends in spite of the flaws of his people.

1. The purpose of Paul. 15:36.

Although their ministry at Antioch was thriving, neither Paul nor Barnabas saw his calling to pastoral care so much as evangelistic outreach. Thus it surely came as no surprise to Barnabas when Paul suggested they revisit the first-journey churches and check on their welfare.

2. A dispute between Paul and Barnabas separates them. 15:37-39.

It apparently did come as a surprise to Paul, however, when Barnabas suggested (assumed?) that John Mark would be part of the missionary team. This young apprentice had started on the first tour only to leave and return to Jerusalem when the group reached Pamphylia (Acts 13:13; cf. p. 153 of these notes). He had "deserted" the work he had committed to do with Paul and Barnabas, and Paul was not of a disposition to risk taking him on another challenging mission.

Barnabas, however, stood his ground for including John Mark in the new venture. One suspects several factors influenced his unyielding position. For

---

**Day 2
Brothers at Odds**

Read Galatians 2:11-21 about conflict between Peter and Paul.

1. What was the issue of dispute between Paul and Barnabas?
2. How do you think the personalities of the two men figured into their dispute?
3. Who do you think was at fault here? How would you have resolved the problem?
4. How does this glimpse into the human frailty

one, John Mark was his nephew (Col. 4:10). For another, it was simply in Barnabas' nature to be forgiving, affirming, and accepting when dealing with others; after all, he had vouched for Paul when the Jerusalem church was reluctant to accept him into its number (Acts 9:27).

It does not take much imagination to visualize Paul as a man of opposite temperament to Barnabas. For all the latter's patience and forbearance, Paul leaves the impression in Acts and in the epistles of a man whose manner was direct, abrupt, and somewhat impatient. He and Barnabas had probably been good working partners by providing balance to each other's natural tendencies. But there would be no short-term resolution for this clash of wills.

Luke lets us know that these two great men, both of whom he clearly admired, let the issue of John Mark become "such a sharp disagreement that they parted company." What effect did their argument have on the Christians at Antioch? Did John Mark hear what the two men said about him? "We are left to think about the Lord's will in all of this matter. Did He intend for Paul and Barnabas to split up? I hardly think so. His intentional will was that they should remain together. His circumstantial will brought good out of the incident in spite of the failure of both men to agree on what to do with someone who had failed. Amazing! And yet, the Lord used the shattered pieces and used the time Mark had alone with Barnabas and then with Peter to help him grow into the mature man who wrote the first Gospel. The Lord could have accomplished that without the tragic break-up of the Paul-Barnabas team. He could have gotten Mark and Peter together for the apostle to give the young man the firsthand account of Jesus' life and message. But our Lord can use our own mistakes to weave the dark threads of failure into the tapestry to highlight by contrast the

of two great men affect you?

5. How did this conflict resolve itself over the long term? What harm may have come from it in the meanwhile?

bright strands of victory." [Ogilvie, *Acts*, pp. 237-238.] Barnabas and John Mark left Antioch for Cyprus, the home of Barnabas (Acts 4:36).

B. Events in Asia Minor. 15:40-16:10.

The sovereignty of God is not only seen here in turning a sharp dispute into two mission projects rather than a single failed ambition. It is also clear in providing Paul a new working partner with whom to begin his journey. A Jewish brother named Silas had come to Antioch after the Jerusalem conference to help deliver and affirm its actions (15:30ff). When the group returned to Judea, Silas chose to remain behind. The guidance of the Holy Spirit often works like this. An unexplainable urge moved Silas to stay longer at Antioch, and he would have been at a loss to make sense of his own actions. But when Paul needed a new partner for evangelistic work, the apostle immediately chose Silas. The right man for an important situation had been provided by the Lord. As a Roman citizen (cf. 16:37), he would be able to move freely through the empire with his fellow-believer and fellow-citizen Paul.

1. Paul and Silas begin the new effort. 15:40-41.

Paul and Silas began retracing the route of the first missionary journey. The reconciliation among estranged parties would happen later. When Paul was in prison at Rome for the first time and as Luke wrote Acts during that period, John Mark was with them and received Paul's endorsement to a church he wrote from Rome (Col. 4:10).

2. Selection of Timothy as a co-worker. 16:1-4.

At Lystra, where a superstitious citizenry had initially tried to deify Paul only to turn and stone him (Acts 14:8-20), Paul visited the church only to find an unexpected new partner for his work. In the year or so since the apostle had been in the city, a young

---

Day 3
God's Providence

Read Romans 11:11-24 about divine providence in Jew-Gentile relationships.

1. What does the term *providence of God* mean?
2. How does this doctrine affirm the fact of divine sovereignty?
3. From the ashes of the Paul-Barnabas division, what good result(s) came?
4. Do these good outcomes prove it was God's will for the two men to have their dispute? Explain.
5. Recall a situation in your own experience where God's providence overruled some foolish thing you did.

Day 4
The Making of Christian Workers

Read Paul's instructions to Timothy at 1 Timothy 4.

1. When and how did Silas become a working partner with Paul?

disciple named Timothy had grown in faith and ability beyond many of his peers. He had a Jewish mother and grandmother who had taught him well from Scripture (2 Tim. 1:5).

Because his father was Greek, Timothy had never been circumcised. This presented Paul with a practical — though not moral or doctrinal — problem. The conference at Jerusalem had settled the matter about *mandatory* circumcision for those who were coming to Christ from the larger population of the Roman Empire. But what about Paul's anticipation of future work not only among Gentiles but Jews? Would he gloat over winning the argument with the Pharisaic Christians and insist on bringing Timothy into Jewish settings without circumcising him? Such an attitude would have violated the spirit of the conclusion reached at Jerusalem. Pointless offense of others is not in keeping with the nature of love for one's fellows. Therefore Paul "circumcised [Timothy] because of the Jews who lived in that area."

As Paul, Silas, and Timothy left Lystra, his working team was back at full strength. Silas had replaced Barnabas, and Timothy was along as the young John Mark had been originally. One wonders if Paul might not have seen Timothy's presence as his chance to make amends for his perceived failure to bring John Mark along as a young disciple-assistant who could eventually shoulder kingdom duties of leadership as Paul grew older or was prohibited from his ministry.

We know that Timothy became Paul's most trusted co-worker. The apostle would later call him "my true son in the faith" (1 Tim. 1:2a), entrust important tasks to him (1 Cor. 4:17), and say he had "no one else like him" (Phil. 2:20).

3. Luke notes the continued progress of the church. 16:5.

As a result of the work this newly constituted team did in the power of the Holy Spirit, the body of

2. Under what circumstances did Timothy join Paul's team?
3. When was Luke added to the group?
4. In what ways were these recruitments alike? Different?
5. What does this tell you about our efforts to create and recruit Christian workers for various ministries?

Christ experienced both qualitative and quantitative growth. "So, the churches were strengthened in the faith and grew daily in numbers."

4. A vision and a new field of labor. 16:6-10.

Paul was apparently pursuing his original purpose of revisiting all the cities he had visited on his first tour. After making his way through Phrygia and Galatia, however, the Holy Spirit intervened. He and his companions intended to go west into Asia but were "kept by the Holy Spirit from preaching the word in the province of Asia." Then, as they tried instead to head northeast in order to enter Bithynia, "the Spirit of Jesus would not allow them to."

The leadership of the Holy Spirit is a promise of the Word of God to believers. "You, however, are controlled not by the sinful nature but by the Spirit, if the Spirit of God lives in you," writes Paul. "And if anyone does not have the Spirit of Christ, he does not belong to Christ" (Rom. 8:9). Some believe this leadership is always clear and dramatic. Others believe it comes more subtly through life events as one prays for sensitivity to the ways and will of God. The truth is that the Spirit's guidance is not confined to a single means, and his communication of his will is sometimes more obvious than others.

When some unnamed circumstance led Paul to conclude the Spirit had forbidden him to enter either Asia or Bithynia, he did not wring his hands and become passive. He knew he was on a mission God had given. From the border of Mysia, he turned in a westerly direction and made his way to Troas. From there his company could have sailed to Greece.

At this point, barriers and prohibitions of the Spirit became an unmistakable call. At Troas Paul had a night vision of a man "standing and begging him, 'Come over to Macedonia and help us.'" The frustrations of the past several weeks were now finished. Paul knew why he had been moved in the direction of

Day 5
Led by the Spirit

Read Romans 8:1-17 about life under the influence of the Holy Spirit.

1. What frustrations did the Holy Spirit create for Paul and his company?
2. Try to imagine yourself as a member of the group. How might you have interpreted repeated closed doors? Might you have quit?
3. When do you think things came clear for Paul about what had been happening?
4. How do you believe the Spirit of God influences and guides your life?
5. What factors give you the greatest confidence about receiving and interpreting the Spirit's guidance?

a seaport town on the Aegean. He and his group began preparing immediately to make the short voyage by sea to Macedonia where they would preach the gospel with great boldness and effectiveness.

The guidance of the Spirit often works this same way in our lives. There will be times of uncertainty and frustration. Doors will be closed that we expected to open. Then God opens the door of his choice and nudges us through it — with a resulting effectiveness that could have come no other way.

A final thing to note here is the change in pronouns that occurs at Acts 16:10. Up to this point, Luke has been writing of Paul and his comrades in third-person terms. At Troas, however, the apostle met and was befriended by another whom God had placed in his life to share his ministry. Luke joins the band of gospel missionaries and the pronouns shift here to first-person plural. "After Paul had seen the vision, we got ready at once to leave for Macedonia, concluding that God had called us to preach the gospel to them." From this point forward, Luke writes most often as an eyewitness and becomes a trusted companion to Paul to the end of his life (2 Tim. 4:11).

Week Twenty-Three

Acts 16:11–17:15 (XI C in Outline)

Day 1
The Lord Opens Hearts

Read Romans 10:8-15 about the role of teaching in salvation.

1. How do you think the Lord "opened [Lydia's] heart to respond to Paul's message"?
2. In what ways have you seen him open the hearts of people to Christ?
3. How was your heart opened to respond to the gospel?
4. Can a human messenger ever take credit for someone's conversion? Explain.
5. Explain John 16:5-11 in light of the experience of Lydia.

Once Paul and his companions reached the conclusion that "God had called us to preach the gospel to [the Macedonians]," they wasted no time. They were at Troas when the vision calling them to Macedonia came (16:8-10), and Troas was an important seaport. Ships left there often for Macedonia and points west. It was probably easy to arrange passage.

C. The Ministry in Macedonia. 16:11-17:15.

1. The work at Philippi. 16:11-40.

Going northwest from Troas, they sailed to the island of Samothrace, overnighted there, and proceeded into Neapolis on the Macedonian coast. From there they traveled the famous Roman highway called Via Egnatia ten miles to Philippi. Luke reports three wonderful stories of the power of God at work in that important Roman colony.

The first account of gospel activity in Philippi focuses on a wealthy Jewish businesswoman whose travels had brought her to the city. Lydia was "a dealer in purple cloth from the city of Thyatira, who was a worshiper of God." In spite of her wealth, sophistication, and pursuit of spiritual things, she needed the salvation that could come only through the knowledge of Jesus Christ. In telling of her conversion, Luke is consistent with the emphasis in his Gospel on telling the stories of women. An Ancient Near-Eastern culture that did not esteem women highly stood over against the ennobling message of the love of God for all. A woman was the first person in Europe to be a Christian.

Following his custom of going first to Jews and then to Gentiles (cf. Rom. 1:16), Paul sought for a gathering of Jews on his first Sabbath in Philippi. The Jewish population there must have been small, for there was apparently no synagogue in the city. It took ten adult males willing to be responsible for the synagogue before one could be organized, so there may have been practically no Jewish community there. In the absence of a synagogue, devout Jews would designate a "place of prayer" — ideally near a body of water that could accommodate the many ritual washings of their faith.

When Paul and his company found the place of prayer, they found a group of women worshiping there. The women likely deferred to the men who had arrived, and Paul used the opportunity to preach the gospel. That conversion is ultimately the work of the Holy Spirit rather than the evangelist is driven home by Luke's comment: "The Lord opened her heart to respond to Paul's message." Since the gospel is the "sword of the Spirit," the response of faith is not won by human agents who speak the message but by the divine agent who empowers it.

Lydia's wealth is attested by the fact that, following her baptism, she invited Paul, Silas, Luke, and others who may have been with them to stay at her home. It could be their base of operation for sharing the Word of God with even more people at Philippi. As one might guess even from the story of the birth of Jesus at Bethlehem, available and safe inns for travelers were not as common in the first century as today. The Christian evangelists accepted Lydia's generous offer, and the woman evidenced the genuineness of her faith by showing hospitality to her teachers.

It would be typically against his practice for Paul to accept financial support and other practical forms of hospitality from people in whose midst he was planting a church (2 Cor. 11:7-9). He made an

**Day 2
Hospitality**

Read Genesis 18:1-19 about Abraham's hospitality to three strangers.

1. What did Lydia's hospitality to Paul's team mean to the evangelists? To Lydia?
2. Why was hospitality an important first-century ministry?
3. Do you think hospitality is a common virtue among believers today? Explain.

4. Reflect on the following texts: Romans 12:13; Hebrews 13:1-3; 1 Peter 4:9.

5. How do you use your home for the practice of this Christian virtue?

exception here because of what he discerned to be the true faith and sincere generosity of her heart. In allowing her to extend him and his partners this courtesy, he permitted her to share in his work and to offer God glory through her virtuous hospitality.

First-century believers were commanded to "entertain strangers" (Heb. 13:2) because evangelists typically depended on such hospitality in their travels (cf. Matt. 10:9-10). Hospitality is fast becoming a lost art (or, perhaps, lost *virtue*) in our culture. Yet those who open their hearts and homes to Christian brothers and sisters, college students away from home, missionaries or evangelists in their city, and the like experience great blessings in doing so. They will hear Jesus say, "I was a stranger and you invited me in" (Matt. 25:35c). When they ask him when such a thing happened, he will reply, "Whatever you did for one of the least of these brothers of mine, you did for me" (Matt. 25:40).

The "place of prayer" beside the river seems to have become the regular place where Paul would gather with people interested in his message. As he was headed there on a given day, he and his friends were met by a "slave girl who had a spirit by which she predicted the future." Exploited by evil men, she told fortunes and they collected a fee. Day after day, she followed the little group of Christians and shouted, "These men are servants of the Most High God, who are telling you the way to be saved." What a strange witness to the gospel and its heralds, but demons have been known to tell the truth on occasion! (Luke 4:34).

Paul eventually tired of the circus atmosphere the girl's shouting created. From this came a second report of the power of God at Philippi. One day he turned and gave an authoritative command to the evil spirit: "In the name of Jesus Christ I command you to come out of her!" This is not the manner of Hollywood for performing an exorcism.

There was no special preparation or elaborate ceremony. Instead, there was a command "in the name of Jesus Christ." In the very instant Paul gave the order, the spirit left her.

When the evil people who had been exploiting that girl's misfortune for their profit found out what had happened, they realized their hope of future profit was gone. So they seized Paul and Silas, dragged them before a Roman public court, and made this charge: "These men are Jews, and are throwing our city into an uproar by advocating customs unlawful for us Romans to accept or practice." Perhaps stirred by their own anti-Semitism, many in the crowd supported the charges. The result was that careless magistrates took the charges at face value, had Paul and Silas flogged, and put them in jail.

The third story of God's power at work in Philippi took place at the jail that same night. The bloodied evangelists were hardly distraught by the events of the day, for "about midnight Paul and Silas were praying and singing hymns to God." As the apostles had done at Jerusalem earlier, they were "rejoicing because they had been counted worthy of suffering disgrace for the Name" (5:41).

Suddenly there was a great earthquake in the prison area. It was clearly a miracle rather than a natural phenomenon, for it both opened the doors of the prison without collapsing it and loosed the chains of the prisoners. When the jailer was awakened by the noise, he saw the condition of his jail and assumed that all the prisoners committed to his care had escaped. Since his own life was security for them, he drew his sword and was about to commit suicide rather than suffer the disgrace of public execution. He must have been startled to hear one of the prisoners shout, "Don't harm yourself! We are all here!"

The jailer was a pagan and did not have the background of either a Saul of Tarsus or Cornelius to

Day 3
Suffering and Civil Rights

Read Acts 22:22-29 to see Paul claim his citizenship rights under Roman law.

1. When Paul was arrested at Philippi, how was he treated by the city magistrates?

2. What crime did the magistrates commit by their actions? What penalty could have been imposed on them?

3. Why do you think Paul insisted on claiming his civil rights as a Roman the next day? Should he have simply suffered in silence?

4. Is it ever *wrong* for a Christian to use police and courts? Cf. 1 Cor. 6:1ff. Give some modern examples that would illustrate your answer.

5. When is it *right* for Christians to claim protection under law today? Give some examples.

interpret what had just happened. Yet he knew this was the activity of God and asked, "Sirs, what must I do to be saved?" Their answer — appropriate to someone who knew no more than he did at that moment — was fundamental: "Believe in the Lord Jesus, and you will be saved — you and your household." Since one cannot believe in a Christ of whom he knows nothing (Rom. 10:14), Paul and Silas "spoke the word of the Lord to him and to all the others in his house." The jailer and his family were baptized that very night.

The next morning, following up on a report that had surely come to them about the night's unusual activity, the city magistrates sent word for Paul and Silas to be released. Given that message by the jailer, Paul refused to be "run out of town on a rail" after being treated so unjustly the day before. It must have sent a chill down the magistrates' spines when Paul underscored his demand to be publicly cleared of the charges lodged against him by stating that he and Silas were Roman citizens. Noncitizens or slaves could be beaten without a trial, but to treat citizens so could have had the most dire consequences for the town's officials. Frightened now, they came personally and requested that Paul and Silas leave Philippi. Not to be hurried, they did so only after returning to Lydia's house, meeting with the converts who had come to the Lord during their brief ministry, and giving them encouragement.

As the group leaves Philippi for Thessalonica, notice that "we" and "us" are replaced by "they" and "them." Luke apparently stayed behind in Philippi to nurture the young church that had just been planted there.

2. The work at Thessalonica. 17:1-9.

The trip from Philippi to Thessalonica would have been made by continuing to follow the Via Egnatia about a hundred miles southwest. For three successive Sabbath days, Paul went to the synagogue, taught from the Hebrew Bible about the role of the Christ (i.e., Messiah), and presented Jesus of Nazareth as the fulfillment of prophetic anticipation. "Some of the Jews were persuaded and joined Paul and Silas, as did a large number of God-fearing Greeks and not a few prominent women."

From the two epistles Paul wrote to Thessalonica shortly after his departure, it seems clear that he stayed in the city for a time considerably longer than the three Sabbath days mentioned in the text.

Made jealous by the fact that some of the synagogue members had been won to Paul's Christ, certain Jews seized on what he had preached about Jesus as "king" and incited a mob to violence. They approached the house of a certain Jason to search for Paul and Silas. Unable to find them, they dragged Jason and some other believers before the city officials and made this charge: "These men who have caused trouble all over the world have now come here, and Jason has welcomed them into his house. They are all defying Caesar's decrees, saying that there is another king, one called Jesus."

The officials appear to have acted responsibly in the midst of an explosive situation. They required Jason and the others to "post bond" — that they would not disturb the peace and/or see to it that Paul and Silas discontinued their preaching — and released them. The crowd was calmed, and no personal violence came to Jason and the other believers with him.

3. The work at Berea. 17:10-15.

In order to help defuse the situation at Thessalonica, the Christians sent Paul and Silas to Berea after night fell on that stressful day of mob turmoil. Berea was about fifty miles further along the Via Egnatia that Paul and his company had been following since arriving in Europe.

Day 4
Discretion and Valor

Read Acts 9:19b-25 to be reminded of the first time Paul ran from his would-be abusers.

1. Retell the story of Paul's work at Thessalonica in your own words.

2. What does Luke say about *reason*, *explanation*, and *proof* in Paul's preaching? What insights should we get from this?

3. What disrupted Paul's ministry at Thessalonica?

4. How did Jason get "caught in the middle" of this turmoil? What was he forced to do?

5. Explain the maxim: "Discretion is the better part of valor." Do you think it applies to Paul's decision to leave Thessalonica?

Day 5
Noble Character

Read Psalm 1 and notice what is said about people who "delight in the law of the Lord."

1. Why does Luke praise the Bereans for displaying

"more noble character" than the Thessalonians?

2. Does the gospel message require *gullibility* of people? Explain.

3. Will the Bible bear close *intellectual scrutiny* from bright people? Explain.

4. Do you think modern teaching methods provide enough intellectual challenge to people? Explain.

5. How may both Christians and non-believers exhibit "noble character" to each other?

Again going to the synagogue, the Christian evangelists found both Jews and a number of God-fearing Greek men and women who were open to the gospel. Neither gullible nor naïve, they "examined the Scriptures every day to see if what Paul said was true." Because of their reasoned examination of Scripture — perhaps using the scrolls from their synagogue to check Paul's accuracy — Luke credits the Bereans with being "of more noble character than the Thessalonians" who reacted with such groundless violence against the messengers of Christ Jesus.

Even so, their work could not proceed unhindered for long. When the people at Thessalonica who had been so determined to search out and put an end to Paul's ministry heard of the success he was having at Berea, they followed him there and began "agitating the crowds and stirring them up." Since it was Paul who was their target, the young church at Berea "immediately sent Paul to the coast" to save him from harm. Yet Silas and Timothy stayed on at Berea to teach and strengthen the believers. They would rejoin Paul at Athens — the city to which Paul's Berean escort carried him.

Week Twenty-Four

Acts 17:16-34 (XI D 1 in Outline)

When Paul left Berea, he must have been wondering about the will of God for his ministry. He had been called to Macedonia by a vision (16:6ff), but now he was headed for Greece and abandoning what appears to have been his original plan. He had been following the Via Egnatia from Philippi to Thessalonica to Berea, and he seems to have been headed all the way to Rome. Only a few years after these events, he would write the church at Rome to say he had often planned to visit there but had been hindered from doing so (Rom. 1:13; 15:22-23).

Several things had combined to alter his plans. There had been a threatening letter from Emperor Claudius in A.D. 41 saying he would take measures against Jews who were "stirring up a universal plague throughout the world" — a threat followed up by the expulsion of Jews from Rome by Claudius in A.D. 49 because of "disturbances" created in the Jewish community by one "Chrestus" (probably an alternative spelling for the word Christ). In A.D. 44, there had been demonstrations in Palestine in the wake of Herod Agrippa's death. And uproar had followed Paul's personal ministry throughout Macedonia. Biblical events happened in the real-world context of politics, intrigue, and setbacks.

D. The Ministry in Greece. 17:16–18:17.

Thus Paul wound up in Athens under circumstances he did not choose. He had planned to wait for Silas and Timothy to join him before beginning a ministry there, but circumstances again altered his plan. Athens was not a large city in Paul's day — per-

Day 1
Paul and the "Real World"

Read Exodus 1:1-22 and reflect on the fact that historical events had direct impact on biblical events.

1. How does this text remind us of the many alterations that had to be made in Paul's travel and preaching plans?
2. Is it hard for you to remember that biblical events took place on a larger world stage? Explain.
3. What historical events had an impact on Paul's ministry in the decade of the A.D. 40s?
4. How have events such as the Civil Rights Movement, Vietnam, Roe v. Wade, etc. affected the life of the church in recent years?
5. What is the single most significant event on the world stage today that is affecting believers? Explain your answer.

haps only about 10,000 people lived there — but its importance was far out of proportion to its size. Athens was the city of Pericles and Zeno, Epicurus and Socrates, Plato and Aristotle. It was the intellectual center of its time.

Day 2
Athens

Read 1 Corinthians 9:16-27 to get Paul's perspective on adapting method to circumstance.

1. What was the status and reputation of Athens when Paul visited there?
2. What names do you associate with the city's history?
3. What one thing about Athenian culture most vividly captured Paul's attention?
4. How did Paul begin his work at Athens? Why was he not more aggressive?
5. What two "styles of preaching" did he use in Athens? Why not use the same method with people at the synagogue as in the marketplace?

1. The events in Athens. 17:16-34.

Paul was undoubtedly exhausted in body, mind, and spirit when he arrived at Athens. Thus, like any first-time visitor to a great city, he walked the streets as a tourist and sightseer. He was an educated and cultured man who had read the poetry of Athenian writers. He knew some of the city's history. So he walked the streets of Athens and saw its temples, statuary, and Acropolis. Yet his appreciation for certain aspects of the city's history, art, and culture could not get him past the fact that most of it reflected and sought to perpetuate pagan idolatry. The Athenian culture was spiritually corrupt and therefore repulsive to Paul.

He became so distressed over the situation that he could no longer wait for Silas and Timothy. So he sought out the Jewish synagogue where he "reasoned" with Jews and God-fearers in attendance. Just as he had done at Thessalonica (17:2-3), he reasoned, explained, and proved from the Law of Moses and the Prophets that Jesus was the Messiah. Neither in Athens nor in any other place did Paul ever ask anyone to make a mindless decision for Christ. God seeks the heart via the mind, and those who have a background of acquaintance with Scripture — as the synagogue audience certainly did — are best taught by the reasoned interpretation of the written Word of God.

a. Paul's daily argumentation with the people. 17:16-21.

But Paul also engaged a non-Jewish segment of the population in discussions about Jesus. He preached both in the synagogue and "in the marketplace [Gk.

agora] day by day with those who happened to be there." The agora was the hub of Athenian life. It was the equivalent of today's suburban shopping mall or downtown commercial district. It was the marketplace and public forum where everyone eventually came. It lay west of the Acropolis and had public buildings, offices, temples, and restaurants.

In the agora, Paul encountered people from a wide variety of religious and philosophical backgrounds. In particular, Luke mentions his dialogue with Epicurean and Stoic philosophers.

Epicurus (342-270 B.C.) had founded a school of thought that argued for pleasure as the chief goal of life. In fairness, he did not define pleasure as we might today — parties and indulgence. Although he would not have denied the existence of the traditional state gods of Athens, he argued very much as a deist would that they take no interest in human affairs. Thus he was a materialist who said one should seek tranquility by avoiding pain, unreasonable desires, and anxiety about death. The notion of the resurrection of the body following death would have been regarded as foolishness by the Epicureans. "Let us eat and drink, for tomorrow we die" could have been the favorite bumper sticker for them.

Zeno (340-265 B.C.) had founded the Stoic school. He and his followers were pantheists. In his view, a "world-soul" — probably to be identified with the principle of reason that Zeno believed to pervade and guide all things — was the divine essence in our cosmos. Humans should seek simply to live by their own reason and in simple harmony with nature, said Zeno, because uncontrollable fate governs everyone's destiny. Zeno committed suicide, and many of his followers advocated the same practice as a "dignified" death.

If the Epicureans and Stoics sound familiar, you should not be surprised. "The prevailing philosophies of the West's post-Christian era — secular human-ism's scientific empiricism and the New Age panthe-istic type of postmodernism — are remarkably similar to the Epicureanism and Stoicism Paul encountered at Athens. Paul's speech becomes a model for how to witness to the educated post-Christian mind, even as it spoke to Theophilus and his fellow seekers with their first-century pre-Christian minds." [Larkin, *Acts*, p. 251.]

Some of the philosophers Paul engaged in conver-sation dubbed him a "babbler." They saw scraps of truth in what he said, but they could not see the coherence of some larger picture Paul might have been trying to paint for them. These people likely lis-tened out of nothing more than curiosity. Others said, "He seems to be advocating foreign gods." That is, they were a bit more interested than the ones who had labeled Paul a mere "babbler," for they saw in him the opportunity to learn about a new god(s) who might be incorporated into their pantheon.

In particular, it seems to have been Paul's em-phasis on the resurrection that caught everyone's ear. It was certainly a frontal assault on the material-ism and fatalism of the Athenian philosophers. Some scholars think that verse 18 points to a mis-taken idea on the part of some that Paul was offer-ing two gods — Anastasis (i.e., the Greek term for resurrection) and Jesus.

Paul was carried to the Areopagus [A-rē-ô´-pə-gəs] to explain his views. The Areopagus was a legislative body for Athens and could credential (i.e., license) a traveling teacher. Paul was going to have to take his doctoral examinations to see whether he would be given the right to teach any longer in Athens' open-air schools! As with doctoral examinations today, interested parties could sit in. And the penchant of people in Athens for talking about and listening to the latest ideas drew Paul a crowd.

Day 3
Babbling

Read 1 Corinthians 1:18-31 about the reaction to the gospel Paul received from Greek intellectuals.

1. Why did some of Paul's Greek listeners call him a babbler"?

2. How does this illustrate what Paul said in 1 Corinthians 1:18ff?

3. Have you ever had anyone indicate he thought the biblical message was trite and shallow? Do you know what created the atti-tude in that person?

4. How do you think the average person has been influenced to think of the gospel in our time?

5. What is the church's best strategy for pre-senting the gospel to this generation? Can you think of any radical change in method we ought to consider?

b. His sermon before the Areopagus. 17:22-34.

Paul's speech before the Areopagus was very different from his sermons in the Jewish synagogue. In the synagogue, he opened Scripture and explained it. Before the Areopagus, quoting Jewish sacred literature would have no positive effect at all — and would likely turn many against his case in a prejudicial way. Without citing Scripture, then, Paul made a case for the existence of a personal God who had showed himself in history as Jesus of Nazareth and through whom alone humankind could be saved. Instead of the Bible, he quoted Greek poets. Doing all he could to identify with his audience without compromising one truth of the gospel, Paul presented his message about Jesus and salvation.

We call this sort of presentation "natural theology." It argues to the existence and nature of God from science and other disciplines of human inquiry. It tells of God's workings among humanity by exploring such fields as history, archaeology, or psychology. And it structures its array of evidence logically and persuasively for the sake of making the strongest possible impression on one's audience (Rom. 1:18ff; cf. 14:14-18). Natural theology stands over against "revealed theology" — the kind of preaching Paul had done at the synagogue by expounding Scripture. Of course, the two ultimately are companions in preaching the gospel to anyone. Even if one begins with natural theology because of a hearer's ignorance of or prejudice against the Bible, the ability to convince him of God's work in Christ leads ultimately to Scripture as divine revelation.

Paul began his sermon by showing respect for his audience. He affirmed their inclination to religious pursuits (i.e., "I see that in every way you are very *religious*" — not the King James Version's insulting "superstitious") and commented on an altar he had observed in the city that was inscribed "To an Unknown God."

Day 4
Natural Theology

Read Romans 1:18-32 for a section of natural theology in the Bible.

1. What is natural theology? Revealed theology?

2. Are natural theology and revealed theology antagonistic to each other? Explain.

3. Why did Paul use natural theology in his Areopagus address?

4. What are some settings today that call for natural theology?

5. How does natural theology inevitably require the introduction of Scripture?

Paul began from this point of identification with his audience to offer them information not about a "new" god but the eternal God of the cosmos who was yet "unknown" to the Athenians.

"Speaking of God in his relation to the world and to men, Paul declares God to be the Creator and the moral Governor of all truths which strike at the very heart of materialism, of pantheism, of polytheism, of atheism, of fetishism, and of idolatry. As to man, Paul proceeds to teach that he is the offspring of God, of one blood, accountable to God and under his providential care; this fact he establishes by a quotation from one of the Greek poets, either Aratas [A´-rə-təs], or Cleanthes [Klē-ăn´-thēz]. As to sin, Paul treats it as an offense against a personal Judge who now demands repentance in view of a new revelation which he has made for the guidance of man. As to the way of salvation, it is through Christ who is the appointed Judge whose real nature is proved by the fact of his resurrection from the dead." [Erdman, *Acts*, pp. 140-141.]

The crescendo of the sermon was reached when Paul came back to the issue that had set up the Areopagus hearing — the resurrection of the dead. In particular, he explained that the redemptive work of God in history had come to fulfillment in Jesus. With so clear a revelation of his person and work, there could no longer be an excuse for idolatry. God is never again to be thought of or represented by stone, gold, or superstitious myth. God has been seen in Jesus of Nazareth! Therefore the ignorance of men that the true God once "overlooked" (i.e., not punishing its practitioners as severely as they deserved, cf. Rom. 3:25-26) is now altogether inexcusable. To reject Jesus is to bring oneself under his judgment. And heaven's authentication of Jesus, the plan of salvation that focuses on his death and resurrection, and Paul's message in all its particulars is the single event of Jesus' resurrection from the dead (1 Cor. 15:12ff).

Because of the mixed reaction to this sermon, some have called Paul's effort at evangelism in Athens a failure and cite 1 Corinthians 2:1-5 as proof that the apostle saw it that way himself. But Paul often received a "mixed reaction" when he preached. No, he did not win over the full council of examiners that day. But these positive results did come from the experience: "A few men became followers of Paul and believed. Among them was Dionysius, a member of the Areopagus, also a woman named Damaris, and a number of others."

Paul's presentation was guided by the Holy Spirit and was used by the Spirit to bring people to faith whose hearts were open to the truth. We ought not shy away from the method he used that day. Indeed, with our world increasingly ill-versed or altogether ignorant of the Bible, we must learn to preach using natural theology, writers from our own time, and current events. These methods can be used to tell the story of Christ faithfully. Indeed, these methods will work better in some settings than verse-by-verse explication of biblical texts. Christians of our time must "do battle with contemporary non-Christian philosophies and ideologies and philosophies in a way which resonates with thoughtful, modern men and women, and so at least gain a hearing for the gospel by the reasonableness of its presentation." [John W. Stott, *The Spirit, the Church and the World: The Message of Acts* (Downers Grove, IL: InterVarsity, 1990), p. 281.]

Day 5
Reaching a Generation

Read 2 Timothy 3:1-9 for a prediction of human lifestyle during the Christian Era.

1. How effective are believers today in communicating the gospel to lost people?

2. Do you know of any outdated techniques of sharing Christ that are being preserved long past their time of usefulness? If so, identify some.

3. What are the most positive and effective methods you know that are being used to preach Christ today?

4. What are the characteristics of our time that are most important to understand in order to reach people with the gospel message?

5. Is your church attempting to communicate with this generation in ways appropriate to its mindset and needs? Explain.

Week Twenty-Five

Acts 18:1-22 (XI D 2 to XI E in Outline)

**Day 1
Discouragement**

*Read Psalms 42 & 43 and
sense another believer's discouragement.*

1. How do we know Paul
   was discouraged when
   he arrived at Corinth?
2. To what do you
   attribute his state of
   mind?
3. What things unsettle
   and discourage you?
4. What elements of your
   spiritual life contribute
   most to your ability to
   overcome discourage-
   ment?
5. Pray for someone you
   know to be struggling
   with discouragement
   and/or depression.

2. The events at Corinth. 18:1-17.

Paul's ministry at Corinth is one of the most significant in his career. For one thing, he spent more
time there than at most other places in his ministries — eighteen months. His work there also
reveals the genuineness of his humanity as his emotions run the gamut from depression to genuine
joy. A church was founded to which he would later
write at least three epistles, two of which are preserved for us in the canonical documents of the
New Testament. Finally, his time in Corinth can be
dated with precision and gives modern students a
fixed point for constructing a chronology for his life
and the events chronicled in Acts.

Paul did not leave Athens as he had been forced
to leave Philippi, Thessalonica, or Berea. There was
no rioting or threat to his life at Athens. He simply
decided it was time to move on or was prompted to
do so by the Holy Spirit.

Nevertheless, he would later confess to coming to
Corinth in a troubled state of mind. He wrote the
Corinthian church: "I came to you in weakness and
fear, and with much trembling" (1 Cor. 2:3). To
what shall we attribute those feelings? He was surely
discouraged by loneliness, for Luke, Silas, and
Timothy were on missions of their own. He was worried about the young Christians he had left in dire
circumstances at Philippi, Thessalonica, and Berea.
He was probably still suffering the physical effects of
the beating he had taken at Philippi. And he was out
of funds. The apostles are not simply figures in
stained-glass windows. They were real men who were

affected by their circumstances. They were as human in their life situations as we are in ours.

Corinth was situated on a narrow strip of land connecting Northern Greece with the Peloponnesus. It was the capital city of Achaia and had a population somewhere between a quarter- and half-million souls when Paul visited there. Because of its strategic position, it controlled north-south commerce via caravan. It even had command of east-west commerce between the Near East and Rome because of the danger of harsh seas around the Peloponnesus. It was safer to land a ship at one of Corinth's two ports — Cenchrea on the east and Lechaeum on the west — and transport cargo overland than to run the risk of navigating treacherous waters. As a business and commercial center, very few cities were its equal. It was a very busy and very wealthy city.

Corinth's enormous wealth brought liabilities as well as benefits. Entertaining so many sailors and other travelers, it had no shortage of entrepreneurs who catered to them. Gambling, prostitution, alcohol and other drugs — all the things we associate with a "wild city" in our own time were available there. Corinth was such an immoral city that the Greeks even coined a word from the city's name. *Korinthiazesthai* meant "to behave as a Corinthian" and was used as an insult to anyone living a depraved and decadent existence.

What religion there was at Corinth centered on the polytheistic gods of Greco-Roman mythology. The worship of Aphrodite, the goddess of love, had a large following. Instead of moderating the moral climate of the city, however, it only made it worse. The priests and priestesses of Aphrodite were cult prostitutes, and the worship center was little more than a brothel.

Day 2
Challenging
Environments

Read 1 Corinthians 6:9-20 to get an impression of life in Corinth.

1. What was the moral and spiritual climate of Corinth in Paul's day?
2. What situations in the city helped create that climate?
3. What parallels do you see in your own city to Corinth? To situations that created Corinth's problems?
4. If you were a missionary looking for a promising location for work, do you think you would have chosen Corinth? Explain.
5. Do you truly believe the gospel is the best solution to the world's ills? If so, explain how that belief translates into practical action in your life.

Day 3
Friendship

Read 1 Samuel 20:28-42 about the great friendship between David and Jonathan.

1. What circumstances led to Aquila and Priscilla being at Corinth when Paul arrived there?

2. What do you think their state of mind was at the time? How might it have paralleled Paul's?

3. What things did Paul have in common with this couple?

4. How did they meet each other's needs?

5. Recall an important friendship that God provided at a critical time in your life.

a. His arrival and association with Aquila and Priscilla. 18:1-4.

Paul arrived at Corinth from Athens in early A.D. 50. Upon his arrival, lonely and in need of money, God met his needs through new friends in Christ. Aquila and Priscilla were also new at Corinth and were there because "Claudius had ordered all the Jews to leave Rome." Suetonius, a Roman historian, tells of Emperor Claudius' edict with these words: "As the Jews were indulging in constant riots at the instigation of Chrestus, he banished them from Rome" [*Life of Claudius* 25. 4.]. This banishment took place in the year A.D. 49 and was likely due to debates and disturbances in the Jewish community similar to those Paul had just experienced himself. Christian evangelists would offer Jesus of Nazareth as the fulfillment of the messianic hope, and a synagogue or neighborhood would be thrown into turmoil. Because of the delicate political situation in the capital city, Claudius put a stop to it by forcing every Jew in the city to leave. Aquila and Priscilla were caught up in the sweep.

In the Lord's providence, however, they were to become friends, business partners, and kingdom workers with Paul. Since all three were tentmakers (Gk. *skenopoios* = tentmaker, canvas worker, leather worker), they shared work and living quarters. In a city with two seaports, they would always be able to find work. The physical labor with new Christian friends would have been therapeutic for Paul in his demoralized state of mind.

b. An eighteen-month period of teaching the gospel. 18:5-11

Attending the synagogue every Sabbath, Paul "reasoned" with those who assembled about the meaning of the Law, Prophets, and Psalms. He held forth Jesus to both the Jews and God-fearing Greeks who were present. At this point, his ministry was apparently limited to those Sabbath discussions.

Since he was expecting Silas and Timothy soon, it would make sense for him to wait for them before starting something more aggressive.

The arrival of his two fellow-evangelists signaled a new enthusiasm for Paul. Healed, rested, and refreshed from his time with Aquila and Priscilla, he was further encouraged to get a good report about the young church at Thessalonica (cf. 1 Thess. 3:6) and a gift of financial support from the Christians at Philippi (cf. 2 Cor. 11:9; Phil. 4:14-15). Now he "devoted himself exclusively to preaching, testifying to the Jews that Jesus was the Christ."

As Paul became more aggressive, his Jewish audience became more defensive and hostile. It was most assuredly the fact that he was having success in converting people to Jesus that upset them. When they eventually "became abusive" — apparently with blasphemous statements about Jesus rather than with physical assaults on Paul — the apostle solemnly "shook out his clothes in protest" and made the Gentiles the primary focus of his ministry in the city.

Paul moved his ministry center from the synagogue to the home of Titius Justus. This Roman "worshiper of God" (i.e., Gentile who revered Yahweh, received instruction at the synagogue, but did not become a proselyte to Judaism) received the apostle and thus allowed his house to be used as a meeting site for believers. Ramsay and others have made a plausible case for identifying Titius Justus with the Gaius whom Paul baptized personally (1 Cor. 1:14) of whom Romans 16:23 says, "whose hospitality I and the whole church here (i.e., Corinth) enjoy."

Another early convert was "Crispus, the synagogue ruler, and his entire household." He is named in the short list Paul later gave of the few at Corinth he had baptized with his own hands. Soon the evangelistic work bore even more fruit, as "many of the Corinthians who heard him believed and were baptized." The man who had come to Corinth in discouragement was now celebrating the powerful workings of God in that city. The final thing that affirmed his ministry and swept away his fears would have been another night vision in which the Lord himself spoke to Paul. "Do not be afraid," he said. "Keep on speaking, do not be silent. For I am with you, and no one is going to attack and harm you, because I have many people in this city." A disheartened beginning turned into a fruitful eighteen-month ministry.

Day 4
Roman Justice

Read Romans 13:1-7 about a Christian's duty to government.

1. What historical facts do we know about Gallio?

2. What circumstances brought Paul before Gallio?

3. What insights and points of law did Gallio apply to Paul's case?

4. Since Luke wrote Acts while Paul was awaiting trial at Rome, why would he have thought this case important to include in the narrative?

5. Pray for Christians who live under governments that either do not protect their rights or aggressively persecute them.

c. Paul brought before Gallio. 18:12-17.

Paul's encounter with Gallio toward the end of his time at Corinth is most interesting. Gallio was the brother of the famous Roman philosopher Seneca and was known himself as a man of wisdom and integrity. The way Luke presents his handling of a situation with the apostle certainly confirms that positive judgment of the man.

Jewish opposition to Paul eventually coalesced into a "united attack" whose plan was to bring him into court, charge him with heresy within the Jewish system, and have him expelled from the city. The province of Achaia was governed by proconsuls, and Gallio had been appointed to that post in July of A.D. 51 and held it for a year. When the charge had been made and as Paul was about to offer his defense, Gallio stopped him and summarily dismissed the case. He ruled that no crime under Roman law had been alleged and that he therefore had no jurisdiction in the matter. It was strictly a matter of "questions about words and names and your own [Jewish] law," and he would not intervene.

After Gallio had all parties involved "ejected from the court," some of the Jews who had attempted to bring the charge must have lingered and grumbled about his ruling. Several of the Greeks who were there appear to have gotten into an insult-swapping altercation that soon escalated into a free-for-all, with a man named Sosthenes getting the worst end of things. Either the co-ruler of the synagogue with Crispus (cf. v. 8) or his replacement, he was the current ruler of the synagogue that the Greek mob held responsible for the frivolous case brought to court. As the mob beat him up, Gallio "showed no concern whatever."

E. The Return to Antioch of Syria. 18:18-22.

After what happened in court, Paul felt no urgency to leave Corinth. So he stayed on "for some time" past that episode. Eventually, however, it was time to move on and he — accompanied not only by his former partners but also now by new helpers Priscilla and Aquila — decided to go back to Antioch of Syria to report on the three years or so of work since beginning his second preaching tour under that church's sponsorship. "The time in Corinth was one of the most strategic in the Apostle's ministry. He preached, taught, wrote the Thessalonian epistles, and was reconfirmed in his call and relationship with the Lord. The time of discouragement was over. The freedom and flexibility of the Spirit returned." [Ogilvie, *Acts*, p. 264.]

Before sailing from that port city, Paul "had his hair cut off at Cenchrea because of a vow he had taken." This indicates that he had previously taken a Nazirite vow (cf. Num. 6), perhaps at the start of his work at Corinth or maybe even as early as the original vision of a man calling him over to Macedonia. The vow would have signaled an earnest plea for the Lord's blessings on him and his work. Now, with the establishment of several new churches behind him and the memory of Corinth still fresh, he signaled the ending of that particular vow by cutting his hair.

His return to Antioch was made by a circuitous route. He arrived in Syria via Ephesus, Caesarea, and

**Day 5
Culture and Faith**

Read Numbers 6 to learn about the Nazirite vow.

1. What was the fundamental purpose of a Nazirite vow?
2. Why did Paul make such a vow in the setting of Acts 18?
3. Some commentators challenge Paul's deed here as inappropriate and perhaps wrong. Why?
4. What is your opinion of his action?
5. When do *culture* and *faith* become irreconcilable?

probably Jerusalem. At Ephesus, he left Priscilla and Aquila to continue a work he could only begin. He left with the promise, "I will come back if it is God's will." From there he sailed to Caesarea. Then, when Luke tells us that Paul *"went up and greeted the church* and then went down to Antioch," the reference is likely to the Jerusalem church. In order to formally end his vow, he would have wanted to present his hair as a burnt offering and offer additional sacrifices at the temple (cf. 21:26) and perhaps celebrate the spring festival of Passover in the Holy City.

With his second missionary tour now complete, he arrived at Antioch of Syria to report what God had done.

Week Twenty-Six

Acts 18:23–19:41 (XII A to XII B in Outline)

XII. The Third Missionary Tour. 18:23–21:16.

Paul's third missionary journey would be the longest — in both time and miles — of the three. It covered the better part of five years (i.e., A.D. 52-57) and involved an extended stay at Ephesus that was apparently punctuated by several quick trips to neighboring places where the gospel could be preached in virgin territory. Paul even made a rushed and painful trip to Corinth to deal with church problems there and wrote two epistles to the Corinthians from Ephesus.

In reporting this third preaching tour, Luke focuses almost exclusively on Paul. We cannot be certain about the participation of Silas, although most assume he was still a co-worker with Paul. Although Titus is not mentioned in the Acts narrative on this tour either, we know he was a participant from references to him in the Pauline epistles (e.g., 2 Cor. 2:13; 7:6,13-14; Gal. 2:1-3; Titus 1:4).

A. Strengthening the Disciples of Galatia and Phrygia. 18:23.

Paul had visited Ephesus briefly on his second tour, received a gracious reception from the Jewish community, and left with the promise, "I will come back if it is God's will" (18:19-21). Intent on honoring his commitment, Paul left Syrian Antioch with Ephesus — 1500 miles to the west — as his goal. He would spend three years there (20:31), the longest

Day 1
Apollos

Read 1 Corinthians 15:1-11 for a summary of the gospel message.

1. What background information does Luke give about Apollos?
2. What message was Apollos teaching the Jews at Ephesus?
3. Was Apollos's message *false*? Was it *bad*? What was the problem with it?
4. What additional information did Apollos need to make his teaching complete?
5. What is the "distinctive" element this new information added to his preaching?

ministry at one place in Paul's career as a Christian evangelist.

As he traveled toward Ephesus, he traversed "the region of Galatia and Phrygia, strengthening all the disciples." These territories would have included such cities as Pisidian Antioch, Iconium, Lystra, and Derbe.

B. An Extended Ministry at Ephesus. 18:24–19:41.

The report of Paul's work at Ephesus is surprisingly brief, especially when compared to the details of much briefer works at a city like Philippi. Some of the surprise is mitigated, however, by the fact that the work at Philippi is among the "we-sections" (i.e., Luke was present as an eyewitness) and the Ephesian ministry is not.

1. Apollos preaches in Ephesus. 18:24-28.

In order to prepare his readers for Paul's arrival at Ephesus, Luke tells of an interesting episode involving Priscilla and Aquila. Paul had left them at Ephesus after his earlier brief visit there (18:19). They met a man named Apollos.

Apollos was a Jew from Alexandria, Egypt, "a learned man, with a thorough knowledge of the Scriptures." Not only was he well-educated, he was also a powerful speaker. But his acquaintance with the story of Jesus was partial, for "he knew only the baptism of John." Communication was not as efficient in the ancient world as it is today. Therefore, although John had been dead for twenty-five years by now, he knew only the "preliminary gospel" that John had preached. He had accepted John's identification of Jesus of Nazareth as the Messiah, but he did not know about Jesus' death, burial, and resurrection or about the coming of the Holy Spirit on the first Pentecost following his resurrection.

The message Apollos was preaching would have gone something like this: Repent, look for the king-

Day 2
A Couple's Response

Read Romans 3:9-31 for another summary of the central message of the gospel.

dom of God, embrace a lifestyle modeled after Jesus' teaching and personal example, and pursue social justice for your neighbors. It was not a bad message, but it was an incomplete message. It did not affirm the necessity of a new birth by the power of the Holy Spirit or explain the basis of justification by means of the cross of Jesus. With all due respect to Apollos, he was preaching the same thing that many sincere men and women in mainline churches teach today. The call for repentance, responsible lifestyles, and social justice is legitimate but incomplete when the story of Christ's atoning death is not preached. If people could be saved by piety, good deeds, and love for their neighbors, there would have been no need for people such as Cornelius or Apollos to hear the gospel.

When the couple Paul had left at Ephesus heard Apollos preach in the synagogue, they had the good sense not to challenge him publicly, embarrass him, or make him defensive. "When Priscilla and Aquila heard him, they invited him to their home and explained to him the way of God more adequately." Their gentle manner and Apollos's teachable spirit achieved an end that glorified God. Apollos "updated" his understanding with fuller knowledge and changed his message accordingly.

With a complete gospel message to preach, Apollos decided to go to Achaia. The Christians at Ephesus had no hesitation about encouraging him to carry through with his intention and even "wrote to the disciples there to welcome him." When he arrived at Corinth, he was a "great help" to the church Paul planted there previously. With his education, knowledge of Scripture, and skill as a public speaker, he engaged Jewish teachers in public discussion. He both "refuted" their arguments and showed himself skilled at "proving from the Scriptures that Jesus was the Christ."

1. What personal background do we have about Priscilla and Aquila? Cf. Acts 18:1-3.
2. How did they meet and hear Apollos?
3. What wise and restrained response did they make to his teaching?
4. What insights should we gain from their approach?
5. Summarize the outcome of their private study with Apollos.

Day 3
A Partial Gospel

Read Philippians 2:1-11 for one more summary of the gospel's core content.

1. What missing elements made Apollos preaching incomplete?
2. Explain the statement from your study notes that many in mainline churches teach a partial gospel today. Do you agree or disagree?

3. If you agree, how do you think that situation came about?

4. What hope do you see for the situation changing? How do you suggest trying to change it?

5. What is the best precaution against our falling prey to accepting an incomplete gospel?

The first four chapters of First Corinthians demonstrate that the church at Corinth held Apollos in high esteem. They also indicate that Paul regarded him as a capable and trustworthy co-worker in the gospel. For example, Paul wrote: "What, after all, is Apollos? And what is Paul? Only servants, through whom you came to believe — as the Lord has assigned to each his task. I planted the seed, Apollos watered it, but God made it grow" (1 Cor. 3:5-6).

2. Paul teaches and wins to Christ twelve men. 19:1-7.

When Paul got to Ephesus, he met a dozen men who presented themselves as "disciples" (i.e., the equivalent term to "Christians" throughout Acts, cf. 11:26). As they discussed their respective experiences of Christ, however, Paul discerned a serious problem. These men did not have a theology that included the Holy Spirit. Since Christian baptism is administered "in the name of Jesus Christ" and is accompanied by a promise of the "gift of the Holy Spirit," Paul knew something was wrong.

Further discussion led to the fact that they had received "John's baptism." As Priscilla and Aquila had done earlier with Apollos — the man who had likely taught these men what they knew of Jesus — Paul taught them the complete story of the gospel. Again, perhaps influenced by Apollos in this regard as well, teachable hearts were eager to know the full truth about Christ and were baptized.

**Day 4
Baptism and
Rebaptism**

Read an important text about baptism at Romans 6:1-15.

1. What is the central meaning of baptism? Why does it naturally follow one's acceptance of the gospel message?

John's baptism was *preparatory* and *partial* by virtue of the fact that it pointed forward to someone yet to come. People such as Peter and the early apostles who received that baptism transferred their allegiance from John to Jesus after Pentecost and were "charter members of the church" without a second baptism. Apollos, for example, appears not to have received baptism after his study with Christian teachers. Yet Paul did baptize the twelve "into the name of the Lord Jesus." The difference in the two cases lies in the fact that in a post-Pentecost world, John's baptism was no longer appropriate or effective. "[The baptism of the twelve men at Ephesus] is no 'rebaptism,' for after the triumph of Easter and the provision of full salvation blessings at Pentecost, a preparatory baptism of repentance is more than incomplete — it is obsolete (Luke 16:16; Eph. 4:5)." [Larkin, *Acts*, pp. 273-274.] Following their baptism, Paul laid hands on the twelve men to impart supernatural power of the Spirit to them. They spoke in tongues and prophesied.

3. Paul's work in the synagogue and the hall of Tyrannus. 19:8-10.

True to his pattern of going first to the Jews, Paul taught in the synagogue at Ephesus for three months. Then opposition to his work there became so intense that some not only "refused to believe" but also "publicly maligned the Way." This sort of public — if not formal — opposition from the synagogue leaders was Paul's signal to find another site to use for conducting meetings. He led the disciples he had converted to the lecture hall of Tyrannus [Tī-răn´-əs] and spent the next two years leading daily "discussions" (i.e., reasoning, give-and-take exchanges) of the Word of God there. Whether Tyrannus was a teacher whose name was attached to the building or the landlord who rented it to the Christians is unclear.

The significant thing about that two-year period is that Paul's ministry was so extensive — both personally and through his pupils — "that all the Jews and Greeks who lived in the province of Asia heard the word of the Lord." The seven churches of Revelation 2 and 3 were likely founded during this period.

4. Extraordinary miracles by the hands of Paul. 19:11-20.

Part of Paul's success at Ephesus surely traces to the "extraordinary miracles" God worked through

2. What was defective about the baptism of the twelve men Paul met at Ephesus?

3. Imagine yourself in Paul's situation with those men. How would you approach their instruction?

4. Were the men *baptized* or *rebaptized* by Paul? Explain.

5. When should someone consider being baptized for a second time today? Would you call such cases *baptisms* or *rebaptisms*?

him in that city. So impressive were these mighty acts that even Jewish exorcists would invoke the name of Jesus in their incantations and ceremonies. Luke's sense of humor is evident in his telling of an episode in which seven men were trying to use Jesus' name as a "magic word" and suffered a terrible (and semi-comical!) fate. A particular evil spirit responded to their improper and illegitimate use of Jesus' name by pouncing on them, beating them up, and chasing them "naked and bleeding" from the house where they had been.

All these events taken together caused both Jews and Greeks in Ephesus to be "seized with fear" (i.e., reverence) and to hold the name of Jesus "in high honor." Some who had already become believers now came forward to confess that they had secretly continued to hold to certain superstitions and to dabble still in sorcery. In a dramatic public display, they brought the scrolls that contained the formulas, incantations, and rites of those evil practices and burned them. Someone calculated that the combined worth of all these parchments "came to fifty thousand drachmas" — a huge sum of money for that day.

5. Paul's intentions for the future. 19:21-22.

The success of an extended ministry at Ephesus led the visionary apostle-evangelist to raise his vision toward Rome. Even so, he felt an obligation to the churches he had founded earlier. So, even before leaving Ephesus himself, he sent Timothy and Erastus back to encourage the churches in Macedonia. He intended to follow them, visit Jerusalem again, and then continue to Rome.

Day 5
Touchy Pocketbooks

Read 1 Timothy 6:3-10 about greed and its relationship to false doctrines about Jesus.

6. Demetrius and the riot at Ephesus. 19:23-41.

Much of the Ephesian economy was built around idolatry. There was a strong Artemis (Latin, Diana) cult in the city. Depicted as a grotesque multi-breasted female deity, Artemis was a fertility goddess. A temple dedicated to her was one of the ancient world's Seven Wonders. Because of this grand temple, Ephesus was a center for tourism, souvenirs, and banking — for ancient temples were frequently used as depositories (i.e., banks) where large sums of money were entrusted to the safekeeping of a deity and its priests.

With so many people at Ephesus being converted to Christ, there was a corresponding decline in the practice of magical arts and idolatry. The decreased number of devotees became particularly worrisome when it touched the pocketbooks of the city's craftsmen. Demetrius, himself a silversmith who made items for veneration, stirred up "workmen in related trades" and created a riot. Combining patriotism, religion, and economics, he made an impassioned outcry against Paul and his work. "Great is Artemis of the Ephesians!" they shouted. Luke, again showing his sense of humor, pictures the confusion of the mob. He writes: "Some were shouting one thing, some another. Most of the people did not even know why they were there."

Paul was willing to try to address the angry crowd, but "the disciples would not let him." Even some friendly provincial officials begged Paul to stay out of the amphitheater where the crowd had gathered. A city clerk eventually quieted the mob enough to address it. He made the common-sense argument that there were no legitimate legal charges to bring against Paul and the Christians and that a riot could cause Rome to come down hard on the city — thus doing even greater harm to its prestige and economy than some of them thought Paul had done. His level-headed advice defused the crowd's potential for violence, and he sent the people home.

1. Demetrius's concern was not really with *theology* but *economics*. Explain.
2. What threat did Demetrius bring to Paul's ministry at Ephesus?
3. How did a level head and common sense bring an end to the riot Demetrius started?
4. Do you think economic issues ever drive religion in our time? Can you cite an example?
5. Compare the spiritual motives of Paul and Demetrius. How did Paul keep himself free of allowing money to become a central issue in his ministry?

Week Twenty-Seven

Acts 20:1-38 (XII C to XII E in Outline)

Day 1
Leaving Friends

Read John 15:1-17 and pay attention to Jesus' statement about friends.

1. What is the saddest farewell you can remember?

2. Can you transfer those feelings to Paul's situation? Describe the situation you visualize.

3. What had caused such a close bond to form between Paul and the Ephesian church?

4. What value do you attach to personal friendships with Christians? How do they bless your life?

5. How do you invest yourself in forming Christian friendships?

A chronology of Paul's missionary tours has been scattered through these study notes as his ministry proceeded. In brief summary, the first tour (13:1–14:28) took place A.D. 46–47, followed by the conference at Jerusalem (15:1-35) in 48. The second journey (15:36–18:21) began immediately after the conference in 48 and continued into late 51 or early 52. The third tour (18:22–21:16) covered the longest period of time and the greatest geographical area; it began in 52 and ended with his arrest at Jerusalem in 57, with approximately 1,500 miles of travel involved.

C. A Visit to Macedonia and Greece. 20:1-6a.

An uproar created by Demetrius and other silversmiths at Ephesus put an end to Paul's three-year ministry at Ephesus. Yet he did not leave that great city in haste and panic. After the situation had quieted down, he "sent for the disciples and, after encouraging them, said good-by and set out for Macedonia."

This must have been an emotionally charged assembly. The Apostle to the Gentiles had been the central figure in the life of the Ephesian church for three years and was now leaving it. The believers knew that his decision was justified in light of the tension in the city, but it must have created fears among them about the future. And Paul's deep affection for these people surely made it painful for him to leave. His close relationship with this body of believers will become apparent at 20:17 where, with several months of travel and work already complete after leaving Ephesus and pressed with a tight schedule for reaching

Jerusalem by Pentecost, he sends a runner from Miletus to Ephesus. While the ship on which he was traveling was tied up at Miletus, he summoned them to meet with him and they came eagerly.

These six verses are easily passed over simply as a travelogue, but one should see a deeper significance to them. As Paul went through Macedonia (i.e., Philippi, Thessalonica, and Berea), his mission was to share "words of encouragement" with the groups of believers he had founded there. It is not enough to lead someone to Christ, baptize the person, and put his or her name on a church roll. New Christians need to be encouraged, taught, and corrected. Paul's pastoral heart recognized that duty in his ministry. Even as he was doing this work of encouragement in Macedonia, he was joined by Titus who had just come from Corinth (cf. 2 Cor. 7:5-16). On the basis of Titus's report on conditions there, he wrote the epistle we know as 2 Corinthians in late A.D. 55 to tell them of his plans to visit them soon (2 Cor. 13:1-4).

When he finally came to Greece (i.e., Corinth), he stayed there for three months — probably because it was winter and his ship was unable to sail. This gave him time to do some additional corrective work in the sin-plagued Corinthian church, to confront some opponents to his ministry who had been undermining him there, and to gather funds from the church for the poor in Judea (2 Cor. 8:1–9:15). Our best evidence is that Paul wrote Romans during this three-month stay at Corinth. All this points to what an intense and busy time this was in Paul's ministry.

Ready now to sail from Corinth in the spring of A.D. 56, he learned that some Jews had hatched a plot to kill him. So he wisely altered his travel plans and gave up ship passage for overland travel back through Macedonia. He was accompanied by a group of representatives from various churches who

**Day 2
Nurturing New Converts**

Read Hebrews 5:11–6:12 about the importance of Christian growth.

1. Why did Paul revisit the churches he had founded in Macedonia?
2. What "words of encouragement" do you think he spoke to those churches?
3. Which do you think is easier: Leading someone to Christ? Nurturing an infant Christian to maturity? Explain.
4. How did Paul disciple young Timothy in the faith?
5. Is there some new or weak Christian who has reached to you for help recently? How are you responding?

had collected money for relief to the church in Judea. He appears to have divided the group, sending some ahead by ship to Troas and taking some with him on the land route.

Interestingly, the second of four "we-sections" begins at 20:5 (20:5-15; cf. 16:10-17; 21:1-18; 27:1–28:16). Luke had apparently been working at Philippi and rejoined Paul as he came to that city in his travels. Paul celebrated Passover (i.e., the Feast of Unleavened Bread) at Philippi and took a ship from there to Troas.

D. A Week's Stay at Troas. 20:6b-12.

At Troas, Paul, Luke, and their companions rejoined the brothers who had sailed there directly from Corinth. The combined party stayed at Troas a full week. The driving reason for a week's delay in a hurried trip seems to have been so they could meet with the disciples in that city on the Lord's Day.

Sunday was a normal workday for the first-century world, so believers had to gather in the evening. They assembled "to break bread" — a reference to the communion of the body and blood of Christ in the Lord's Supper (cf. 2:42) — and Paul used the gathering as his opportunity to instruct and encourage the church. Because it was night, "many lamps" were in use in the upstairs meeting room. The heat and oxygen loss in a crowded room with many lamps burning surely contributed to what happened next. As the long-winded Paul "talked on and on" in the hot room, a young man (note: the Greek term *pais* in v. 12 denotes a person between seven and fourteen) named Eutychus appears to have moved as close as he could get to an open window. Even if he was fighting sleep, he could not win. He went sound asleep, fell from the third-story window, and brought a sudden halt to the church meeting. Paul and the others rushed downstairs and found him dead.

Day 3
The Lord's Day

Read about a Lord's Day worship experience at Revelation 1:9-20.

1. Why did Sunday come to be called "The Lord's Day" by Christians?
2. Why is Sunday the special day for Christian assemblies and worship?
3. What appears to have been the primary reason for the assembly in Acts 20?
4. How do you sanctify Sunday to the Lord?
5. Poor Eutychus! What is the funniest or most unsettling thing you ever saw in a church meeting?

In a scene that reminds a Bible student of Elijah and Elisha (cf. 1 Kgs. 17:21; 2 Kgs. 4:34-35), Paul "threw himself on the young man and put his arms around him." He told the crowd that all would be well. Eutychus was restored to life by the power of God, and Paul exclaimed, "He's alive!" The group returned to the third-story room, ate a snack to help everyone deal with the late hour and physical exhaustion, and continued listening to Paul until daylight broke.

E. Paul's Meeting with the Elders from Ephesus. 20:13-38.

"The farewell address of Paul to the Ephesian elders, more than any other passage of The Acts, reveals the heart of the great apostle, his tenderness, his sympathy, his affection, and his tears. No other paragraph contains more direct and practical advice for Christian ministers and missionaries; furthermore, its guidance and inspiration are such as to aid every follower of Christ in the conduct of life and in the fulfillment of duty." [Erdman, *Acts*, p. 156.]

1. Travel from Troas to Miletus. 20:13-16.

Luke and others in Paul's group left Troas by ship and sailed for Assos. Paul, apparently wanting to spend as much time in Troas as possible, made the short twenty-mile trip overland to board the ship there. Sailing from there, Paul chose "to sail past Ephesus to avoid spending time in the province of Asia, for he was in a hurry to reach Jerusalem, if possible, by the day of Pentecost." Another emotional farewell with the entire Christian body in that city would require time and energy the apostle simply did not have.

2. A call to the elders at Ephesus. 20:17.

Yet Paul wanted one final contact with the church with which he had invested three years of his

Day 4
Church Leadership

Read Paul's counsel to church leaders from 1 Timothy 3.

1. Explain the importance of good leadership in churches.
2. How did Paul encourage the development of leaders in the churches he founded?
3. What are some of the ongoing things a church should do to develop leadership in its ranks?
4. What leadership development options does your church provide?
5. What are your personal ambitions about leadership in the church?

life. Therefore he sent a messenger from Miletus [Mī-lē´-təs] to Ephesus — a distance of approximately thirty-five miles — to ask the elders of the church to come to him. The clear purpose of his request was not simply that he might have a convenient-for-him social time with friends. The apostle wanted to speak to the leaders of the Ephesian church in order to encourage them for their responsibilities in steering a safe and fruitful course for the Christians under their charge. Paul's plan was to conduct a brief leadership seminar for the Ephesian presbyters.

3. Paul's address to the elders. 20:18-38.

Although we have a few of Paul's sermons to unbelievers recorded in Acts, this is his only speech to Christian leaders. It follows an organizational pattern similar to some of his epistles. First, he reviewed his career and defended the legitimacy of his ministry; this may indicate that in Ephesus, as at Corinth, some critics had attempted to undermine confidence in the apostle. Second, he explained his present activities and travel plans. Third, he encouraged the elders from Ephesus to faithfulness in their task.

The first section (vv. 18-21) recalls Paul's integrity of ministry at Ephesus. He had worked among the people of that city by giving freely of himself. There had been humility, tears, and testing to be endured. He had proved his love for the people of God in the city by enduring all these things for their sake. More significantly still, he had preached the salvation message to all who would hear him: "I have declared to both Jews and Greeks that they must turn to God in repentance and have faith in our Lord Jesus."

The second section (vv. 22-24) explains that his current travel is part of the same Spirit-compelled mission that had originally brought him to Ephesus. He was headed for Jerusalem, convinced that the Holy Spirit wanted him to go there. Yet the same Spirit had also warned him that "prison and hardships" lay ahead for him. His only concern, he insisted to his friends, was not protecting himself but "the task of testifying to the gospel of God's grace."

The third section (vv. 25-38) focuses on the future. Paul expressed his conviction that he would likely never see these men or work among the believers at Ephesus again. So he sought to impress upon these church shepherds that the future of the body in that city lay with them, not him. He challenged them to trust in the Lord and to be as faithful in leading the Ephesian church as he had been in filling his role in planting and strengthening it during the early days of its existence. As "overseers" and "shepherds" of the church, it would be their duty to guard the flock from false teaching and apostasy. At Ephesus false teachers were likely to come from both the right and left; the legalism that certain people with Jewish backgrounds were inclined to import into the church would have its counterpart in the indulgent lifestyle that many from pagan roots would favor. It was the duty of these men to see that no one was allowed to "distort the truth" by veering to either of these errors. Therefore they were challenged, "Be on guard!"

The keys to their faithfulness in these duties would be a commitment to sound theology and a lifestyle of principled behavior. Thus Paul concluded his address by a blessing that committed the Ephesian elders "to God and to the word of his grace, which can build you up and give you an inheritance among all those who are sanctified" and urged them to follow his example among them of serving the church without thought of any material reward.

At the end of his charge, Paul knelt with them and prayed. The men who had been called to Miletus were overcome with emotion. Luke describes the scene and the motivation behind it in these words:

**Day 5
An Overseer's Duty**

Read about the qualifications of an overseer-elder at Titus 1:1-16.

1. List the key terms used in the New Testament for an overseer.
2. What is the special significance of each of the terms you listed?
3. Name three things you think should be priorities for an overseer.
4. Is there some special word of encouragement you need to speak or write to one of your overseers?
5. Write a prayer for your church's elders. Pray also for him to raise up additional godly leaders for the church.

Week Twenty-Eight

Acts 21:1-16 (XII F to XII H in Outline)

F. A Brief Visit to Tyre. 21:1-6.

As Luke traces Paul's travel route from Asia Minor to Jerusalem, he gives us significant insight into both the character of Paul and the devotion of the apostle's friends. After a tearful departure from Miletus, Paul and his company sailed on successive days to the islands of Cos and Rhodes. Their next stop was Patara, a major port city of the province of Lycia. Its harbor was a favorite haven for large ships traveling between Asia Minor and Syria, Palestine, or Egypt. Here the Christians changed ships and boarded one of the oceangoing craft headed in the direction of Jerusalem.

When the ship completed its voyage of several days from Patara to Tyre, the once-proud capital of the Phoenician Empire, Paul found a church in the city. Likely founded as a result of the persecution following the death of Stephen (cf. 11:19) and perhaps already visited once previously by Paul (cf. 15:3), these believers hosted the Christian travelers in their midst for seven days.

The statement that they urged Paul "through the Spirit" not to continue to Jerusalem has made some wonder if the apostle disobeyed God in this situation. In view of the fact that Paul had originally formed his determination to go to Jerusalem under the Spirit's prodding (cf. 20:22), this hardly seems reasonable. "Probably . . . we should understand the preposition *dia* ('through') as meaning that the Spirit's message was the occasion for the believers' concern rather than that their trying to dissuade

Day 1
The Spirit's Leading

Read John 16:1-16 for Jesus' promise of the Holy Spirit to his apostles.

1. What evidence can you offer that Paul sought and was conscious of the Spirit's leading in his life?
2. Do you think the Spirit gave Paul contrary guidance through his friends here? Explain.
3. Do you think Paul made the right decision in going on to Jerusalem against his friends' advice?
4. Have you ever had to make a decision against the wishes of people you loved and trusted? What came of the decision?
5. How do you experience the guidance of the Holy Spirit in your life?

Day 2
Suffering for Christ

Read Paul's comments about his sufferings for the gospel at Philippians 1:12-30.

1. Should Christians be surprised at suffering in their lives? Explain.
2. Is God unjust to allow righteous people to suffer? Defend your answer.
3. What values sometimes come to people through suffering?
4. What lesson has an event of suffering taught you that otherwise you might have missed?
5. Did Paul think it unjust that he should have to suffer for Christ? Cite proof for your answer.

Paul was directly inspired by the Spirit." [Longnecker, "Acts," p. 516.] That some interpretation along this line is correct is supported by the events that will shortly occur in connection with Agabus. The point of revealing Paul's suffering in advance was less to dissuade him from taking risks than to allow him to fortify his will for bearing faithful witness to Christ under persecution.

The question of whether Paul was obedient or disobedient to the Lord in going to Jerusalem is settled decisively after the fact. After he was arrested, threatened by a mob, and taken before the Sanhedrin, the Lord appeared to the apostle at night and said, "Take courage! As you have testified about me in Jerusalem, so you must also testify in Rome" (23:11).

When the ship on which they had taken passage was finished with its cargo at Tyre and ready to sail, the apostle and his group left the city. They were escorted to the dock by the believers who had been their hosts. Men, women, and children saw them off. One can easily sense the passion of the scene.

G. Paul Travels to Caesarea. 21:7-14.

From Tyre, the ship sailed some twenty-five miles to another Phoenician seaport named Ptolemais [Tŏ-lə-mā´-əs] and met with some Christians during a one-day layover. The ship then sailed to Caesarea, just over thirty miles south of Ptolemais.

Caesarea had been built by Herod the Great to be the port city for Jerusalem. It had a magnificent harbor and had been designated the provincial capital of Judea by the Roman government. The city was Herod's most colossal work of self-expression that was built as a monument to certify his fame. He built Caesarea in the dozen years between 22 and 10 B.C., naming it for Caesar Augustus. An aqueduct that required tunneling through four miles of solid rock brought water from Mount Carmel to its Roman baths and fountains. He built a harbor in the open sea without any protective bay or peninsula. Using a concrete mixture that hardened when it came into contact with water, his engineers surpassed anything the Romans had ever done with the concrete construction techniques they had invented two centuries earlier. At least one hundred ships of the time could anchor in its protected waters at one time.

1. The arrival and association with Philip. 21:7-9.

When Paul and his companions reached Caesarea, they appear to have made immediate contact with Christians in the city. Paul had, after all, visited the city at least two times prior to this (9:30; 18:22). Philip, one of the seven men appointed earlier in Acts as a deacon for the congregation at Jerusalem (6:5), was now living at Caesarea. He offered his house for lodging and hosted the group for the several days of their visit at Caesarea. Luke makes the observation in passing that Philip "had four unmarried daughters who prophesied." The fact that he says nothing further about them may indicate that they were widely known in the early church.

2. The prophecy of Agabus. 21:10-14.

It was neither Philip nor his prophesying daughters who figured most prominently in the events of Caesarea, however, but a prophet who arrived from Judea during their visit. We have already been introduced to Agabus in the Acts narrative. Luke tells us that it was he who predicted to the church at Antioch a famine that would shortly affect the Roman world. In response to his message, the Gentile church at Antioch decided to send relief help to their Jewish brothers and sisters in Judea. This unifying act of charity was implemented through the hands of Barnabas and his new associate at that time, Saul of Tarsus (11:27-30). Now, more than a decade later,

Day 3
The Prophet Agabus

Read Amos 3:7 and 7:10-17 for insight into the role of a prophet.

1. What does the word "prophet" mean? How does the word relate to telling the future?
2. In what setting have we seen Agabus already in Acts?
3. How did Agabus communicate his revelation from the Lord?

4. What was the effect of
   his message?

5. Why do you think God
   gave this message to
   Paul in advance of his
   Jerusalem experiences?

**Day 4
Paul's Determination**

*Read about Jesus' determined
trip to Jerusalem from Luke
9:51-62.*

1. Do you see Luke's par-
   allelism between the
   journeys of Jesus and
   Paul to Jerusalem? Why
   do you think he devel-
   oped this idea?

2. How did Paul react to
   his friends' pleas that he
   not go to Jerusalem?

3. Did the apostle have a
   "martyr complex"? Why
   was he so resolute about
   going there?

4. How did Paul's friends
   signal their acceptance
   of his decision?

5. Can you identify a situation in which your stub-
   born determination to
   do what you believed
   was right made a holy
   difference?

Agabus reenters Paul's life with a message about his
personal future.

The prophecy was delivered in dramatic fashion.
Agabus took Paul's belt (i.e., a long sash or cord that
would have been wrapped around his tunic several
times at the waist) and tied the apostle's hands and
feet with it. He then said, "The Holy Spirit says, 'In
this way the Jews of Jerusalem will bind the owner of
this belt and will hand him over to the Gentiles.'"

In response to Agabus's prophetic revelation,
everyone present — including Luke (cf. the "we" of
20:12) — sought to discourage Paul in his plan to go
to Jerusalem. "Why are you weeping and breaking
my heart?" he asked them. "I am ready not only to
be bound, but also to die in Jerusalem for the name
of the Lord Jesus."

"The difficulty for Paul was that he had to digest
the information about what the Jews would do to
him and at the same time deal with his grief-stricken
friends who wanted to keep him out of danger. It is
not easy to fly in the face of a host of friends, all of
whom believe your decision or direction is wrong.
They had all prayed their prayers and Paul stood
alone in the guidance he received. How can we
account for these counterconvictions? The Spirit
had not given different guidance; Paul and his
friends interpreted the guidance differently. It is
what the friends and Paul added to the guidance
that made the difference. Paul added the resolute-
ness of previous clarity; his friends added the reserve
of tender affection for the Apostle.

"Through Luke's eyes, we are given an inside
look at the warm and caring relationship between
Paul and his friends. They really cared about the
Apostle. He was not only the spiritual and intellectual giant we meet on the pages of Acts and in the
epistles; he was also a man capable of receiving and
giving deep affection. Christ in him had softened his

rigid, cold Pharisee's heart and made him able to share in profound friendships in the family of faith." [Ogilvie, *Acts*, p. 297.]

When his friends realized that they would not be able to alter Paul's determination to go to Jerusalem, they ceased arguing with him. In what should be read as an affirmation of the apostle rather than mere resignation, they said, "The Lord's will be done." Contrary to the spirit of some Christians today, Paul understood that God's will may entail suffering for the sake of righteousness. One is not affirmed of God only when everything works out pleasantly. Affirmation may also come in suffering.

At this juncture in the narrative, it is interesting to notice the parallel construction that seems to mark Luke's description of Paul's journey toward Jerusalem. The highlight features of the Savior's final trip into Jerusalem in the Gospel of Luke have counterparts in Paul's trip to Jerusalem in Acts that can hardly be accidental. In both cases, there is (1) a plot by the Jews, (2) a handing over of the central figure to the Gentiles, (3) predictions along the travel route of what was ahead, (4) protestations by friends, (5) an unshakable determination to carry through with a holy purpose, and (6) a submissive spirit to the will of God.

H. The Company Arrives at Jerusalem. 21:15-16.

With the decision made that Paul would go to Jerusalem, some of the Christians from Caesarea traveled the sixty-five miles southeast to the Holy City with him and his companions. More specifically, they escorted the group to the home of a disciple named Mnason [Nā´-sən] where they knew the company would be received graciously. This was no small matter, for Paul's traveling companions included both Jews and Gentiles. A disciple who had

Day 5
The Lord's Will

Read James 4:1-17 about submitting to the Lord's will.

1. What did Jesus mean when he prayed, "Your will be done," in Gethsemane?
2. What did Paul's friends mean when they told Paul, "The Lord's will be done"?
3. How is accepting the Lord's will different from a fatalistic resignation to fate?
4. In what ways is "the Lord's will" the same for all people? In what ways distinctive to each person?
5. How do you determine the Lord's will for your life in difficult situations?

outgrown his racial prejudice to the degree that he would be willing to have the group stay in his house would have to be found. The Caesarean believers knew that Mnason, "a man from Cyprus and one of the early disciples" would be the appropriate person to receive them.

From this initial base of operation, a remarkable series of events would unfold for Paul in the city that had once been friendly to him as a persecutor of Christians. Now he would become the object of persecution himself.

Week Twenty-Nine

Acts 21:17–22:29 (XIII A to XIII C in Outline)

XIII. Paul Made a Prisoner at Jerusalem. 21:17–23:30.

The content of Acts from this point forward deals exclusively with the experiences of Paul the prisoner. Following his arrest at Jerusalem in the spring of A.D. 57, Luke traces him from there to Caesarea to Rome. Luke wrote Acts at Rome during the time of the apostle's house arrest that ended with his release in A.D. 62.

A. A Meeting with James and the Elders. 21:17-26.

1. Paul relates the success of the gospel among Gentiles. 21:17-19.

After Paul and his party had been received at Mnason's house, the word appears to have spread quickly that he was in the city. A number of Christians came to the house and received him and his friends warmly. On the day following that informal reception at the home of Mnason, Paul took the initiative to seek out the leaders of the Jerusalem church in a more formal way. This was no mere act of courtesy but a desire to share with them how the Lord had affirmed the decision of the conference held in that city about the propriety of preaching the gospel of God's grace to the Gentiles (cf. 15:1ff).

Paul sought out James — not the apostle (cf. 12:2) but the half-brother in the flesh of our Lord — who was one of the "pillars" of the Jerusalem church (Gal. 2:9). He, Luke, and the others who had trav-

**Day 1
Accountability**

Read Acts 15:1-35 to be reminded of Paul's previous visit with James and the Jerusalem elders.

1. What was the issue Paul discussed with James and the Jerusalem elders on his last visit to the city?
2. What had been the resolution of that discussion?
3. Paul's visit with James and the elders in Acts 21 gave a report of his experiences in preaching under the mandate he had carried from his previous visit. How does this demonstrate accountability?
4. In what way can spiritual accountability be helpful to Christian growth? To whom are you accountable?
5. How can one keep accountability from degenerating into legalism?

eled with them from Asia Minor met with James and "all the elders" of the Jerusalem church for two purposes. First, they "reported in detail what God had done among the Gentiles" through the ministry of Paul. Second, they surely presented to James and the church's elders the collection of money from the Gentile churches that had been gathered for the saints in Judea. This, after all, was the driving force behind this trip to Jerusalem (cf. 1 Cor. 16:1-4; Rom. 15:25-28). It was the second such contribution of relief funds Paul had delivered to the Jerusalem church and was a further affirmation of the solidarity of the body of Christ.

Day 2
Essentials and
Nonessentials

Read Romans 14 about the freedom Christians are supposed to grant each other.

1. Does salvation remove cultural distinctions among people? Is this good or bad?
2. What were some of the cultural distinctives that Paul practiced but would not allow to be bound on Gentiles as conditions for salvation?
3. Did Paul believe that Jews had to give up circumcision, kosher food, and holy day celebrations to accept Christ as their Messiah? Explain his position.
4. What modern parallels to this honoring of one's cultural roots come to your mind?
5. How do you distinguish a gospel essential from a nonessential?

2. A vow of purification to demonstrate Paul's attitude toward the Law before certain critical Jews. 21:20-26.

The response from James and the elders was that they "praised God" for his mighty work among the Gentiles through Paul's preaching missions. Yet they also advised Paul of a problem that would confront him in their city. Malicious rumors about Paul and his ministry were circulating in Jerusalem and would make it hard for some of the Jewish brothers there to receive Paul. "They have been informed that you teach all the Jews who live among the Gentiles to turn away from Moses, telling them not to circumcise their children or live according to our customs."

The report that was circulating in Jerusalem about Paul was, of course, untrue. Yet it was just close enough to the truth that it could be told believably by the apostle's enemies who had followed him all along his ministry path. It was *true* that Paul had rejected the Law of Moses as a means to justification; right-standing with God was available only through faith in Jesus Christ. It was *untrue*, however, that Paul had repudiated Moses or rejected the lifestyle (i.e., circumcision and other Jewish customs) of his people. Though he was the Apostle to the Gentiles, Paul was himself a Jew who loved his racial and religious heritage, who observed its ceremonies and rituals, and who was eager not to offend his countrymen (cf. 1 Cor. 9:19-23).

What could be done to counter the malicious reports about Paul? How could James and the elders help the apostle gain acceptance by the larger Jerusalem congregation? How could they protect themselves from needless suspicion about their relationship to Paul as leaders of the Jerusalem church? James and the elders suggested that Paul be proactive against such falsehoods by assisting four Jewish Christians in the completion of a Nazirite vow they had recently taken. Since Paul himself had taken the same vow at Corinth (cf. 18:19), such a thing would not have been problematic for him. In this case, he was not planning to join the four men in their vow of thanksgiving and/or consecration. Instead he was going to "pay their expenses" for the several animals that would be required for sacrifice at the termination of their vow, at which time they would signify its end by shaving their heads.

Paul agreed to the plan suggested by the leaders of the Jerusalem church. In turn, they repeated their commitment to the decision that had been reached and published earlier at Jerusalem about the inclusion of Gentiles into the church without their having to adopt the Law and its customs. The plan seemed reasonable to all parties concerned, and it was hoped that its execution would allay the fears some had about Paul based on misinformation.

Before Paul could participate in the ceremony that would bring the four men's Nazirite vow to an end, he would have to be ceremonially pure himself. Having just come from Gentile territories, he would need to undergo a seven-day purification ritual. Thus he went into the temple precincts with the four men on the following day to inform the priest of his intention about paying their expenses. He also

Day 3
Malicious Rumors

Read some passages about malicious talk: Leviticus 19:15-16; Proverbs 11:13; 20:19; and Romans 1:29-30.

1. What slander was being circulated about Paul by his enemies at Jerusalem?
2. What kernel of truth made their lies believable?
3. What strategy did James and the elders suggest to quash the malicious rumors?
4. Have you ever been the target of slander or malicious rumors?
5. If so, how did you handle and survive them?

would have informed the priest about his own purification process and made arrangements to return at intervals over the coming week to undergo the rituals involved in his purification. He was not to get the chance to carry through with his plan.

B. A Temple Uproar and Paul's Arrest by the Romans. 21:27-36.

As the week of Paul's own purification proceeded, he would have needed to make several trips into the temple courtyard in order to carry out certain rites. Near the end of the week, some Jews from the Roman province of Asia created a riot by seizing Paul and telling onlookers, "Men of Israel, help us! This is the man who teaches all men everywhere against our law and this place. And besides, he has brought Greeks into the temple area and defiled this holy place." The charge was false. Paul was simply reaping the hatred against Christ and the church that his enemies had long wanted to bring against him. He had not violated the Law or desecrated the temple. To the contrary, he was in the process of demonstrating his loyalty to both.

The situation turned violent almost immediately. The charges of apostasy and blasphemy circulated quickly through the people in the vicinity of the temple. The mob attacked Paul, dragged him to the Court of the Gentiles, shut the gates into the inner precincts of the temple, and were ready to kill Paul. At that point, Paul was rescued by Roman soldiers.

On the north side of the temple precincts stood the Fortress of Antonia. Built by Herod the Great, it overlooked the temple courts and served as a command post for Roman soldiers in the city. Although the police who patrolled the temple area were Levites accountable to the Roman officials, their commander and the effective military presence in the city were themselves Romans. Seeing the riot in progress, the commander rushed down with soldiers, waded into the crowd, and restored a semblance of order. The beating of Paul was stopped and his life spared.

Focusing on Paul, the commander arrested and chained him. He then began asking what his prisoner had been doing to cause such an uproar. Unable to get a consistent story about Paul, he ordered him taken to the Fortress of Antonia for personal interrogation. The crowd reacted to the idea that Paul might escape its grasp by pressing their cries and trying to get at Paul. The violence became so intense that Paul had to be "carried" — more likely we should translate "dragged" — by the soldiers up the steps to the fortress. The mob was shouting, "Away with him!"

C. Paul is Allowed to Address the Crowd. 21:37–22:29.

In this section of text, Paul makes the first of five speeches that he will make at Jerusalem and Caesarea to defend himself from false charges. In each case, he turns the defense speech into an opportunity to proclaim Christ.

1. He receives permission to speak. 21:37-40.

As the soldiers were about to drag Paul into their barracks, he spoke to the Roman commander Claudius Lysias (cf. 23:26). To that point, the commander in charge of Paul had assumed he was an outlaw. Specifically, he thought he was a Jew from Egypt who had instigated a revolt against Rome earlier that had involved "four thousand terrorists" who eventually were driven into the desert. Paul shocked Claudius Lysias by speaking fluent Greek and letting him know that he was from the Roman free city of Tarsus in Cilicia.

With the commander's permission, Paul stood on

Day 4
A Personal Testimony

Read another account of Paul's conversion from his own lips at Acts 26:1-23.

1. What does the expression "personal testimony" mean?
2. What is the value of telling other people one's story of conversion to Christ?
3. Try to share the story of your conversion with someone this week who is already a believer.
4. Ask the person with whom you share your story to help you make it into a true testimony to Christ's saving power that could affect someone who is an unbeliever.
5. Begin praying for God to lead you to someone

221

within the next two weeks who is not a Christian and with whom you can share your personal testimony.

the steps of the fortress-barracks and made a speech to the mob assembled below. He addressed them in their native language, Aramaic, for the sake of getting their attention and being understood clearly by them all.

2. He relates his background and conversion to the people. 22:1-16.

Speaking in their language and showing respect to them (i.e., "Brothers and fathers"), Paul addressed the crowd. They became quiet and listened attentively as he related his Jewish heritage, training under Rabbi Gamaliel, and previous opposition to Christianity himself. But the experiences on the Damascus Road had changed his mind and heart. He saw a vision of Jesus of Nazareth and received instructions about going into Damascus and waiting for further information.

That information came to him through Ananias, "a devout observer of the law and highly respected by all the Jews" in Damascus. Ananias spoke of a choice made by "the God of our fathers" (i.e., Yahweh, the God of Israel) to have Paul see "the Righteous One" (i.e., Messiah) and to bear witness to him to all men of what he had seen and heard.

3. He tells of his commission to preach to Gentiles. 22:17-21.

After his baptism, Paul reported, he came back to Jerusalem — probably the visit made three years after his conversion (cf. Gal. 1:18) — and was "praying at the temple." The Lord spoke to him and told him to leave Jerusalem. Paul had protested, he said, believing that his previous involvement in opposing the Christians could make his testimony all the more effective. But God had other plans.

To this point, notice how skillfully and tactfully Paul has told his story. He affirmed his Jewishness and zeal for the Law of Moses. He spoke of "devout"

Ananias and his prayers at the temple. Indeed, Paul was no enemy to Moses and would not think of desecrating the temple. As he completed his story, however, he could not avoid the word that would reignite the mob's passion.

Why had the Lord not allowed him to stay in Jerusalem earlier? "Go; I will send you far away to the Gentiles," he told Paul. At the mention of being directed by God to reach out and to include Gentiles in the covenant blessings, the riot began all over again.

4. The crowd again enraged and Paul rescued by his captors. 22:22-29.

"Until he said this" about the Gentiles, the crowd had listened quietly. But that pushed them over the edge, and the rioters began to scream, "Rid the earth of him! He's not fit to live!"

The garrison commander who could not speak Aramaic and who had no idea what Paul had said to throw the courtyard into turmoil again rescued Paul a second time. Taking him into the fortress, "he directed that [Paul] be flogged and questioned in order to find out why the people were shouting at him like this." He was ready to employ the dreaded *flagellum* that had been used previously on Jesus at his trial before Pilate and that was often used to beat confessions out of prisoners. So terrible a punishment was a beating with the *flagellum* that a Roman citizen could not be flogged prior to a trial and a guilty verdict. Paul appealed to the protection of citizenship by asking the centurion in charge of carrying out Claudius Lysias's order, "Is it legal for you to flog a Roman citizen who hasn't even been found guilty?"

Startled and frightened, the centurion reported Paul's question to Claudius Lysias. The Roman commander came and asked Paul about his citizenship. Perhaps by means of documents he carried with

Day 5
Speaking to Enemies

Read Jesus' predictions and warnings at Matthew 10:1-25.

1. Why do you think the Roman commander allowed Paul to speak to the mob?

2. How did Paul try to identify with his hearers in a positive way?

3. What subject threw the crowd into an uproar again?

4. How did Paul escape harm at the hands of the mob? At the hands of the Roman commander?

5. Have you ever been forced to speak before a hostile audience? Witnessed such an event? What was the outcome?

him, Paul convinced the man in charge of him that he was indeed a free-born citizen of the Roman Empire. Claudius Lysias was alarmed at that point, for a citizen was not only exempt from the *flagellum* without a trial first but also the humiliation of being bound with chains. This case would require further careful investigation.

Week Thirty

Acts 22:30–23:11 (XIII D to XIII E in Outline)

One of the important things about the Christian religion that is neglected by moderns is its Jewishness. Christianity was born from the womb of Judaism.

This is not to say that Christianity is a Jewish sect or merely an evolutionary offshoot of Judaism. It is to claim that there is a fundamental continuity to biblical religion. The *proto evangelium* of Genesis 3:15 is the earliest biblical glimmer about the Redeemer who was to come. In preparation for his presentation to the world, Abraham and his descendants were selected by God's grace to be the Chosen People through whom the Lord's Anointed (i.e., Messiah) would come. The Law was given through Moses, himself a type of the Redeemer who would eventually come on the scene (Deut. 18:15-18). The prophets bore anticipatory witness until John the Baptist. Then Jesus of Nazareth appeared to bring all the promises scattered across history to fulfillment. Indeed, the Christian religion was — by sovereign design and the will of God — born from the womb of Judaism.

Antisemitism not only forgets but denies Christianity's Jewish roots. Most of today's Christian community does not deny but does overlook its Jewish origins. Paul was keenly aware of this important fact, and — as Stephen had before him (Acts 7:1ff) — testified before the Sanhedrin that his faith was not a repudiation of Moses, the Law, or the temple but a flowering of all the hopes embodied in them.

Day 1
Christianity's Jewishness

Read Romans 10:1-21 and sense Paul's passion for his fellow Jews.

1. What does it mean to say: "Christianity was born from the womb of Judaism"?
2. What is the relationship between Moses and Jesus? The Old and New Testaments?
3. What is your view of the antisemitism that has evolved in some "Christian" cultures?
4. On what basis can Jesus be presented to Jewish persons most effectively?
5. What rites of Christian worship can you trace to Jewish roots?

Day 2
Fulfillment

Read Hebrews 10:1-18 and pay particular attention to the theme of fulfillment.

1. What does the term "fulfillment" mean in its biblical setting?

2. In what sense did early Christian evangelists present Christianity as the fulfillment of Jewish hopes?

3. Is it correct to say that Jesus "repudiated" or "abolished" the Law of Moses? Explain.

4. Explain the meaning of Matthew 5:17-18.

Day 3
Civil Rights

Read Romans 13:1-14 for Paul's view of civil governments.

1. When and why did the Roman government come to Paul's aid in the temple precincts?

2. Why did Claudius Lysias decide to flog Paul?

3. How did Paul's status as a citizen of the Roman

D. Paul Examined before the Sanhedrin. 22:30–23:10.

The speech Paul made on the steps of the Fortress of Antonia had left the Roman commander Claudius Lysias more bewildered than enlightened. For one thing, the commander did not understand the Aramaic language in which Paul has spoken to the crowd. For another, even if Paul had chosen to speak in his fluent Greek, Claudius Lysias likely would not have grasped the issues involved; the speech was about theology and the interpretation of Scripture, not Roman law.

Luke takes great care, however, to present the commander as a fair and diligent official. Claudius Lysias "wanted to find out exactly why Paul was being accused by the Jews." This had become all the more important in light of his discovery that Paul was a Roman citizen and entitled to certain rights under the law. Since Paul was a citizen, the commander could not "beat the truth out of him" or leave him under arrest without a charge being specified. So he used his authority to call the chief priests and the Sanhedrin to assemble in order to examine Paul and determine why his presence in Jerusalem had precipitated a riot.

The Sanhedrin was Judaism's highest court. Made up of seventy members plus the High Priest, it was granted considerable freedom to function on behalf of the nation. Its decisions were always subject to review by the Roman officials, and it could not impose a death sentence without the sanction of the procurator (e.g., Jesus' trials before both the Sanhedrin and Pilate). In order to retain its stature and authority, the Sanhedrin had become concessive to the Romans. Since the Sadducees were far more willing to play this sort of game than the Pharisees, the court's membership was taken predominantly from the Sadducee party. The high respect given the orthodox Pharisees by the Jewish populace meant that they could not be completely shut out of the Sanhedrin, but they were clearly in the minority and could not have the decisive word on matters for Israel.

Brought before the high court, Paul began his speech with a respectful salutation and a bold statement: "My brothers, I have fulfilled my duty to God in all good conscience to this day." No sooner were these opening words out of his mouth, however, than the high priest Ananias "ordered those standing near Paul to strike him on the mouth."

This Ananias — a common Jewish name of the time — is known to us from sources outside Acts. He was the son of Nedebaeus [Nĕ-də-bē´-əs] and reigned as high priest from A.D. 48-59. He held his position by being staunchly pro-Roman in policy and by pilfering temple assets in order to lavish gifts on the Roman officials who could protect him. Both the Talmud and Josephus speak of his greed. We also know that he was a brutal man who used violence whenever he thought it would serve his purpose. Whether he had Paul hit simply to show him who was in charge or in response to the claim that he could possibly have a "good conscience" after embracing Christianity is unclear. In either case, Ananias was doing nothing out of character for the person we know him to have been.

Paul responded to the blow with an outburst of temper. Appealing to the principle in the Law of Moses that one was to be presumed innocent until proved guilty, he said, "God will strike you, you whitewashed wall!" It was wrong for Paul to react as he did here, yet many of us would be hard pressed to say that our own humanness might not reply just as he did. Yet Christians have been taught to turn the other cheek to insults (Matt. 5:39) and to imitate the example of our Lord who did not respond in kind to taunts and humiliation (1 Pet. 2:23). Paul lost control for a moment, and

Empire save him from the commander's intentions?

4. What rights as a citizen of your country do you value most?

5. Do you know of situations where people are denied their civil rights? If so, explain your reaction to those situations.

**Day 4
Paul's Apology**

*Read 1 Peter 2:13-25 about
one's response to personal
insults.*

1. What caused Paul to
   "lose his cool" before
   the Sanhedrin?
2. Does it diminish your
   respect for Paul to see
   his human weakness on
   display here? Explain.
3. Do you find any com-
   fort in seeing that Paul
   could be as human as
   you? Explain.
4. How did Paul take
   responsibility for what
   he did?
5. Recall a time when you
   did something similar to
   this. How did you take
   responsibility for it?

that loss of control put him at a disadvantage for all that would follow.

Someone standing near Paul said, "You dare to insult God's high priest?" Paul then apologized for what he had just done: "Brothers, I did not realize that he was the high priest; for it is written: 'Do not speak evil about the ruler of your people.'" Ananias had come to his position well over a decade after Paul had left Jerusalem, and we ought not be surprised that he did not know him. The larger truth here is that Paul should not have responded to call down God's wrath on anyone in that setting. Again, however, we are looking back at a situation through the eyes of reflection and hindsight. Paul was dealing with a tense situation the likes of which most of us will never face.

Paul immediately resumed his address to the assembled group. He went from a defensive posture to an offensive one, putting the matter of the resurrection on the floor for consideration. "My brothers, I am a Pharisee, the son of a Pharisee. I stand on trial because of my hope in the resurrection of the dead." He was unable to go further in his speech, for the words "resurrection of the dead" threw the room into turmoil. The Sadducees were the materialists of Judaism and flatly rejected the notions of resurrection and life after death. On the other hand, the Pharisees believed in both — along with angels and spirits, which the Sadducees also rejected. With the subject of resurrection on the floor, the members of the Sanhedrin resumed their old battles over it. There was a "great uproar" as the dispute became more and more heated. Eventually Claudius Lysias thought that Paul was in jeopardy of his life in that setting, sent troops to rescue him from the Jews a second time, and brought him back into the barracks.

"Is this only a clever diversionary ploy? Is Paul simply trying to divide the assembly, so that they cannot agree to request and be given this prisoner for trial and certain execution? No, Paul's confession focuses on that aspect of the gospel that will be central to his apologetic throughout his trial witness (24:15; 26:6-8; compare 28:20). It tells the truth about the ultimate reason for his arrest by the Jews. For Paul and Luke, resurrection, especially the resurrection of Messiah Jesus, is the key issue that determines the nature of the continuity and discontinuity between Jews and Christians as part of the true people of God. . . . Paul finds himself on trial because of the Messiah's resurrection and the new realities it introduced. For if Jesus had not risen from the dead, he could not have appeared to Paul on the Damascus Road, or in the temple, and commissioned him to take the gospel to the Gentiles (Acts 22:15, 21). Paul would, then, not have promulgated a message or lived a lifestyle that his fellow Jews would have opposed." [Larkin, *Acts*, pp. 328-329.]

While this is true of the issue's importance to Paul and the gospel he preached, the Pharisee-Sadducee debate over the issue did not address the issue of Jesus. It simply pitted old adversaries against each other once more. The Pharisees wanted to protect Paul from harm and insisted that he had done nothing wrong. "What if a spirit or angel has spoken to him?" they asked. The Sadducees were now resolutely set against Paul, for they had heard him confess his own party background within Judaism and affirm the resurrection of the dead. Claudius Lysias was wise to get Paul out of the Sanhedrin chamber, for there easily could have been a repeat of the fate that befell Stephen in a similar setting.

E. A Communication from the Lord. 23:11.

What was Paul's state of mind after the day's events? He had come to Jerusalem only as he had felt "compelled by the Spirit" and had admitted to

**Day 5
Resurrection**

Read Matthew 22:23-33 for background to Sadducee-Pharisee conflict over this issue.

1. What was the Sadducee view of the resurrection of the dead? The Pharisee view?
2. What statement from Paul threw the Sanhedrin into turmoil?
3. Why do you think Paul introduced this subject?
4. Why is the resurrection of the dead the central doctrine of Christian faith?
5. Explain Paul's statement at 1 Corinthians 15:17-19.

his friends that he did not know what would happen to him there (20:22). The apostle's worst apprehensions of what might happen to him there looked like they were going to come to pass. And what would come of his dream of carrying the gospel to Rome? (cf. Rom. 15:31). He may have been demoralized beyond words after the past two days. But the Lord would not leave him without assurances.

On the night following Paul's presence before the Sanhedrin, the Lord appeared to him in a vision. Although he was locked in a Roman cell, the apostle was not alone. The Lord "stood near Paul" and gave him this message: "Take courage! As you have testified about me in Jerusalem, so you must also testify in Rome." The effect of this night must have put new resolve into his heart. "This assurance meant much to Paul during the delays and anxieties of the next two years, and goes far to account for the calm and dignified bearing which seemed to mark him out as a master of events rather than their victim." [F.F. Bruce, *Acts* (Grand Rapids: Eerdmans, 1954), p. 455.]

Week Thirty-One

Acts 23:12–25:12 (XIII F to XIV C in Outline)

F. A Plot against Paul's Life is Thwarted. 23:12-30.

1. The scheme formulated. 23:12-15.

On the day following Paul's stormy hearing before the Sanhedrin, a group of "more than forty men" — likely most of them Jews from Asia Minor who had tried earlier to kill him in the temple precincts — joined in a murderous vow. The depths of their perversity is exceeded only by that of the chief priests and elders of Israel to whom they revealed it. They told the Jewish leaders of their plot in order to secure their assistance in carrying it out.

The assassins would need to get Paul in the open again. So they asked the chief priests and elders to request another interview with the Christian evangelist before the Sanhedrin. Their plan was to ambush Paul in Jerusalem's narrow streets and kill him before he reached the Sanhedrin chamber. The Jewish rulers were willing to be party to the evil plan that had been laid out before them.

2. The plan found out and told to Paul's captors. 23:16-22.

The plot was thwarted when Paul's nephew, the son of his sister, somehow learned of it and reported it. There is no information about the apostle's sister and nephew beyond this passing reference to them. Most of us take Paul's comment about having "lost all things" for the sake of Christ and the gospel (Phil. 3:8) to include his family. While it is possible that his sister was a Christian and sympathetic to him, it seems unlikely. Indeed, his nephew likely

Day 1
Evil Schemes

Read Ecclesiastes 5:1-7 about hasty or wicked vows.

1. What evil scheme was plotted against Paul?
2. What oath did the men take who plotted against him?
3. How long do you think those men waited before they ate a meal?
4. What does the word "fanatic" signify to you? Does it fit here?
5. Give some examples of fanatical schemes from our own time.

learned of the plot only because word of it was spreading among the Jewish people who were unsympathetic to Paul and the church.

Regardless of these unknown factors, Paul's nephew went to his uncle with the news he had. Paul called one of the centurions in charge of security and told him that the boy had important facts that needed to come to the attention of Claudius Lysias. When he was presented to the Roman commander, the young man told everything he knew — including the assassins' "oath not to eat or drink until they have killed him." The boy was sent away with instructions not to tell anyone that he had reported the plot.

Claudius Lysias clearly took this information very seriously. Without further investigation, he knew how passionate the mob had been against Paul and how unscrupulous Ananias and his associates were. He took the warning at face value and began making arrangements to fulfill his duty to protect a Roman citizen under his care from a murder threat.

3. Preparation for Paul's safe conduct to Caesarea. 23:23-30.

The Roman commander knew that the safest place for Paul now would be the garrison town of Caesarea. It was the official residence town for Governor (i.e., Procurator) Felix and was well-fortified with trained Roman soldiers. The small detachment under him at Jerusalem was hardly equipped to deal with a mob action that could easily involve thousands of angry Jews.

Lysias wasted no time. He called two centurions and ordered them to assemble a detachment of two hundred infantrymen, seventy cavalry, and two hundred spearmen (or "light-armed troops," NEB) to escort Paul out of the city.

The letter sent by Claudius Lysias to Felix is interesting for two reasons. First, its form — writer's name, recipient's name, formal greeting, issues of concern —

is typical for all first-century letters. It is the same form used in all the New Testament epistles, except Hebrews and 1 John. Second, it displays the common human practice of laying out the facts of a case in the way most favorable to oneself. Lysias had not, in truth, rescued Paul because he had "learned that he is a Roman citizen." It was only when he was about to have Paul flogged that he had learned the frightening fact that the man he had pulled out of the temple mob was a Roman with rights under law (cf. 22:25-29). As the commander's letter was entered into the record at Caesarea, Paul surely laughed to himself about the way its author had presented himself in the most favorable light possible.

XIV. Paul a Prisoner at Caesarea. 23:31–26:32.

A. Paul's Delivery to Caesarea under Roman Guard. 23:31-35.

The detail in charge of Paul left Jerusalem around nine in the evening, went about thirty-five miles to Antipatris [An-tĭ´-pə-trĭs], and stopped for the night. This leg of the trip appears to have been without incident. The next morning the infantrymen and spearmen returned to Jerusalem, and the seventy cavalry escorted him the remaining twenty-five miles to Caesarea.

Felix read the letter Claudius Lysias had sent with Paul. Upon learning that Paul was from Cilicia, he decided to hear the case personally. Cilicia was a "free city" and not part of a puppet kingdom in the area. Thus there was no client king to placate or protocol he feared violating. A procurator could hear and decide such a case himself. He informed Paul that he would conduct an investigation when his accusers arrived from Jerusalem and ordered him kept in custody.

Day 2
Shading the Facts

Read what Jesus said about factualness at Matthew 5:33-37.

1. How did Claudius Lysias "shade the facts" in his report?
2. Why did he change the facts of the case?
3. Do you know anyone who tends to do this sort of thing? Can you cite an example?
4. How do you guard your own integrity against the temptation to shade the truth?
5. Imagine you are Paul and listening to Lysias's report. How do you react?

B. Paul before Felix. 24:1-27.

Antonius Felix was the procurator of Judea from A.D. 52 to 59. He had been born a slave and had been granted his freedom by Antonia, mother of the emperor Claudius. His tenure as a Roman governor was characterized by constant disturbances among the Jewish people. His brutal measures of suppression only made him more hated by the people and stirred up more unrest in the region. One of the most frequently quoted comments about the man comes from Tacitus. The Roman historian says that Felix "practiced every kind of cruelty and lust, wielding the power of a king with all the instincts of a slave." [*Histories* 5.9.] The description of a man without principle certainly fits the character Luke describes in his narrative.

Day 3
Flattery

Read Psalm 12:1-8 and notice what David says about flattery.

1. What does the term flattery signify?

2. How is flattery different from a legitimate compliment?

3. Who was Tertullus? What was his task in this setting?

4. What was his flattering introduction? How close was it to a genuine compliment?

5. Are you ever tempted to flatter and manipulate other people? Explain.

1. The accusations made against him. 24:1-9.

Paul was kept in custody for five days until the high priest Ananias, some of the Jewish rulers, and a lawyer named Tertullus [Tər-tŭl´-ləs] arrived. Tertullus is a common Greek name, and this lawyer was most likely a Hellenistic Jew who had been hired to make the case against Paul in a way appropriate to the Roman courts. The opening lines of his speech constitute a laughable lie intended to flatter the unscrupulous Felix. To hear their lawyer say that Judea had "enjoyed a long period of peace" under him and to imply that his "reforms in this nation" were appreciated among Jews must have gagged the religious leaders from Jerusalem who were paying his fee. Yet, for the sake of trying to win Felix to their side, they likely nodded or spoke their assent.

When Tertullus finally got to the matter of making a charge against Paul, there were essentially three. First, he charged him with political sedition by calling him a "troublemaker" and accusing him of "stirring up riots among the Jews all over the world."

Second, he lodged a charge of heresy against the apostle by calling him "a ringleader of the Nazarene sect." Third, he accused him of attempting to "desecrate the temple." While the first of the charges was the most serious in the court of Felix, the second and third were designed to make it more believable. This procurator had put men to death before for disturbing the peace that Rome wanted everywhere in its territories, and Tertullus was clearly hoping to get a death sentence against Paul.

2. His defense. 24:10-21.

With the charges lodged against him, Paul was permitted to speak for himself. Refusing to begin with his own version of Tertullus's lying flattery, he simply acknowledged that Felix had ruled the Jewish territory long enough to know how to weigh the charges that had just been made. So he launched directly into a point-by-point rebuttal of the three things Tertullus had claimed.

First, Paul had only come to Jerusalem twelve days earlier — hardly time enough to organize anything that could pass for sedition against Rome. Indeed, he had gone to Jerusalem to worship rather than to agitate the people. "My accusers did not find me arguing with anyone at the temple, or stirring up a crowd in the synagogues or anywhere else in the city," he said. Second, he freely confessed to being a Christian (i.e., "a follower of the Way"). He was a believer in Christ precisely because he believed the Law and the Prophets, not because he was heretical in rejecting them. Although he differed with Ananias and his colleagues about their interpretations of the Scriptures, his conscience was clear before both God and mankind. Third, he was in the temple area to bring gifts to the poor among the Jewish people and to present offerings for his ceremonial purification. Neither charity nor purity is a desecration of the temple.

After this terse and devastating response to the false charges Tertullus had made, Paul proceeded to explain what was really at stake in the anger Felix saw directed at him from the Jewish leaders. When the high court of Judaism had examined him, the sticking point had been his belief in the resurrection of the dead. That belief — particularly as it focused on Jesus — was at the root of the personal rage and unjust charges brought against him.

3. Felix discontinues the case. 24:22-23.

Felix was able to see immediately that Paul was innocent of any crime. He knew enough about "the Way" to be assured that the whole issue boiled down to religious controversy rather than violations of Roman law. So he adjourned the proceedings, promising to rule on the case when Claudius Lysias arrived in Caesarea. As proof that Felix knew Paul was no criminal and in keeping with his rights as a Roman citizen, he kept the apostle under arrest but gave him permission to visit with his friends and associates who had come to the city.

4. Another interview before Felix. 24:24-26.

Luke tells us of a series of informal interviews that Felix conducted with Paul. The first of these was only a few days after the formal hearing just related, and the Roman governor brought his wife along. Drusilla was Felix's third wife, the youngest daughter of Herod Agrippa I. Felix had seduced her away from her husband, and the young woman had responded in hope of sharing the brighter prospects of a rising Roman official. When Paul came before this immoral pair, he left the matter of his defense to preach to them about "righteousness, self-control and the judgment to come." Felix had enough conscience to feel afraid, but he simply stopped Paul from preaching rather than being moved to repentance. Drusilla was apparently outraged at the preacher's impudence,

Day 4
Corrupt Officials

Read Exodus 23:1-9 for instructions about integrity.

1. What do you know about the character of Felix?
2. Did Felix have any doubt of Paul's innocence? Explain.
3. Why did Felix retain Paul under arrest?
4. How much confidence do you have in public officials? Explain.
5. What factors in our culture make public officials subject to corruption? Suggest ways to deal with these factors.

for there is no indication she ever saw or heard him again.

Felix had no intention of acting on Paul's case when Lysias arrived. He was hoping instead for Paul or his friends to offer him a bribe to set the evangelist free. So he left him to rot in jail, sending for him frequently in hope of the bribe offer he wanted.

5. Festus succeeds Felix with no disposal made of Paul's case. 24:27.

Nero recalled Felix to Rome sometime during A.D. 59, and we know nothing of him or Drusilla past that time. He was succeeded by Porcius Festus and left for Rome with Paul still in jail as a concession to the Jews.

C. Paul and Festus. 25:1-12.

Festus was a man of higher character and greater competence than Felix. His brief encounter with Paul sets the stage for an appeal to Caesar and a trip to Rome.

1. Festus visits Jerusalem and hears charges against Paul. 25:1-5.

Only three days after arriving in the region, Festus visited Jerusalem to meet with the leaders of Judaism. The hatred these men still harbored for Paul quickly became evident when they pressed for him to be brought back to Jerusalem. Their plan — likely involving many of the same assassins who had once taken an oath not to eat until Paul was dead — was to ambush the apostle en route to the city. Festus did not fall for their trap and invited them to come to Caesarea where he would conduct a hearing on the matter.

2. Festus returns to Caesarea and examines Paul. 25:6-9.

A tired ritual repeated itself when Festus held the promised trial. False charges were made, full and convincing answers were given, and the Roman offi-

Day 5
An Appeal to Rome

Read about the Cities of Refuge at Numbers 35:6-34.

1. Why do you think Paul made the appeal to Caesar?
2. In what ways does Paul use his rights at a Roman citizen in Acts?
3. What fundamental civil rights do you treasure most? Explain.
4. Do you affirm those rights for others? Explain.
5. Pray for Christians who live in situations where they have no protection under law.

cial was unwilling to act under the law. As Felix had before him, Festus wanted to find a way to wash his hands of Paul without making the Jewish rulers angry at him.

3. Paul appeals to Caesar. 25:10-12.

Paul sensed that this process could go on forever, so he exercised his final option as a citizen of Rome. A citizen who believed he was being denied justice under a provincial official could appeal to Caesar for a trial in the imperial court at Rome. Paul made his appeal, and an embarrassed but perhaps relieved Festus had no choice. "You have appealed to Caesar," said Festus. "To Caesar you will go!"

Week Thirty-Two

Acts 25:13–26:32 (XIV D in Outline)

D. Paul and Agrippa. 25:13–26:32.

One of the most dramatic scenes in all of Holy Scripture takes place in this text. In the longest and most artfully crafted of Paul's five defense speeches in Acts of the Apostles, the gospel is presented brilliantly by an apostle in chains. The setting for the speech is a hearing arranged by Festus in a final attempt to formalize a charge against Paul that will not be ludicrous when received at the imperial court of Rome.

1. Agrippa and Bernice visit Festus and learn of Paul's case. 25:13-22.

Only a few days after Paul had made his appeal to Caesar, Festus was visited by a neighboring ruler and his sister. Because of the background in Judaism his guest possessed, Festus thought it might be a good thing to ask his help in framing the document he would send with Paul to Rome.

The "King Agrippa" of this text is Herod Agrippa II, the son of the Herod who beheaded James and imprisoned Peter in A.D. 44 (cf. 12:1ff) and the great-grandson of Herod the Great. Agrippa II had lived in Rome and had been a favorite of Emperor Claudius in his younger years. When his father died under the circumstances related earlier in Acts (12:19b-23), he would have been only seventeen years old. Beginning around A.D. 50, various territories north of Judea began to be assigned to him until he had a "kingdom" to rule. At the outbreak of the Jewish revolt against Rome, he sided with Rome and was rewarded with a larger area to govern. At his

Day 1
The Audience

Read 1 Corinthians 1:18-31 about Christian evangelism.

1. Who were the primary persons in Paul's audience?
2. What special spiritual need did each of those persons have?
3. What part of Paul's message do you see directed to those persons and needs?
4. What are the greatest needs you see in our culture that are addressed by the gospel?
5. Explain the meaning of 1 Corinthians 9:19-23 to Christian evangelism.

death in A.D. 100, the Herodian dynasty came to an end. With Festus only recently appointed as the new procurator for Judea, Herod Agrippa II came to Caesarea to meet (and ingratiate himself to!) the more powerful Roman authority whose territory adjoined his own.

With King Agrippa was his sister, Bernice. She was a year younger than her brother and had previously been married to her uncle, Herod of Chalcis. When she was widowed in A.D. 48, she came to live with her brother and began an openly incestuous relationship with him. What an unholy pair they made.

Festus explained to King Agrippa that he had a problem involving a prisoner left over from the rule of his predecessor, Felix. He explained that the Jewish leaders in Jerusalem had greeted his initial visit there with charges against the man and "asked that he be condemned." So he told of his arrangement for a hearing in Caesarea at which the prisoner had been charged not with violations of Roman law but religious heresy. His summary of the issue he found to be at stake is fascinating. He explained that the Jewish leaders "had some points of dispute with him about their own religion and about a dead man named Jesus who Paul claimed was alive."

Festus confessed being "at a loss how to investigate such matters." So he had suggested the possibility to Paul that he go to Jerusalem to face his accusers there. It was then, he explained to Agrippa, that Paul appealed to Caesar. And while that appeared to take the Christian evangelist off his hands, it had simultaneously created a problem as to how Festus could explain Paul's case in the documentation he would need to send with him.

Whether as a courtesy to Festus or out of personal curiosity, King Agrippa said, "I would like to hear this man myself." With what must have been a sigh of relief, Festus replied, "Tomorrow you will hear him." Thus was the stage set for one of the most fateful confrontations in the history of Christian evangelism.

2. Paul brought before Agrippa. 25:23-37.

With great ceremony, Festus, Agrippa, Bernice, along with a number of "high ranking officers" and some of the "leading men" of Caesarea, assembled for the hearing. When all was in readiness, the prisoner was brought into the hall. In rehearsing the background for what was about to take place, Festus both exonerated Paul of any capital crime under Roman law (i.e., "I found he had done nothing deserving of death") and candidly confessed his own predicament (i.e., "I have nothing definite to write to His Majesty about him. Therefore I have brought him before all of you, and especially before you, King Agrippa, so that as a result of this investigation I may have something to write").

3. Paul's defense and presentation of the gospel. 26:1-29.

Agrippa invited Paul to speak for himself, and the apostle lifted his manacled hand (cf. 26:29b) to get the attention of his audience. He began by expressing legitimate gratitude for finally having the chance to make a defense before someone "well acquainted with all the Jewish customs and controversies." The Talmud informs us that Agrippa II's mother, Cypros, had taken an intense interest in the religion of the Jews. Perhaps her son followed her in some of that interest and therefore had particular knowledge that would make it possible for him to follow Paul's address. Perhaps Paul was simply expressing the lesser confidence that he had lived in Jewish territory and therefore would know more of these issues than Festus could possibly grasp.

"Paul's address before Agrippa is much more

**Day 2
The Message**

Read Paul's summary of the gospel at 1 Corinthians 15:1-11.

1. What parts of Paul's speech were defense comments?
2. To what two issues did Paul trace his problems with the Jewish leaders? Explain.
3. How did Paul turn his defense speech into an evangelistic opportunity?
4. How did he summarize the gospel message in this speech?
5. Why do you think Paul handled this situation as he did?

than a defense of his own innocence or a review of his personal religious experience; it is a superb statement of the very essence of Christianity, and as one reads this historic speech two or three of its propositions should be especially noted. Paul insists that faith in a risen, divine Christ is the very heart of Christianity, that the resurrection is attested by competent human witnesses and by inspired Scriptures, and that the message of salvation through Christ is intended for the whole race of mankind." [Erdman, *Acts*, p. 183.]

Day 3
Personal Experience

Read an earlier account of Paul's conversion from Acts 9:1-19.

1. What details of his early life did Paul tell? Why were those facts important to his defense?
2. Why did Paul tell of his history of persecuting Christians?
3. What event changed his life? Why?
4. Is there a single event to which you trace monumental changes in your life?
5. What is the most powerful personal testimony you have ever heard a believer give?

Paul began his defense by informing Agrippa of his personal background in Judaism. He had been a strict Pharisee and had nothing in his background that would have predisposed him toward Christianity. As a matter of fact, he had been an ardent foe of everything associated with it. "I too was convinced that I ought to do all that was possible to oppose the name of Jesus of Nazareth," he said. "And that is just what I did in Jerusalem. On the authority of the chief priests I put many of the saints in prison, and when they were put to death, I cast my vote against them."

Although a Pharisee and therefore one who believed in the resurrection of the dead (i.e., "Why should any of you consider it incredible that God raises the dead?"), he would have none of the Christian claim that Jesus of Nazareth had risen from the dead. So he had enlarged the scope of his opposition to those who made such a claim about him. He went from one synagogue to another and even to foreign cities and "tried to force [Christians] to blaspheme."

All that came to an end for Paul when he was confronted, challenged, and commissioned by Jesus on the Damascus Road. There was no denying the resurrection of Jesus after he saw him alive that day! Not only did that experience persuade Paul that

Jesus was the Messiah, but it also convinced him that the gospel of salvation in Jesus was to be preached to Gentiles as well as to Jews.

Notice that Paul attributed his trouble at the hands of the Jews to two things in this speech — the resurrection of the dead in general (and of Jesus in particular) and his ministry to Gentiles. "And now it is because of my hope in what God has promised our fathers that I am on trial today. This is the promise our twelve tribes are hoping to see fulfilled as they earnestly serve God day and night. O king, it is because of this hope that the Jews are accusing me. Why should any of you consider it incredible that God raises the dead?" (26:6-8). "First to those in Damascus, then to those in Jerusalem and in all Judea, and to the Gentiles also, I preached that they should repent and turn to God and prove their repentance by their deeds. That is why the Jews seized me in the temple courts and tried to kill me" (26:20-21).

Yet, Paul insisted, these two doctrines were imbedded in Jewish Scripture. He was not rejecting or speaking against Moses in making these claims. He was claiming the fulfillment of all that Moses had predicted and for which he had longed.

At that point in Paul's speech, Festus could sit still no longer. All of this was sheer nonsense to him, so he interrupted and said, "You are out of your mind, Paul. Your great learning is driving you insane." Practical, world-centered Romans had no place in their belief system for the notion of the resurrection of the dead. Paul's brief and respectful reply to Festus was simply to disclaim madness and to affirm that what he had said was both "true and reasonable." He then turned from the Roman procurator to the man who, because of his knowledge of Scripture and recent Jewish history around Jerusalem, would be in a better position to follow his argument. He

Day 4
The Response

Read Matthew 13:1-23 about different responses to the gospel.

1. What was Festus's response to Paul's defense sermon? Explain.
2. What response did Agrippa have to what he had heard? Explain.
3. How has Agrippa's response been misinterpreted by some?

243

4. How did Paul reply to Agrippa?

5. Was Festus's heart hard, shallow, or thorn-filled? Agrippa's?

**Day 5
"Almost Persuaded"**

Read 2 Peter 3:1-10 about the fate of those who scoff at the gospel.

1. How does the King James Version mistakenly translate Agrippa's response to Paul?

2. What misunderstandings have been produced by the KJV reading?

3. Can you think of other translation problems that have produced similar misunderstandings?

4. Why do you think Agrippa scoffed at Paul's speech?

5. Have you ever witnessed a similar response by someone you knew? If so, explain.

expressed the confidence that King Agrippa was familiar with these issues and that he had heard of the events involving Jesus.

With both boldness and pleading in his voice, Paul turned to his primary hearer. "King Agrippa, do you believe the prophets?" he asked. As if to signal that his question was purely rhetorical, he then added, "I know you do." Agrippa seems to be embarrassed by this direct appeal. How dare Paul ask someone of his position to engage in a personal discussion of spiritual issues in a public setting! So the king sought to cut Paul off by saying, "Do you think that in such a short time you can persuade me to be a Christian?"

Unlike the King James Version's "Almost thou persuadest me to be a Christian" and all the sermons preached from that rendering, Agrippa most assuredly was not brought to the brink of faith that day. His response was a cynical retort. It was an affirmation of unbelief rather than an admission of interest.

Paul's response to being put off by Agrippa was restrained. He merely said, playing off the king's own words, "Short time or long — I pray God that not only you but all who are listening to me today may become what I am, except for these chains." "How tragic is Agrippa's sophisticated avoidance of a confrontation with the risen Christ! At least Festus looked at it directly and called it madness. Agrippa sets conditions that the evangelist cannot meet. To all those who say, 'It will take more than this to make me a Christian,' Paul warns, 'Your conditions are irrelevant in the light of the supreme importance of the salvation this gospel offers. Don't let your requirements prevent you from receiving God's provision.'" [Larkin, *Acts*, pp. 364-365.]

4. Private reaction of the Roman officials to Paul's defense. 26:30-32.

With the hearing concluded, the procurator and

king talked privately about the prisoner. They agreed that Paul had done nothing worthy of either death or imprisonment. "This man could have been set free if he had not appealed to Caesar," said Agrippa. While Festus had the authority yet to set him free, political considerations made it impossible for him to do so. There would be too many explanations to have to make to the Jewish leaders. He would have to account for not honoring Paul's appeal to the imperial court. And he would have to explain to himself how he could set a "madman" free without admitting that his message was something other than madness, without admitting that it was the truth that could set men free from sin.

Week Thirty-Three

Acts 27:1–28:16 (XV A to XVI B in Outline)

Day 1
How Character Is Revealed

Read James 1:1-12 about the formation of Christian character.

1. How does one's reaction to a crisis reveal character?
2. What did this crisis show about Paul's character?
3. What situation in your life most dramatically *shaped* your character?
4. What recent situation has most dramatically *revealed* your character?
5. Pray for God to strengthen your character where it is weakest.

XV. The Prisoner's Journey to Rome. 27:1–28:10.

Luke's account of Paul's fateful voyage to Rome is the last and longest of the four "we-sections" of Acts of the Apostles. There is a minuteness of detail about ancient seamanship that has been noted even by those who do not regard Acts as God-breathed Scripture. This is the story of a natural disaster that Luke experienced along with Paul and their associates. The events at hand show Paul as a man of faith, courage, and practical good sense. He certainly earned the respect of the ship's crew and his Roman guard by the way he handled himself in this crisis.

A. Initial Incidents of the Voyage. 27:1-8.

Ancient documents other than the Bible tell us that the part of the Mediterranean Sea navigated in this story became treacherous in mid-September and was considered impossible to navigate after mid-November. Because this trip was attempted "after the Fast" (v. 9; i.e., Yom Kippur) — which falls at the end of September or early in October — this was not a good time to be on the sea. But irregular schedules and the opportunity to board a ship at Caesarea that was headed for Italy before winter dictated Paul's circumstances. His Roman keepers put him and some other prisoners on the ship. A centurion named Julius was in charge of the prisoners.

Julius clearly showed Paul some unusual kindnesses. For one thing, both Luke and Aristarchus

[Ar-ĭs-tär´-khəs] (cf. 19:29; 20:4) were allowed to travel with Paul. That Paul was a Roman citizen who had not yet been convicted of a crime likely gave him this privilege. When the ship stopped some seventy miles north of Caesarea at Sidon to take on cargo, Julius permitted Paul and his friends to visit with the church in that port city. This was not a normal privilege of a Roman citizen traveling under arrest; it reflects the personal respect Julius had for the apostle.

The initial voyage was slow and tedious "because the winds were against us." Sailing northwest and hugging the shoreline of Asia Minor, the ship eventually reached Myra in Lycia. Here the centurion arranged passage for his fellow-soldiers and their prisoners on a larger grain ship headed to Rome from Egypt. The grain ship moved slowly, taken off its course by winds that forced its captain to navigate "to the lee (i.e., southern coast) of Crete." The stressful voyage finally came to a small bay called Fair Havens.

B. Paul's Counsel to the Men in Charge. 27:9-12.

The hard decision facing the ship's owner and the Roman centurion aboard his grain vessel had to do with wintering at Fair Havens versus trying to reach a better port before winter shut down the sea lanes. Incredibly, Paul was apparently a participant at some level on those discussions. He expressed his opinion that it would entail disastrous consequences to sail at this late date. But the people in charge made the decision to try for the larger, safer port of Phoenix on the opposite side of Crete. They did so in the knowledge that navigating around the island would expose them to potentially dangerous winds from the north.

Day 2
Good Advice

Read Proverbs 12:1-15 and notice what is said about advice.

1. What advice did Paul give in two situations in this text?
2. What did experience prove about the advice he gave?
3. Why would Julius listen to Paul's advice about anything?
4. Who is your most trusted counselor? Why?
5. How does one become the person whose advice others will seek?

Day 3
Shipwreck

Read Mark 16:8-20 about the signs to accompany Christ's apostles.

1. Describe the dramatic details of Paul's ship-wreck.
2. What happened at the bonfire on Malta?
3. What had Jesus said about such events?
4. What was the effect on the inhabitants of the island?
5. Do you see God's providence at work in these events? How?

C. The Storm at Sea. 27:13-38.

1. The ship in a violent storm. 27:13-20.

When "a gentle south wind began to blow," the ship weighed anchor and began moving along the coast toward Phoenix. The ship had not been long out of harbor, however, when a violent "wind of hurricane force" caught it and started driving it toward the open sea. Paul and his sailing companions were helpless before its power. With the greatest of difficulty, the sailors pulled in the lifeboat as the ship was being driven by the tiny island of Cauda.

In the grip of the furious Northeaster, the sailors did everything they knew to do to save the vessel and themselves. They reinforced the ship with ropes and dropped the sea anchor in hopes of being spared a wreck on the sandbars of Syrtis. They lightened the ship so it could ride higher in the water by dumping cargo overboard. They eventually even tossed the ship's tackle into the churning waters. The ship was tossed and battered by the Northeaster for two full weeks (v. 27), and all aboard it "finally gave up all hope of being saved."

2. Paul encourages the men aboard the ship. 27:21-26.

Although Paul himself had apparently given up hope, an angel appeared to him in the night and made him a promise. "Do not be afraid, Paul," the angel had said. "You must stand trial before Caesar; and God has graciously given you the lives of all who sail with you."

As Paul began relating his vision to the sailors, soldiers, and other prisoners, he began by reminding them of his earlier advice about staying in port. In context, it is far more likely that he referenced his previous counsel for the sake of his credibility for what he was about to say rather than as an I-told-you-so form of rebuke. At any rate, he told everyone what the angel had said. The ship would run aground on an island and be destroyed, but no lives would be lost. Paul affirmed his attitude toward the Lord he served by saying, "So keep up your courage, men, for I have faith in God that it will happen just as he told me."

3. The ship approaches land. 27:27-32.

On the fourteenth night of their ordeal, the sailors sensed — perhaps by the sound of breakers — that they were approaching land. Soundings proved they were right. Fearing that the ship would be broken apart on the rocks, the crew put out four anchors from stern and longed for morning. In a panic, some of the sailors launched the ship's lifeboat. Pretending that they were going to drop some additional anchors from the bow, they were going to try to save themselves at the expense of the others. Paul discovered (or had revealed to him) their deceptive plan and went to the centurion. "Unless these men stay with the ship, you cannot be saved," he warned. Every able-bodied man would be needed tomorrow, so no one could be allowed to flee.

4. More encouragement from Paul. 27:33-38.

As the day was about to dawn, Paul reminded everyone that they had not eaten during the two weeks of fighting the storm. Because everyone would be challenged to the fullest by what lay ahead, he encouraged that everyone should break his fast and eat. After he assured them again that God would save them from the water, he took some food, gave thanks to God for it, and started to eat as an example to the others. Everyone among the total of 276 souls onboard ship ate what he wanted. Then everything that remained — including the remainder of the cargo of wheat — was thrown overboard in a final effort to allow the ship to sit high in the water.

D. The Shipwreck. 27:39-44.

1. The vessel runs aground and breaks up. 27:39-41.

When the sun rose and the sailors saw land, they decided to hoist the foresail and try to beach the ship. It ran aground on a sandbar and began to be pummeled by the waves. It broke in half and started to sink.

2. All the ship's passengers escape to land. 27:42-44.

Following standard procedure for such a situation, the soldiers were ready to kill all the prisoners. They would have to answer with their own lives, if they escaped. Julius had come to hold Paul in such high regard that he gave the order to spare the prisoners and told them to try for land the best way they could. All of the 276 people who had been on the ship survived, just as the Lord had assured Paul they would.

E. The Time Spent at Malta. 28:1-10.

1. The group is warmly received. 28:1-2.

The land the sailors had not recognized at daybreak that morning (cf. 27:39) turned out to be the island of Malta. It is located about sixty miles south of Sicily, below the boot of Italy. The people of the island were kind and hospitable to those who had survived the wreck. They built a fire to warm them against the cold and rain.

2. Paul is bitten by a viper. 28:3-6.

As Paul was helping gather more sticks to keep the fire going, he was bitten by a viper. The natives of the island saw the snake bite and hang onto his arm, and their superstitious assumption was that "fate" had judged Paul for some serious crime he had committed. When Paul shook the viper off his hand and suffered no injury from the bite, their new conclusion — again rooted in their superstition — was that he was "a god."

3. Numerous healings at the hand of Paul. 28:7-10.

After what the people of Malta had witnessed, they insisted that Paul and his immediate entourage go with them to the home of the island's chief man. Publius received them warmly and held a three-day banquet in Paul's honor. Learning that Publius's father was sick with fever and dysentery, "Paul went in to see him and, after prayer, placed his hands on him and healed him." This established the apostle as a healer, so sick people from across the island came to him over the three months he was there and were healed. We are given no information about preaching the gospel on Malta or the establishment of a church. We are simply told that Paul and his company were "honored" in many ways when they left the island and were supplied with the things they would need to resume their voyage.

XVI. The Prisoner's Arrival at Rome. 28:11-31.

After the high drama of the storm, shipwreck, and events on Malta, Luke relates the conclusion of Paul's journey to Rome in brief fashion. He is principally concerned to show the reception given him in the capital city of the empire — first by the church, then by the officials of the Roman government, and finally by the Jews.

A. Arrival and Reception by the Disciples. 28:11-15.

When the spring came and the seas were safe to travel again, Julius put his soldiers and their prisoners on another Egyptian grain ship that had wintered at Malta. Sailing north-northeast, the ship made the east coast of Sicily and put in at Syracuse for three days. From there the ship went to Rhegium, a harbor

**Day 4
Everyone Needs
Encouragement**

Read what Paul said about discouragement in 2 Corinthians 1:1-11.

1. As Paul neared Rome, who came out to meet him?
2. What was the impact of this greeting on him? Explain.
3. Describe a time when someone encouraged you in a stressful situation.
4. Do you know anyone who is under great stress today?
5. How can you encourage that person during the next week?

city on the toe of the Italian boot. The next day a wind from the south carried them almost two hundred miles up the coast of Italy in only two days to Puteoli. It was the port city of Neapolis (modern Naples) and one of the two main ports for grain ships from Alexandria.

The party under Julius's command disembarked at Puteoli to travel the final 150 miles to Rome by land. A community of believers in the city invited Paul to spend a week there. Perhaps Julius had duties to tend to that allowed his prisoner to have this time of refreshment with fellow-Christians. Perhaps he showed a courtesy to the man of God through whom he had been delivered from death on the seas. At any rate, during the week at Puteoli, word traveled from there into Rome that the Apostle to the Gentiles would soon be in the city.

The route from Puteoli to Rome would have carried Paul and his party along the famous Appian Way. As he walked toward the city, delegations of believers walked from the city toward him to welcome him and to encourage their brother in chains. Some came as far as the Forum of Appius and others to the Three Taverns Inn — forty-three and thirty-three miles outside of the Imperial City respectively. "At the sight of these men Paul thanked God and was encouraged."

B. Paul's Situation under a Roman Guard. 28:16.

Upon Paul's arrival in the city itself, the charged-but-still-unconvicted citizen was allowed to live in private quarters. Although living in a house at his own expense, he was still guarded by a Roman soldier at all times and "bound with a chain" (cf. v. 20). For the next two years, Paul received guests, taught the gospel, and wrote letters as he waited for his case to be heard in Caesar's court.

Day 5
The Best of a Bad Situation

Read Romans 8:28-39 for an assurance of God's concern for his people.

1. What arrangements did the officials allow Paul to make for himself at Rome?
2. How did Paul make the best of his situation for two years as a prisoner?
3. How did Paul's presence help the church at Rome?
4. What is the greatest problem in your life today?
5. Pray for God to show you how to make the best of your situation.

Week Thirty-Four

Acts 28:17-31 (XVI C to XVI E in Outline)

For several years, Paul had dreamed and prayed about going to Rome to preach the gospel. The circumstances under which he spent two years there were hardly those he would have chosen. As he awaited his trial, he was under house arrest in the city but free to receive guests. His Christian brothers and sisters had received him warmly, and the Roman officials had treated him fairly. But he wanted an audience with the Jewish leaders in the Imperial City.

C. An Initial Meeting with Jews at Rome. 28:17-22.

Three days after his arrival at Rome, the apostle "called together the leaders of the Jews." His purpose was to explain the reason for his imprisonment and impending trial. He knew it was altogether possible that word had already reached these men about him and that his situation had been misrepresented. For the sake of his desire to preach Christ among those of his own ethnic background in the city, he did not want to be thought of as a disloyal Jew who had repudiated Moses or the Law.

When the leaders had assembled with him, he assured them, "I have done nothing against our people or against the customs of our ancestors." He quickly explained that he had been arrested in Jerusalem and judged innocent of any crime by the Roman authorities. He would have been released except for objections lodged by his Jewish accusers. And what had been the issue they had raised? "It is

Day 1
Rome at Last!

Read Paul's statement of desire to visit Rome from Romans 1:1-17.

1. Why had Paul wanted to visit Rome?
2. How was this consistent with his strategy for evangelism?
3. Contrast Paul's plan with the reality of his arrival in Rome.
4. What "dream" are you praying about most fervently?
5. Are you ready for God to answer your prayer in some strange way? Explain.

because of the hope of Israel that I am bound with this chain," Paul explained. In other words, the point of sharp contention between Paul and his accusers was their interpretation of the messianic hope of Israel; he had offered Jesus as the personal fulfillment of that hope, and the Jewish leaders at Jerusalem had both rejected Jesus and turned against Paul with charges of disloyalty to his people.

The reply of his hearers must have startled Paul. They said, "We have not received any letters from Judea concerning you, and none of the brothers who have come from there has reported or said anything bad about you." Some writers see this as a "polite lie" by the leading men of the Jewish community at Rome. Perhaps that is so, but it seems altogether possible that their ignorance of Paul's problems at Jerusalem was real rather than pretended. Claudius had banished the Jews from Rome about ten years before this (cf. 18:2), and they were only now getting reestablished there. Perhaps their links of communication with Jerusalem were still weak enough that word had not reached them about this Christian from Tarsus.

At any rate, even if they had no word about Paul, the Jews of Rome had certainly heard about the Christian church and had opinions about it. They knew it was being spoken against by their Jewish brethren everywhere as a "sect." Yet they indicated their willingness to give Paul a hearing so he could explain his views to them.

Day 2
A Magnanimous Spirit

Read Paul's passion for his fellow Jews at Romans 9:1-18.

1. Where had Paul's principal opposition come from during his missionary journeys?

D. Great Numbers of the Jews Hear Paul Again. 28:23-29.

Without having to face an overt prejudice from his fellow Jews over his faith in Jesus as the Messiah, Paul was able to arrange a second meeting with the Jewish leaders. The second meeting was considerably larger. Again, the group had to come to Paul's quarters because of his confinement to house arrest. Without giving details of the things Paul said, Luke writes: "From morning till evening he explained and declared to them the kingdom of God and tried to convince them about Jesus from the Law of Moses and from the Prophets."

The sermon that day was likely similar in content to his synagogue sermon at Pisidian Antioch (cf. 13:17ff). There was surely a great deal of debate and intense discussion of critical texts from Scripture. At the end of the day, several converts had been made. Some were "convinced" by Paul's explanations and arguments, but others — presumably the majority — "would not believe."

The apostle apparently came to a point where he thought everything that could be accomplished in such a setting had been done. So he made a "final statement" that he knew beforehand would bring the discussion to a close with some. He affirmed that Isaiah had predicted Jewish unbelief and hardness of heart against the Messiah which had led, in turn, to the sending of "God's salvation" to receptive Gentiles.

The passage cited from Isaiah 6:9-10 had been used by Jesus himself to explain Jewish unbelief toward his message of the kingdom of God (John 12:40). "Paul's point was to show the leaders that they had come to the dreadful stage of religious dullness. They heard words but did not understand; they saw truth but would not respond; their emotions were insensitive; and their ears were weary of great ideas which they had not lived. The tragic result of their faithless familiarity was that they were no longer able to receive truth and order their lives around it. Most of all, traditions and customs, rules and regulations had been substituted for God. They had resisted so long, they could not receive. There was no longer a desire or a need for God's healing

2. If Paul had abandoned preaching to the Jews altogether, would you have blamed him? Explain.
3. What does his seeking of an interview with the Jewish rulers of Rome tell you about Paul?
4. What was the result of his day-long discussion with the Jews?
5. What should be the attitude of Christians toward Jews today?

Day 3
"Faithless Familiarity"

Read Matthew 23:1-39 to be reminded of how religion can blind people to God.

1. Explain the statement of Isaiah 6:9-10.
2. How did Jesus use this statement during his ministry?
3. How did Paul apply it in his situation?
4. Have you ever seen religion get in someone's way who was seeking God?

5. How may we keep our eyes, ears, and hearts sensitive to God while being religious?

love and forgiveness. Status as the people of God had excluded God!" [Ogilvie, *Acts*, p. 360.]

We sometimes express amazement today at the eagerness an "unchurched" person shows toward the gospel as opposed to the nonchalance of some church members with that same message. Has familiarity bred contempt? Does the startling nature of God's salvation escape those who have heard it discussed throughout their lifetimes? As surely as the habits, trappings, and discussions of religion among the Jewish leaders of the first century were allowed to blind them to what God was doing among them, so might the same thing happen among us.

Paul certainly did not say or believe that the Jews had been rejected. After all, he was a Jew himself. He was simply observing what his own experience had taught him about the relative joy with which Jews and Gentiles were responding to the gospel at that point in history.

**Day 4
Paul's Final Years**

Read Philemon for an interesting episode from his two years at Rome.

1. How did this two-year imprisonment end for Paul?
2. What did he do after his release?
3. How did Paul's career and life end?
4. What is your estimation of Paul's career as a Christian missionary?
5. How do you expect to spend your final years? How will that time honor the Lord?

E. The Progress of the Gospel at Rome during Paul's Two-Year Imprisonment. 28:30-31.

Luke has now told us the essential features of Paul's arrival at Rome as responded to by the church, the Roman government, and the Jewish leaders. The Christians had received him warmly and enthusiastically by traveling out to welcome Paul and his companions. The Roman officials had treated him graciously by allowing him to receive people and teach all who came to his rented house. For the most part, at least, the Jewish community rejected Paul's view of Jesus as the Messiah. The pattern has been the same throughout his missionary tours.

"Though there may be incarceration, the Word of God is not bound. Luke has fully demonstrated that the implementation/application portion of the salvation message is indeed true (Luke 1:4; 24:47). And if his readers in any day embrace that message, they will soon find themselves embodying it, proclaiming repentance to the forgiveness in his name to all the nations 'with all boldness, unhindered.' So may it be till Jesus comes." [Larkin, *Acts*, p. 393.]

Thus Luke's brief summary of Paul's two years at Rome ends his second volume of the beginnings of the Christian faith. Why does he not give us more details? Why are we not told what became of the apostle? For one thing, the strategy of the book in showing the gospel's spread from Jerusalem through Judea and Samaria and eventually to the "ends of the earth" (1:8) has been brought to its grand climax by Paul's arrival in Rome. For another, Acts of the Apostles is not a Pauline biography and never had as its purpose the setting out of the details of the apostle's life.

From the angel's assurance to Paul during the terrible storm and shipwreck, readers of the book were to understand that a trial would take place in the Imperial Courts (cf. 27:24). Acts was surely written during the two years following Paul's arrival at Rome in the spring of A.D. 61. Some have even suggested that it was intended to be part of the defense brief submitted to the government. During the same two-year period in which Luke was writing this volume, Paul himself wrote at least four epistles that are preserved for us in the New Testament — Ephesians, Philippians, Colossians, and Philemon. A number of insights about the apostle's experiences can be gleaned from a close reading of those letters.

Paul's accusers from Jerusalem would have had eighteen months under Roman law to appear and present the particulars of their case against him. Whether they ever arrived is unclear. His "trial" may have consisted of nothing more than a formal dismissal of charges against him because of a lack of evidence. At any rate, our best information is that Paul was released from house arrest at the end of the two years mentioned by Luke.

Day 5
Acts 29

Read the promise of God to be with his church from Luke 24:36-53.

1. Did God's work in his church end with the writing of the New Testament? Explain.

2. The Holy Spirit is clearly the agency of power in Acts. Do you see him working in your life today? Your church?

3. How do you see your church attempting to implement the Great Commission?

4. What signs do you see of a spiritual revival in your lifetime?

5. Write a short 29th chapter of Acts by focusing on the dreams you have for your church.

After his release, Paul continued his evangelistic travels and revisited many of the churches he had founded in Asia Minor. Tradition has it that he realized his desire to visit Spain during these travels (cf. Rom. 15:23-24). This would have carried him to the fringes of the world known to his contemporaries. First Timothy and Titus were written during this period.

The apostle was arrested a second time around A.D. 67 and returned to Rome. This time there was no rented house but a dank dungeon for him. Second Timothy, written during this final incarceration, reflects no expectation of release (cf. 2 Tim. 4:6-18). The difference in the two imprisonments and their outcomes was the persecution begun under Nero. The tradition is that Paul was tried, condemned, and beheaded during that awful time.

The work of the Holy Spirit that Luke chronicled in Acts of the Apostles is still going on among the people of God. The gospel is preached, souls are saved, and lives are transformed. The people who have fallen in love with Jesus band together in churches where, in turn, they fall in love with one another. Such churches are outposts of holiness in an unclean world. They function as lights to a world floundering in darkness.

No higher honor comes to modern Christians than that we should be included in the work God started on that first Pentecost following the resurrection of Jesus. May we continue to bear faithful witness to him until he returns to claim his church-bride.

Printed in the United States
110372LV00002B/77-106/A